Welcome

Congratulations: picking up this book is the first step towards what could be a life-changing experience. I've built and run a number of businesses in the past decade, and have had my share of failures as well as successes. This book distils what I've learned in that time, along with the best practice of some of the industry's leaders.

The aim of this book is to set you on the right path towards running your own successful online business. It covers four essential areas: coming up with the right product; building a platform to sell that product; the mechanics of successful selling; and connecting with the right customers.

You don't need to be an IT expert to launch an online business, and this book reflects that. What you do need is imagination, open-mindedness and determination.

Nor is this a "get rich quick" book. It's a realistic guide to setting up in business, and pulls no punches about the hard work and stamina required.

The good news is that it's possible to set up an online business on a low budget. You don't need premises or high levels of stock. It also opens up a potentially huge audience to sell to, and you can be up and running much more quickly than a traditional business.

You can see this in practice: in tandem with the writing of this book, I built a real, working business at www.makingyourowncandles.co.uk. This updated edition covers new ways of using social networks to market your business and how to set up a free online shop, and covers the lessons learned in our first three years.

Best of luck!

Kevin Partner is a writer, coder and entrepreneur and has been a Contributing Editor to PC Pro magazine since 1996.

He is the creator and manager of MakingYourOwnCandles (www.makingyourowncandles.co.uk), Scribbleit Ltd (www.scribbleit.co.uk), PassYourTheory Ltd (www.passyourtheory.org.uk), NlightN Multimedia Ltd (www.nlightn.co.uk) and FixedPriceWebsite.co.uk.

Scribbleit provides writing, marketing, editing and publishing services. MakingYourOwnCandles launched in 2009 as part of the development process of this book and is now the UK's leading supplier of candle making kits. PassYourTheory provides driving theory test training and NlightN Multimedia is an independent publisher of iPhone, iPad and Android apps. FixedPriceWebsite provides custom business websites for a low, fixed cost.

Go to www.kevinpartner.co.uk to find out how to follow him on social networks or visit www.pcpro.co.uk/author/253598/kevin-partner to read his recent columns.

Contents

PART 1 Planning

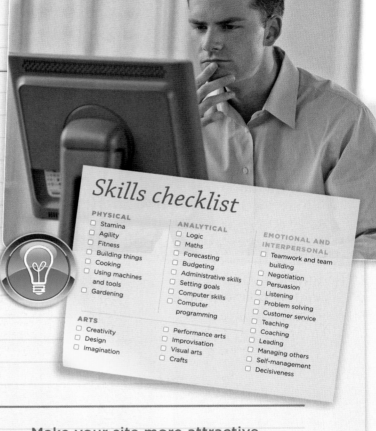

Skills checklist

PHYSICAL
- ☐ Stamina
- ☐ Agility
- ☐ Fitness
- ☐ Building things
- ☐ Cooking
- ☐ Using machines and tools
- ☐ Gardening

ANALYTICAL
- ☐ Logic
- ☐ Maths
- ☐ Forecasting
- ☐ Budgeting
- ☐ Administrative skills
- ☐ Setting goals
- ☐ Computer skills
- ☐ Computer programming

EMOTIONAL AND INTERPERSONAL
- ☐ Teamwork and team building
- ☐ Negotiation
- ☐ Persuasion
- ☐ Listening
- ☐ Problem solving
- ☐ Customer service
- ☐ Teaching
- ☐ Coaching
- ☐ Leading
- ☐ Managing others
- ☐ Self-management
- ☐ Decisiveness

ARTS
- ☐ Creativity
- ☐ Design
- ☐ Imagination
- ☐ Performance arts
- ☐ Improvisation
- ☐ Visual arts
- ☐ Crafts

PART 2 Building

PART 3 Selling

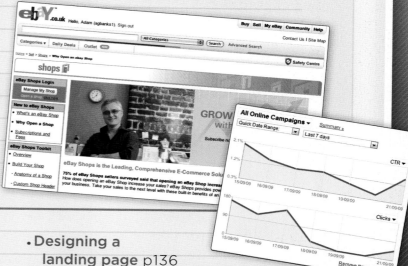

PART 4 Marketing

Google AdWords

Attract more customers

No matter what your budget, you can display your ads on Google and our advertising network. Connect with potential customers at the magic moment they're searching for your products or services, and only pay when people click your ads.

Want a hand creating your account? Have one of our team help you get started.

You create your ad…

You choose keywords, set your budget and decide where your ad will be displayed…

People click on your ads and connect with your business!

PART 1 Planning

Start the right business

Going into business

Before you begin working on your business, you need to work out what you want to get out of it. Think carefully; the answers you come up with might surprise you. Creating a business from scratch can be exciting and rewarding, but it also involves time, effort and money. So it's essential to understand why you're doing it: a clear sense of purpose will help propel you through what is likely to be a demanding process.

In many cases there will be a specific trigger that kicks this process off. In some cases it's a change in circumstances. This could be something traumatic, such as being made redundant, or even something more positive, such as coming into money.

For most people, however, the underlying reason for starting their own business is a desire for freedom. This might be the freedom to do something you enjoy; freedom from the tyranny of the corporate structure; or the freedom that money brings. There's also a natural appeal in being your own boss, especially if you're able to base your business on skills you've previously employed as part of your job. There's no doubt that working for yourself gives you a level of self-determination that simply doesn't exist within an organisation. If you have a good business, after all, you can pick and choose your clients.

consequence of this is that many people don't believe they have what it takes to start up a successful business because they're not like that.

Now, I don't doubt that such entrepreneurs exist (you can hardly get away from them on TV, after all), but I can tell you that in my ten-plus years as a business owner, the only people I've met like this have been working within blue-chip companies. Real business owners are real people. The only difference between them and people who don't work for themselves is that they have, for one reason or another, decided to go into business. There's no qualification process, there are no entry requirements – just a decision followed by action.

However, there are certain qualities that successful businesspeople tend to have. Fortunately, they're not uncommon, and all of them can be learned:

"For most people, the underlying reason for starting their own business is a desire for freedom."

 HAVE YOU GOT WHAT IT TAKES?
Think of business startups, and images of *Dragon's Den* and *The Apprentice* inevitably spring to mind. People such as Alan Sugar, Peter Jones and Deborah Meaden matched up against nervous and often self-deluded prospective entrepreneurs begging for hundreds of thousands of pounds of investment. This could hardly be further from the reality for most small-business owners.

The real problem here is the very term "entrepreneur". Thirty years ago, American businessman Michael Gerber tackled this in his book *The E-myth: Why Most Businesses Don't Work and What to Do About It*. A common perception of an entrepreneur is a smart-suited, Mercedes-driving, fast-talking, maverick risk-taker with a highly inflated view of their own self-worth. The

 DETERMINATION Above all else, you need to have the stamina and drive to finish what you start. For every business that launches, I reckon a thousand expire before they see the inside of anyone's wallet.

 HUMILITY Not a quality you might associate with business, but the ability to recognise that you don't know everything is essential. If you know that you don't know, you'll do your research and remain flexible enough to change direction in response to evidence. You'll also have a mind open to learning new things, every single day. Arrogance is a business-killer.

 DECISIVENESS Nothing gets done unless you make decisions. Developing a business is

a repeated process of information-gathering followed by decision-making. You must also be prepared to take personal responsibility for your decisions. Once you do this, you take control of your own destiny, rather than feeling dependent on the state of the economy, other people or the weather.

4 **AN ANALYTICAL MIND** You need to be able to evaluate every aspect of your business and the market in which it operates. At every stage of developing and running your business, you need to be analysing whether things are working as they should and how to improve them. The best business owners have minds that think laterally and aren't afraid to change radically the way they do things – based on good analysis, of course.

People like this don't generally make headlines. They're just quietly going about their businesses; supplying goods and services, paying taxes and providing jobs for more people than all the big corporates put together.

FROM LITTLE ACORNS Unless you're sitting on a big pile of cash, the safest way to start up a business is to run it while you're still working for someone else.

For many people, this is exactly how their business will stay: a profitable sideline and diversion from the tedium of their regular job. For others, the business will start small but their hope is to eventually grow it enough to allow them to give up the day job and run it full-time.

By starting small, you can test and adjust your product and make sure it's profitable before expanding. My aim when I'm evaluating the viability of an idea is to ask whether I think it's capable of generating £500 per month net of all costs and tax within a month or two of starting the business. This may not sound like a lot, but get a few of these going and you'll quickly earn enough to replace a full-time income. Also, a business that can generate £500 net per month can often be upscaled by increasing marketing exposure and widening the audience.

IS THIS THE RIGHT TIME? The economy's taken a pounding over the past few years, but that doesn't mean you should delay your plans until things improve. The key issue is whether *you* are ready, not the economy. The essential truth is that most businesses are poorly run, and a recession will tend to expose the weaknesses of these firms. This produces holes in the market that you – if you choose the right product or service and then implement and market it effectively – can exploit. By following the steps in this book, you'll be better prepared than the vast majority of other startups. Yes, it's true that 50% of all new businesses fail within three years. But that means that half succeed: you just need to ensure you're in the successful half.

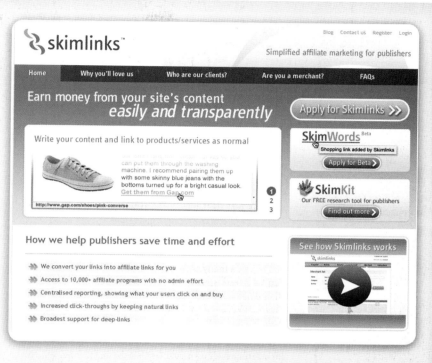

Q&A

Alicia Navarro is founder and CEO of Skimbit and Skimlinks www.skim links.com).

Q: What was the moment of inspiration for Skimbit?
A: After years of working for big companies like IBM and Vodafone, I knew I didn't want to work for a big company again. Then I got offered a job interview at Google. I didn't want the job – Google, despite its "fun factor", was very much a big company. I went for it anyway, and in the interview they asked me to come up with a business idea and say how I would market it.

I'd had the idea for Skimbit.com a while before, but it was in that moment, trying to convince Google it was a good idea, that I realised it *was* a good idea. I started the company the very next day.

Q: Lots of people have ideas for businesses but very few follow them through. What was it that enabled you to push the business through to, and beyond, launch?
A: I had nothing to lose. I didn't have a mortgage, I was single, and I'd had a burning urge to start a company all my life. I had deliberately chosen jobs that taught me the skills I would need to run a business, and at that point in my life I deliberately took a flexible job so I could work four days and have a day off to work on my business. I was willing and able to go from earning a healthy stable income to becoming a penniless entrepreneur.

I won't lie to you, it's the hardest thing I've ever done, and it isn't the right thing for many people. But the world has shown us lately that job stability is an illusion anyway. If it's in your blood to start a business, don't wait until you know everything, because you never will; but when the inspiration hits you, throw yourself completely into it.

Why an internet business?

It's one thing to decide to set up a business, but now consider the advantages of doing it online. Some have compared the advent of the internet with the invention of the printing press. In the same way that printing made books cheap enough to be distributed to the masses (at least to those who could read), the internet allows a businessperson in their broadband-connected bedroom to connect with billions of buyers.

In many ways, direct mail was the forerunner of the internet as a distribution channel, and much of the best practice established by direct marketers is still valid today. Let's take a look at the benefits of doing business online.

LOW STARTUP COSTS With both direct mail and internet, there's no need for the financial commitment of renting a shop, which reduces the risk. The costs of premises are replaced by server hosting costs; shop fittings and infrastructure by a simple electronic shopping cart; and adverts in the local press make way for Google AdWords with a worldwide audience. So the internet doesn't just lower the cost of starting up your business, it also offers an opportunity to sell to the world. Whether you take this up depends on the nature of your product and the level of your ambition.

LONG OPENING HOURS An internet business can be open 24 hours a day, 365 days a year. If you're selling a downloadable product, in fact, the sales side can take care of itself. The dream of many aspiring internet entrepreneurs is to wake up in the morning, turn on their computer and gaze adoringly at the mountain of automatically fulfilled orders as their PayPal balance grows. The promise of the internet is a business that, once set up, can be left to run itself as an efficient, low-maintenance, money-making machine. Whether it lives up to that promise is another matter.

TESTING The internet also lets you quickly and cheaply test the performance of different product lines and the effectiveness of marketing approaches. Imagine you had an idea that there was a

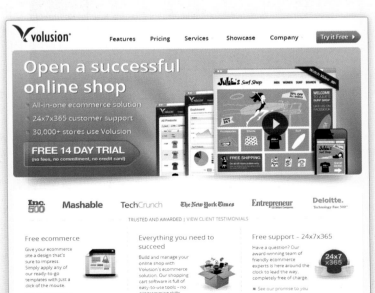

Companies such as Volusion make it possible to set up an online shop in minutes in a way that would have been impossible just ten years ago.

On a larger scale, Amazon is a business that could only exist online and has become one of the most famous brands in the world.

demand for 100% natural puppy-training treats. Twenty years ago your choices would boil down to either selling them yourself or finding a distributor. It clearly wouldn't be practical to rent a shop to sell one product, so you'd have to go into the general pet trade or, perhaps, hire a market stall. Finding a distributor would be little easier, involving lots of negotiations and committing to a large production run.

Fast-forward to the present day. Within a couple of weeks you can have a website up and running with a low-cost shopping cart, payment handled by PayPal, and production limited to whatever you can handle in your kitchen. If there turns out to be enough demand, you can then ramp up production, increase your marketing spend and enhance the shopping experience.

✓ **SCALE** Because of this flexibility, internet businesses can often be scaled to suit you. For example, they can be run alongside a normal job, either permanently or until you want to increase the income generated and go full-time. They can also take up much less time than traditional businesses, because so much of the work normally done by human beings is handled by software.

✓ **COMPETING WITH THE BIG BOYS** The final major benefit of the online business is that it's possible for the smallest concern to compete on more or less equal terms with global corporations. Since you have no physical shop, your customers can't necessarily tell how large your business is. A well-designed, smoothly running website can, without misleading customers, appear just as polished and trustworthy as Amazon or Tesco.

For example, 37Signals is a small team of around 15 people spread around North America. Over the past few years, it has developed a series of web-based organisational applications. These include Basecamp, the online project-management service; personal organisation software Backpack; and Highrise, a web-based contact management system. They have over three million users; 200,000 customers per employee, which isn't a bad ratio.

✗ **THE OTHER SIDE OF THE COIN** There are, of course, some downsides to doing business online. The fact you can get a business up and running quickly means your potential competitors can do the same. Indeed, the likelihood is that whatever sector you choose, there will be companies servicing it already. You're taking advantage of the fact that you can go from idea to working business in a few weeks, so you must expect others to see the same opportunity. Fortunately – and this is a theme you'll see popping up regularly throughout this book – the vast majority of your existing and future competition won't be taking the same care as you.

In enabling a new form of communication, the internet has been likened to the printing press. Now customers are easy to reach no matter where they live.

Q&A

What is PayPal?
PayPal is an internet-based payment system, owned by eBay, that can handle both tiny transactions and large ones. There is a cost involved to businesses, but not to consumers, so it's an attractive and secure way to pay for goods without the consumer having to worry about giving out their credit card details.

Think about your experiences of shopping online. My experience is that it can be like trudging through treacle. Many sites actively put barriers in the way of buying. I came across one recently that couldn't even tell me what the shipping cost of my order would be until after I'd committed to buy. Apparently they would weigh the goods when packing them and email me to let me know what it would cost to post them. Given that the most basic ecommerce packages let you incorporate shipping costs by specifying the weight of each item, this is hideously amateurish – and that company didn't get my order.

So there are opportunities in both new and existing markets to exploit the inadequate performance of competitors. My company's site, www.passyourtheory.org.uk, is an example of this. Since we launched in 2005, many others have spotted the potential for driving theory test training and have gone through the process of setting up a rival service. However, all of them have fallen by the wayside, either going out of business or ceasing advertising (usually a good sign of a business that doesn't work).

Why? Because Passyourtheory has been an ongoing project since its inception; always getting better, always learning how to market more efficiently, finding out from its customers what they want on a regular basis. Newcomers don't have this advantage – indeed, you'd be amazed at how many don't do any research at all, and the services that existed when we launched weren't doing it either. The internet gives you all the tools you need to constantly improve and reinvent your product; the issue is whether you actually do it.

What are you good at?

Before you start to generate specific ideas, it helps to look at what sort of enterprise would suit you. There's an almost infinite range of possible ventures, and the first step is to narrow these down. You owe it to yourself and your customers to build your business around your skills and interests. By working out what these are, you can both eliminate ideas that fall outside that list and use it as a springboard for generating ideas.

It's rarely a good idea to start a business that sells something you have no interest in or knowledge of. After all, you'll naturally do better when spending your time working in areas you're familiar with and interested in. Furthermore, there are a number of fundamental skills needed for all businesses. You need to be clear about which of those you have, which you can learn and which you will outsource.

We suggest using a spreadsheet to help organise your thoughts. Begin by listing your skills. Remember, a skill is something you *do* rather than something you *know*. The skills checklist opposite is by no means exhaustive, but it should get you started. Add any skill in which you think you are better than average. For example, if you keep going when others give up, you might add "stamina" to your list.

 RATE YOUR KNOWLEDGE You can now break down the skills you have into the knowledge you use to carry them out. As an example, if you've selected "Computer Programming", the knowledge that supports that skill might include PHP 5, Apache, CSS and XHTML – along with a whole raft of other, more general knowledge. For each of these aspects of your knowledge, you now need to rate your level of expertise.

Keep in mind that you should be above average on everything, since these are supposed to be your strengths. You might, therefore, choose a scale of 1 to 3, where 1 is "above average" and 3 is "exceptional".

For further inspiration, try the survey at www.pcpro.co.uk/links/yourstrengths. The survey you want is the VIA Signature Strengths Questionnaire. You need to answer 240 short questions, and the result will give you a real insight into what you're good at. Shaping your business around your top five strengths makes it much more likely that you will stick with it in the long run.

SKILLS EVERY BUSINESS OWNER NEEDS

Michael Gerber, author of the *E-Myth* series (www.e-myth.com), defines three roles that the business owner must fulfil: the entrepreneur, the manager and the technician. One way or another, a successful business requires all these roles. For many small businesses, all three might be fulfilled by one person (you!) – and your success will be largely determined by how well you balance the three.

THE ENTREPRENEUR is the ideas person. Without the entrepreneur, the manager and technician would have nothing to do. The entrepreneur needs to be creative, innovative and on the lookout for opportunities at all times. Did your five top VIA Signature Strengths include "Creativity" or "Judgement, critical thinking and open-mindedness"? If not, you might well need someone to help you with ideas generation. The entrepreneur has his or her eyes on the future all the time.

THE MANAGER is the organiser. The manager sets targets, organises resources, solves problems. The manager is the pragmatist and needs administrative, organisational, marketing and communication skills. In many ways the manager is the "face" of the company and is most likely to be the role that comes into contact with customers most often. Remember, all three roles might be a single person; it's a case of wearing the right hat for each situation.

THE TECHNICIAN actually gets the work done. The entrepreneur thinks up the idea; the manager puts the

"There are three roles that the business owner must fulfil: the entrepreneur, the manager and the technician."

system in place and imposes deadlines; the technician builds the product. Without the entrepreneur there would be no ideas, no innovation. Without the manager, the technician would just do what he or she wanted whether or not it achieved any long-term goals. Without the technician, nothing would actually get built.

Anyone who's run a small business will probably recognise the technician in themselves more than any other. This is because most small businesses are set up by people good at something who decide they could make more money by doing it for themselves rather than an employer. The problem is that they then end up doing what they like rather than what is profitable and efficient. I've already mentioned the statistic that 50% of all businesses fail within five years. Michael Gerber would argue that this is because most businesses are "technician-driven" rather than having a balance between the three.

Action: You need to take an honest look at your list of skills and interests. Which of the skills within the three roles do you have at present, which are you prepared to learn, and which do you have no interest in?

Of the three, the manager is the easiest to outsource either to individuals (for example, your spouse) or to technology (for example, Backpack or Basecamp – more on these later in the book).

In my case, I was the typical technician. All I wanted to do was to spend days at a time coding away. However, to make a success of my businesses, I recognised the importance of the other two roles. I've therefore spent a lot of time adding to my entrepreneurial skill set, mainly through reading management books and the autobiographies of innovators. I've also developed my marketing skills through education and practice. Those skills I don't have and am not interested in – there are, after all, only so many hours in a week – I outsource.

In the first part of this book, we're focusing largely on the entrepreneur skill set as we go about identifying and assessing one or more business ideas. In the second part, the skills are largely those of the technician as we build the product and the technology to support it. In the third and fourth, the skills will be those of the manager as we market the product. A successful business depends crucially on spending time on each stage, rather than simply jumping in at stage two and hoping for the best.

Q&A

Lisa Gosling built an award-winning business (www.daisys dogdeli.co.uk) around her own skills and interests.

Q: What inspired you to start your business?
A: I am a qualified chef, so I decided to combine my two passions in life: dogs and food.

Q: What do you see as your main strengths when it comes to the business?
A: Passion and drive. You need bundles to keep you going, especially at busy times such as Christmas. Last year I baked for 36 hours without sleep!

Q: Did you originally intend the business to be your main occupation?
A: I've always worked in full-time employment, so it was a big decision to leave the security of a monthly pay cheque, but I took the plunge just over a year ago to concentrate on the deli. Best decision I ever made.

Q: What have been your main challenges?
A: Fitting everything in! There's never enough time – I always need at least another five hours in the day.

Q: What advice would you give to someone considering starting up an online business?
A: Really research every aspect. It can mount up, all the different services you need – hosting, payment gateway and so on – and you're sometimes tied into a year of payments. Also, spend as much money as you can afford on photos: I ended up wasting money trying to do it on the cheap, and it's such an important aspect of the website; customers are drawn further in by the way the first page looks.

Last but not least, before you "go live", get as many different types of people as possible to try out the website to make sure it's user-friendly.

Skills checklist

PHYSICAL
- ☐ Stamina
- ☐ Agility
- ☐ Fitness
- ☐ Building things
- ☐ Cooking
- ☐ Using machines and tools
- ☐ Gardening

ARTS
- ☐ Creativity
- ☐ Design
- ☐ Imagination

ANALYTICAL
- ☐ Logic
- ☐ Maths
- ☐ Forecasting
- ☐ Budgeting
- ☐ Administrative skills
- ☐ Setting goals
- ☐ Computer skills
- ☐ Computer programming
- ☐ Performance arts
- ☐ Improvisation
- ☐ Visual arts
- ☐ Crafts

EMOTIONAL AND INTERPERSONAL
- ☐ Teamwork and team building
- ☐ Negotiation
- ☐ Persuasion
- ☐ Listening
- ☐ Problem solving
- ☐ Customer service
- ☐ Teaching
- ☐ Coaching
- ☐ Leading
- ☐ Managing others
- ☐ Self-management
- ☐ Decisiveness

Which kind of internet business are you?

Finding out which category of business you fall into will help you shape your plans. Broadly speaking, the internet can facilitate businesses in three ways: supporting an existing bricks-and-mortar business; selling physical goods and services; and finally, selling online services and information.

Any business that doesn't have a supporting website is missing a trick. If nothing else, a well-designed site establishes credibility with your customers and tells them how to get in touch with you. Note that qualification: the site must be well designed, or at the very least it mustn't look as though it's fallen out of a £10 "build a site in a minute" box from PC World or been put together in PowerPoint using every available font and colour.

Many businesses depend entirely on the internet. It's the world's biggest product catalogue, and the majority of ecommerce is now conducted through companies who have no physical shop front.

SELLING GOODS It's in the selling of physical goods that the real-world benefits of using the internet as a marketing channel become so obvious. For example, if you wanted to set up your own small supermarket, there's no way you could compete with the integrated systems – both electronic, physical and marketing – that the big players such as Tesco now

employ. The cost of fitting out a store in an attractive way, adding the stock management and EPOS (electronic point of sale) systems and then employing enough staff is a huge investment that excludes almost everyone.

Compare this with setting up an online retailer. All the infrastructure – including stock management, product display and payment processing – can be purchased or rented at a low price. This makes it perfectly possible to give your visitors (almost) as effective an experience as they might have at, say, Play.com. Indeed, with services such as eBay shops and Amazon Marketplace, you can use the infrastructure of these companies to sell your products. That so few small online retailers actually create efficient sales processes is a pity, but it opens up gaps that you can exploit.

However, simply putting together a slick, efficient "sales funnel" (the process from choosing a product to paying for it) is not nearly enough to ensure success. If the product isn't right, the best shop in the world won't succeed: what having the right software does ensure is that you don't lose sales you should otherwise get.

Working with – or being – a web developer to create your own site from scratch (left) means you can make it more distinctive and professional than a ready-made shopfront within a service such as eBay (above). The result should be a more personal and compelling experience for your customers.

SELLING DOWNLOADS AND ONLINE SERVICES

The advent of the internet, and specifically broadband, has given rise to a whole range of new commercial products. The internet itself is the natural home for these, and in many ways they represent the ideal online business. Having no physical products means you don't need to buy any stock, store it or dispose of it if it doesn't sell. It becomes possible to keep an enormous range of products at no cost.

In fact, a whole new economy has been built around this "long tail", in which it's possible to make money by selling tiny quantities of thousands of different items, adding up to profitable revenue. Amazon is the most obvious case in point: it makes much of its profit from obscure books that aren't found in high-street bookshops.

There's also a huge market for online services. 37Signals (www.37signals.com) has made an entire business out of providing online organisational software, including its flagship Basecamp project-management service. Online accounting software FreeAgent (www.freeagentcentral. com) is, in my view, the most elegant UK-developed web application. Like Basecamp, FreeAgent is one of those rare software products that has radically altered how I work: in this case it has reduced the length of time it takes to keep my accounts up to date by around 90%.

You might also use the internet to sell your own internet-related skills. For example, if you're a copywriter, web designer or Google AdWords specialist, you'll use a website to sell your services. This can be similar to the website of a bricks-and-mortar business, but will need to be much more sophisticated and to reflect current trends, because as well as being a brochure it's a living, working example of your abilities. If you're a web developer, for example, you'd better make sure your site looks good. If you're an AdWords specialist, you'd better have an effective AdWords campaign of your own and plenty of further examples online.

Identifying the nature of your business is a crucial step in putting together your plan.

> "A new economy has been built around making money by selling tiny quantities of thousands of items."

Organisational tools such as 37Signals' Basecamp can help the smallest of businesses work efficiently enough to rival much larger companies.

SELLING INFORMATION

Enrol in almost any internet marketing guru's training course, and one method of making money will be pushed more than any other: information products.

These really do have a lot going for them. Usually created in the form of PDFs (such as eBooks), MP3s (such as seminars) or videos (the sky's the limit), they tend to be products that can then be sold for years with minimal change. They can be very quick to get into place, and they can be naturally slotted into Google's search engine so that you know the people visiting your site are actually looking for the information you want to sell.

Having said that, information products have their problems. The most fundamental of these is that web users increasingly expect information to be free. To charge for a product, you need to convince potential customers you can offer information that's not freely available elsewhere and that you're an expert in the relevant field.

One of my sites, www.passyourtheory.org.uk, can justify charging for access to our materials because the driving theory test database has been specially written so that it is very similar to the actual test – a task that took several months to complete. We also filmed our own set of Hazard Perception video clips that, again, are similar to those the learner will see on the day. The learner driver, then, is paying for access to those valuable resources – resources that are not available outside the site.

Our UK citizenship test site, on the other hand, failed because the information it sold could be found elsewhere. Furthermore, the expectations of your potential customers are getting more sophisticated, so the cost and time required to create your materials is going to be greater.

However, if you have specialist knowledge that you believe others will pay for – after all, this is the proposition behind most books, including the one you're reading now – then an information business can be easy to set up and highly profitable.

GOING YOUR OWN WAY

Given the sophisticated systems and ease of setup offered by eBay and Amazon, why would you want to go your own way and set up your own independent website?

The first and most important reason is that you get complete control of the setup, configuration and marketing of your site and its ecommerce software. For some businesses, this could be seen as a disadvantage – a barrier preventing you from simply getting started. If you wanted to start a business selling second-hand books, for example, Amazon Marketplace is the perfect platform to use. The margins per item are likely to be pretty low, but you get high-quality infrastructure, guaranteed traffic and specialised stock-management tools. ➡

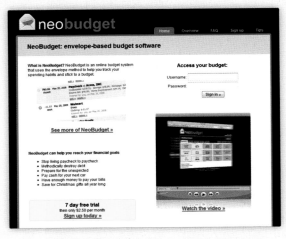

NeoBudget, an online personal finance service, uses the Spreedly customer service system to handle its recurring subscriptions.

→ However, for many product types, the choice is between an eBay shop and one of your own (or, indeed, evolving from one to the other, or even maintaining both). There's only so much customisation you can do to an eBay shop, and whatever you do, your shop will never feel like an entirely independent entity either to yourself or your customers. A substantial business will achieve greater credibility by appearing to be more professional and by being able to offer greater functionality with its own site – though exceptions will apply.

Daisy's Dog Deli (www.daisysdogdeli.co.uk) is a case in point. Compare the home page (see p12) with the Holistic Pet World store on eBay (also on p12). Although both are functional, I know which one I think looks more credible and professional. Lisa Gosling, creator of Daisy's Dog Deli, has been able to customise the design to suit her business, decide what additional information to include, and choose which ecommerce partner to work with; in this case, Actinic Express. Lisa's options when it comes to online marketing are much wider than if she had an eBay shop, as is her ability (or that of her web developer) to optimise the site for Google searches.

By creating your own site, you can implement a more sophisticated marketing strategy. When we get into Part 3 of this book, you'll see why this is so important.

 PAYMENT SOLUTIONS If you create a software product or download, you can either integrate your own shopping cart in a similar way to selling a physical product or you can use a specialist third-party application.

Digital River's share-it, for example, offers a complete ecommerce and delivery system. You can either have share-it store your software and supply a link to the purchaser or store it on your own server. Many different shopping carts include some support for downloadable products, but systems such as share-it offer sophisticated features such as registration key generation and trial versions, so if you're selling software there's little reason to look elsewhere. Costs range from 4.9% to 8.9%. You'll need your own website to publicise your product and act as a link into the share-it system.

This is also the case if you're planning on selling information products and online services. An information product can be delivered using most standard ecommerce products, but billing for an online service can be rather more complicated.

Most online services are paid for on a rolling basis, usually monthly, so your payment system needs to take account of this. For most service providers, this has traditionally meant writing their own recurring billing software, which is hideously complicated. The system needs to handle refunds, pro-rata payments, trial periods and changes of payment details along with a whole host of less usual occurrences – and this, on its own, is one of the major barriers between a great idea for an online service

> ## "You have a choice between an eBay shop and one of your own. A business will achieve greater credibility with its own site."

and its realisation. In fact, there's a significant danger that the subscription management system could take longer to perfect than the online service itself.

However, a service called Spreedly (www.spreedly.com) offers a solution by sitting between your service and a range of payment providers and handling repeated billing for you. Once integrated into your website, Spreedly will present the subscription options to your customer and you'll be able to retrieve that customer's current subscription status using the Spreedly API (the "application programming interface" that lets you connect a solution to your own software). While this isn't a simple process, it's much easier than doing it from scratch. At the time of writing, Spreedly charges $49 per month plus 40 cents per payment transaction, which is a fair price to pay for the rich functionality it offers.

If you plan to create your site using WordPress then there's a range of plugins available that enable you to add membership functions easily. The best of the bunch is WishList Member (http://member.wishlistproducts.com) which costs $97 for a single site and offers just about every feature you might need for a membership site.

Planning Start the right business **1**

Shops that sell for you

eBay

If you've decided to sell a physical product, you have two main choices when it comes to how you supply the infrastructure. The first is to hook into an existing provider's system. This is how eBay shops work: as an eBay "shop owner", you are simultaneously adding your goods to the search-based interface used by most shoppers, while also having a more traditional catalogue-style shop that your customers can browse.

The advantages of having an eBay shop, compared with listing each product individually, include the credibility, and thus the trust, they generate. Buyers are more likely to buy from a business than from a private individual, particularly for higher-value items. Your shopfront further reinforces this and makes it more likely that you'll get follow-up sales as buyers browse your shop.

All this results in a potentially increased conversion rate: the percentage of visitors who end up buying. Again, of course, it depends on exactly what you're selling.

The cost of running an eBay shop is a minimum £14.99 per month rental. You then pay an insertion fee and final value fee, all of which are very similar to the prices paid by private sellers for standard auction sales. However, you get a big discount on "Buy It Now" listings, where any buyer who decides to pay the stated price wins the item immediately, without having to wait for an auction to play out. Given that most shops operate almost entirely using this type of listing, big savings can be made.

You'll still need to sell a fair amount to recover your monthly rental in savings. However, if you decided to build your own site, you'd probably need to hire your ecommerce system, and the monthly eBay rental compares quite favourably with that expense.

Finally, along with eBay's fees you'll also be charged by PayPal for processing your customers' payments. All this needs to be borne in mind when you price your products.

As an example, let's say you want to sell a CD with a "Buy It Now" price of £9.99. You would pay an insertion fee of 10p and, if sold, a 9.9% Final Value Fee (99p). Then there's PayPal's processing fee of 3.4% + 20p: 54p in this case. So, ignoring any profit to be made on postage and packing, assuming you had only a single picture for the item, ignoring any VAT implications and not taking into account your rental fee, you'd be left with £8.36 net.

Amazon

Amazon's Marketplace offers many of the same advantages as the eBay shop system, but works in an entirely different way. First, you can only sell items that already appear in the Amazon system. This makes the process of adding items simple and intuitive: you simply search for the product in the usual way and click the "I have one to sell" button. You then specify its condition and set a price (Amazon Marketplace is not an auction).

Amazon charges a "completion fee" of 86p per item plus a "closing fee" of 17.25% of the sales price. Bear in mind that this includes what you would otherwise pay out as a payment processing fee, as Amazon uses its own system. Finally, Amazon also takes a "variable closing fee", which is deducted from the postage price that the buyer pays, the remainder going to you as a postage credit.

As an example, let's say you've sold a book at £9.99. You'll pay an 86p completion fee, a £1.72 closing fee and a 49p variable closing fee. However, you'll be credited with £2.75 to cover postage, leaving £9.67. Given that you only have to send books by second-class post, and this might cost less than £1, so – as with eBay – you can make a profit on that as well.

This explains why you'll see paperbacks advertised at 1p. The seller is paying only the completion fee and the variable closing fee, and making a profit on the postage. But you need to sell an awful lot to make that pay.

Businesses will want a Pro Merchant account. This has a £28.75 monthly fee (£25 if you're VAT registered), but the completion fee is waived, making it worthwhile if you sell more than 30 items per month. You also get inventory management tools to help upload and edit stock details.

> **"Buyers are more likely to buy from a business than from a private individual. Your shop-front reinforces this and makes it more likely you'll get follow-up sales."**

Coming up with your business idea

It's time to come up with that million-dollar idea. And it's all about you. Having gone through the exercise on pp10-11, you should by now have identified what you're good at. The extra dimension you need to add is how much each of these areas of skill or expertise really appeals to you.

In most cases, you'll probably find that those things you're particularly good at also happen to interest you, but it's important to put both of these factors together to arrive at a list of potential opportunities. Your chances of establishing a successful business are much, much greater if you develop it based on your skills and interests.

Let's take an example. In my case, "creativity" is at the top of my VIA Signature Strengths (see p10). I also think I'm good at making things, cooking and gardening. Immediately, then, I'm thinking about businesses that involve creating things. This might be a business that creates things itself, or a business that enables others to create those things. For instance, my love of cooking might push me towards opening a restaurant or starting a business developing recipes to help people produce wonderful food for themselves.

I also notice that no-one is advertising in Google with those keywords. If you see this in your own results, it's worth keeping a note, as this can mean one of two things: either there's no market, or you've spotted a market that no-one else has been able to exploit yet. Food for thought – pardon the pun – either way.

TURN ON THE RADAR In my view, most of the best business ideas come out of frustrations or opportunities spotted in everyday life. The idea for Passyourtheory.co.uk came about when standing in the queue in WH Smith behind someone buying a driving theory test CD-ROM. It suddenly occurred to me that it must be possible to offer this service online. The candle-making business idea came out of my extreme

"If no-one is advertising with your keywords, either there's no market, or you've spotted a market no-one else has exploited."

It may be that your own list of strengths doesn't immediately cause an idea to leap to mind. That's fine, because the purpose of this list is to make sure the ideas you do come up with fit in with what you're good at and what interests you.

One technique for generating business ideas is simply to Google your interests. If I Google "creative cooking", I get results including www.creativecook.co.uk (a spice company), creative cooking holidays, menu suggestions for men, ethnic cooking ideas and even how to cook creatively for people with medical conditions.

McDonald's Ray Kroc didn't invent burgers, but he saw a better way to run an existing business.

disappointment at the quality and cost of the retail kit I bought. Similarly, 37Signals' Basecamp product came out of their frustration, as a web design agency, with the email ping-pong that characterises web development projects.

Ray Kroc, founder of McDonald's, so admired the efficient way in which schoolchildren could turn out identical burgers like clockwork that he bought out Dick and Mac McDonald and established the biggest restaurant franchise in the world. Now, I'm not suggesting you'll necessarily want to take the approach of buying out an existing company (although, if done with care, that can be very successful), but you can be aware of what one company does well and apply it to another industry. Indeed, the McDonald's principle has been applied to many other businesses with great success.

I call this phase "turning on the radar", and it's more a frame of mind than anything else. For the next few weeks, critically analyse every commercial interaction you have. Look out especially for those that frustrate or disappoint you. Don't overanalyse, don't eliminate any at this point: the aim is to get a list of ideas to work on.

BRAINSTORMING We're all familiar with the technique of brainstorming, although it's rarely practised properly. The idea is to put analysis of the suggestions completely on hold at this point and simply generate ideas. Your skills and interests would be a good starting point. Contrary to popular belief, in my view, this is best done on your own. Human nature being what it is, it's next to impossible not to react to someone else's "stupid" idea, and this inhibits the process. The purpose here is to generate as many ideas as possible and not to allow snap judgements or instant decisions to veto them.

Here are the ideas I came up with at the end of my idea-generation phase:

1. **A daily Sudoku puzzle emailed to each customer's inbox every morning for printing**

2. **A "garden in a bucket" kit for people with limited garden space**

3. **A service to help migrants to the UK to pass their citizenship exams**

4. **A business selling kits enabling buyers to make their own candles**

EVALUATING YOUR IDEAS The mistake many, many business owners make is to fasten on to the first or most obvious idea and build a business around that. This is hugely risky, and is probably the main reason behind the high failure rate among small businesses: if your product doesn't have an audience, it doesn't matter how well you run your company or market the product, it will fail.

Equally, if you've generated a lot of ideas, there's no point in subjecting them all to a full market analysis, or you might end up wasting so much time that you never actually get started. So, as a first step, you need to apply the following criteria to your crop of business ideas:

CAN YOU MAKE MONEY AT IT? This may seem like a banal, obvious question, but you must honestly and objectively feel that there is a market for your idea. Unless you are truly confident that there is a market, reject the idea right now – however emotionally attached to it you might be. →

Affiliate schemes

You don't always need an original idea. One option is to find someone who's already operating in a market and become an affiliate. Typically, this involves creating and publicising a website that drives traffic to your partner. You receive a percentage of each sale. In a sense, this works in the opposite way to the traditional approach of developing businesses around what frustrates you about existing offerings: in this case you're looking for examples of excellent products and services.

You might imagine you'd find it irritating to be promoting someone else's product, but this is a quick and relatively painless way to start, and some schemes are extremely generous. The only cost to you (apart from web hosting) is marketing, usually via Google AdWords, and this can be controlled at a very fine level of detail.

Expert eye

Larry Heiman, Senior E-Myth Business Coach (www.e-myth.com), says your business should be built around your "Primary Aim".

"YOUR PRIMARY AIM IS YOUR DEFINITION OF yourself – the qualities you manifest when you're at your best. As coaches, we often describe it as your 'personal bumper sticker'. The Primary Aim is the process of finding the words to describe that essence of who you are; the source of your passion and drive.

"Once you have discovered your Primary Aim, your business should be a vehicle to nurture and fulfill that passion. Maybe there is something in the nature of the business itself that directly feeds that passion, so showing up every day completes the circuit. Or it may be that the business is simply the source of the fuel to provide you with the time, energy and wherewithal to be more completely living as your best self.

"Just as your business is a vehicle for your Primary Aim, the force of the Primary Aim is what drives you to visualise and build the business that will allow you to truly live your passion. It allows you the ability to put your life in perspective and helps you make conscious choices that are consistent with what is most important to you."

1 Planning Start the right business

Focus on what your potential customers are worth over a full 12 months. For example, a Basic plan on Basecamp is worth an initial payment of only £14.50, but over a year the customer will pay £175. This makes all the difference in the world to your marketing budget!

➜ Do you personally know people who'd buy your product or service? Do you know that lots of people might use it? For example, in the case of www.passyourtheory. org.uk, it was obvious that there was a big potential market since I knew that lots of people take their driving test every year. Other "good ideas" I've had don't pass this test: indeed, for every ten ideas, I only proceed to analyse one of them.

Action: Reject all ideas that you're not confident will make money – even if you love them.

HOW MUCH IS EACH CUSTOMER WORTH? Think about how the pricing of your product or service is likely to work. How much income can you expect from each customer per annum? If at all possible, pick a product or service that means you can establish a long-term relationship with your customers. You want to be able to sell repeatedly to them, since it's much cheaper to sell to existing customers than to find new ones.

As a general rule of thumb, you should be looking for an income of between £25 and £100 per customer per year. Why? Because it's almost always a mistake to try to occupy the low end of any market and compete on price alone. Remember, the income you're looking for is spread over a whole year, and knowing that your typical customer is worth, say, £100 per year means that your marketing budget can be set with this in mind. If your typical sale is only £10, you may baulk at the idea of spending £10 in AdWords

to attract that customer; but if you anticipate that the customer will then go on to spend another £90 in the first year, that £10 investment looks a bargain.

How do you know how much a customer will be worth? The simplest way is to look at any existing services: pick a value in the mid-range to get the level of a single sale.

Action: Reject all ideas that won't generate at least £25 per annum per customer. Be very wary of any idea that involves a single sale with no follow-ons.

CAN YOU SUM IT UP IN A SENTENCE? The famous "elevator pitch" is a great way of establishing if you have a focused, sellable business idea. Unless you can summarise your idea in a single sentence, you should be wary. First, you must communicate your business and what it offers in the limited space available in Google AdWords. Second, your website will get just a few seconds to grab a visitor's interest before they head elsewhere: it's rare that a potential customer who doesn't immediately "get it" hangs around long enough to buy.

Action: Reject any idea that can't be summed up in a single sentence.

GREAT BUSINESS WEBSITES

1&1 MyWebsite has been created to allow any business to have an attractive and functional website. With professionally written text and images relevant to your business, along with many other interactive and professional features, 1&1 MyWebsite is the perfect solution for getting your business online today.

1&1 MYWEBSITE FOR OVER 120 BUSINESS SECTORS

1&1

Call **0800 171 2631** or buy online

www.1and1.co.uk

Your business 0.1

It's possible that you'll reach this stage with no viable ideas left. That's fine – you've just saved yourself a fortune by eliminating your non-commercial business concepts. You now need to go back to the drawing board, give it a little time, and generate some more ideas to put through the same process.

Assuming you do have an idea or two left: well done. It's now time to give your nascent business a name. Isn't this a bit premature? After all, your more detailed research might still rule this business out before it even launches. However, your business name is essential to your marketing, so you need to know it before you can evaluate the size of the potential market.

Begin by looking at your "elevator pitch". Here's mine for the candle-making business:

> ## "A business selling high-quality, reusable and customisable candle-making kits to beginners."

Your elevator pitch will give you some initial Google search keywords that your potential customers will find you with. Indeed, if you've got it right, your one-sentence description should give you the most important keywords straight away. If not, are you sure it truly describes your business?

My prime keywords are "candle-making", "kits", "beginners" and "high-quality", in roughly that order of importance. Because of the way Google works, both in its "natural" search listings (those that aren't paid for) and AdWords (sponsored listings), you're automatically rewarded if your domain name includes the search terms used by your potential visitor. This manifests itself as a higher natural ranking for your site and/or lower AdWords costs.

The practical consequence of this is that your business domain name must include your most important keywords, and it also makes sense to name the business itself the same way. "What about Amazon?" I hear you cry. Neither its company name nor domain name include the word "book", after all. But stand by for a reality check: you *aren't* Amazon! Don't make your life more difficult by working against Google.

In my case, I settled on www.makingyourown candles.co.uk. My personal preference is for my domain names, where possible, to include a verb. So why not "makeyourowncandles"? That would have been easier on the ear, but remember, my keywords are "candle *making*".

The other ideas from my list that have made it this far are www.freesudoku.co.uk and

Case study 1: The idea

If you've read the introduction to this book, you'll already know that while writing it I created a real, functioning online business, which you can see at www.makingyourowncandles.co.uk. This idea came about when I bought a candle-making kit from a major craft-product retailer and was massively disappointed by the contents.

The product cost £11 and I estimated, after a little research, that the contents would have cost the manufacturer around £1.25. The fact that such kits exist at all is prima facie evidence of a market, so it ticks that box. Given the retail cost of the kits, it's not unreasonable to expect to be able to make £25 or more per year from the initial purchase and refills.

The "elevator pitch" is simple enough: a business selling high-quality, reusable and customisable candle-making kits to beginners. From that, I can generate my Google keywords and choose my domain name: www.makingyourowncandles.co.uk.

The idea for my business came from the shortcomings of a candle-making kit that I bought for my own use.

Is there a market for your business idea?

You've come up with some ideas: now you need to see if the market is there. It doesn't have to be huge, because you can succeed by hitting the right niche. The internet has many unique properties, but one of the most important is that it opens up a truly global market to anyone with a product or service.

The consequence of this is that products that wouldn't be viable within a single town, region or even country may have a big enough audience across the world. Some, of course, are specific to a country – PassYourTheory being one – and it's rarely a good idea to go global from the start, since marketing will need a different approach in each territory. Attempting to reach too broad a market too early is one of the prime reasons for online business failure, as your cash disappears into the Google AdWords black hole.

 YOUR NICHE The specific market you're targeting is your "niche". You should have some product or service ideas by now, and the next step is to consider who, exactly, is likely to be your target audience. This is an inexact science at this stage, since to some extent you can't predict exactly who is going to be attracted to your service or product enough to buy it. However, it should be possible to get a reasonable idea, which you can then amend as your business grows.

Remember, you should already believe that your business can make at least £25 per customer per annum and is based on your own skills and interests. You should also have your one-line "elevator pitch".

SO WHO IS IT AIMED AT? Think about your market and specifically look at:

1 The likely age range
2 Whether they're more likely to be male or female, or if there's no gender preference
3 Their interests and, most importantly, what other websites they're likely to visit

---

Web Show options...	Results 1 - 10 of about **235,000**

Litter **Training** your **Rabbit**
Litter **Training** Your **Rabbit** by Emma Magnus MSc. Over the past few years an increasing number of people have moved away from the traditional idea of keeping ...
www.apbc.org.uk/article7.htm - Cached - Similar

How to Train a **Rabbit** - wikiHow
If you want to teach your **rabbit** to come when called, start her **training** by ... Avoid overfeeding your **rabbit** during **training** sessions, and avoid using ...
www.wikihow.com/Train-a-**Rabbit** - Cached - Similar

Training Your **Rabbit** with a Trio of Tricks - For Dummies
If you let your **rabbit** run in a large area of the house, you may want her to come when you call her name. It will allow you to find her if she's hiding and ...
www.dummies.com/how-to/content/**training**-your-**rabbit**-with-a-trio-of-tricks.html - Cached - Similar

Rabbit Training - barneyandjemima.co.uk
How to train your **rabbit**: Toilet litter box **training** and behaviour **training**.
www.barneyandjemima.co.uk/**training**.html - Cached - Similar

If you have an idea for a rabbit-training product, there doesn't seem to be much competition. But is there a market for it?

Your product or service needs to be marketed in such a way that it feels natural to your target audience. If you personally represent that audience fairly well, look at the sites you visit on a regular basis. Look at the site design, language and graphics used and how they achieve a sale.

SIZE ISN'T (THAT) IMPORTANT It is possible to select a market that's too big. You'll find it hard to target your marketing and you'll be competing with large companies. You should be looking for a niche that, while it's big enough to sustain a business, is small enough to provide an opportunity for you to dominate. Even with a global market, some niches are too small to be worthwhile, and the purpose of this stage is to work out where your business fits.

YOU DON'T HAVE TO BE ORIGINAL One of the great myths that prevents many people from starting their

---

"Aim to find the weaknesses of your rivals and provide an experience at least as professional as the best big-name competitor."

own business is that you need a completely novel idea. Looking at a market, it's easy to feel intimidated by the competition. After all, these companies must be doing something right, surely? Not at all. The fact is that most businesses are poorly run, whether in terms of their core product, marketing, management, customer service or the conversion process. In difficult economic times, such businesses get weeded out as they cut down on marketing and product development (the very things that improve your chances of success), thus leaving gaps for you.

The key is to be better than your competition. In some markets this is easier than others, and the only way to find this out is to evaluate the quality of your competitors. You can make money by being better than your rivals if you:

1 Have a better product or service
2 Do better marketing
3 Offer supreme customer service
4 Produce at a lower cost

I recommend concentrating on the first two in this list. Unless customer service is built into your product and measurable (for example, if you're a delivery firm), it's hard to convince potential customers that your service is much better than their existing supplier – phrases such as "passionate about customer service" have been paid lip service too often by big corporations.

Producing at a lower cost is also something to avoid if at all possible; it's certainly not the basis of any business I'd be involved in. Margins are squeezed, and you're vulnerable to a big player coming into the market and undercutting you due to economies of scale.

You have the best possible chance of success if your product or service is measurably better than the competition and you employ better marketing techniques.

CHECK OUT THE COMPETITION You should know your main keywords as part of the process of coming up with a business name. Google them and see what comes up in the sponsored listings. Only pay attention to the first page, as this is where the real competition is.

Look at the ads. You're mainly interested in those that include the keywords you typed within their body, title and domain name. These ads have probably been created by a marketer who knows at least the basics of Google AdWords optimisation. Take a look at their website. Do they *only* sell a product or service like yours, or is it one of a big range? If you find a market where no-one is concentrating on selling a product like yours, but where many sell such a product alongside others, give that product a big tick.

Spend some time getting to know the sites and, specifically, the shopping process, of your competitors.

Case study
2: Search check

My main key phrase is "candle-making kit". Typing this into Google, I can see the number one position in the Sponsored Listings is occupied by Fred Aldous (a bricks-and-mortar craft retailer) with an ad that is not optimised and is therefore likely to be expensive. In the number two position is a general online craft retailer. Number three is a US-based craft retailer. Due to the cost of shipping heavy wax, this is unlikely to be a competitor.

Number four, bizarrely, is a Swedish castle specialising in weddings; heaven only knows which of my keywords triggered that! Number five is Amazon. Finally, number six is a gift retailer (and a potential supplier of our candle kits).

You'll also notice the Product Search results summarised above the natural listings. These are added by submitting your product to Google's Merchant Center (www.google.com/merchants). If you can achieve a high rank here, you're getting a lot of visibility for nothing.

My main conclusion from this is that none of my competitors is running a site dedicated solely to candle making (let alone candle-making kits), although there are companies selling kits among a range of products. These tend to be the cheap products that inspired MakingYourOwnCandles.co.uk, so there could well be a market for a higher-quality version supplied by us.

Given all this, it should be possible to create a highly optimised Google campaign, focused entirely on candle-making kits, that won't cost the Earth.

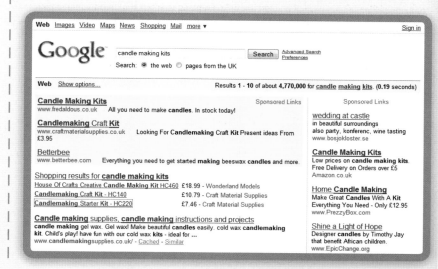

Concentrate first on the good-quality ads, identified using the criteria we described just now, but also take a look at those that appear in the top two positions in the Google results. It is possible to get a top position with a poor ad simply by paying a lot, so positions one and two are often occupied by big names. Take a look at this phase in our case study, above, for an example analysis.

Your aim is to find the weaknesses of your rivals so that you can provide an experience that is at least as professional as the best big-name competitor while being focused, personal and mercilessly efficient.

Analysing the market and the competition

As we've said, no matter what type of business you intend to set up, it's vital to analyse whether there's a market for your product or service and who's already in that market. But how? The simplest way is to estimate the number of Google searches that people are initiating for the relevant keywords.

Too many searches suggests your keywords are too broad and competition is likely to be fierce. Too few and the market might not be big enough. All you need to count them is a Google account. If you don't have one, sign up at www.google.co.uk: click Sign in, then Create an Account.

1 GET AN INSIGHT Go to www.google.com/insights/search to start Google Insights. This shows how search terms compare in terms of traffic over time as a percentage of total searches. To see this in practice, type in your two or three most important

keyword phrases, set your regional options to reflect your intended market, and click Search.

In my example, "candle making" has roughly five times more search volume than "candle making kits", but they tend to peak at the same time. The peak in April 2009 is in all likelihood due to the TV programme *Kirstie's Homemade Home*, in which Kirstie Allsopp made candles for her new house. Overall, the trend for both has been slightly negative until this year when, perhaps surprisingly, both have begun to trend upwards. One word of warning: remember the peaks and troughs are as a *percentage* of

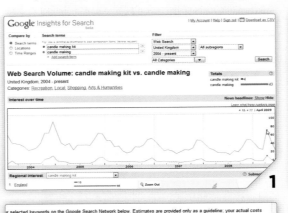

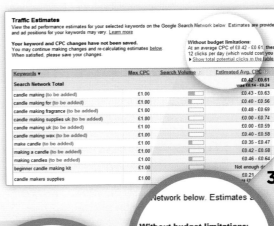

Google AdWords' Keyword tool gives you a rough idea of how many people will click on your advert and what it will cost you.

overall searches. They don't tell you whether the actual number of searches has risen or fallen, but rather whether your topics are relatively gaining or losing popularity. In this case, I'm happy they're holding up well over time.

2 **THE KEYWORD IS ADWORDS** We'll use the Google AdWords Keyword tool to estimate the number of clicks we'll get when we advertise. You need a Google AdWords account for this: see p128 to create it. Once you've signed up, go to the Keywords tool and type in the same keyword phrases you used for Insights.

The principle of Google AdWords is that you pay for your ad to appear in the Sponsored Listings whenever people search for a given keyword. Rather than paying a fixed fee up front, you pay each time a user clicks on your ad. (This takes the user to your own website, where it's up to you to persuade them to buy your product or service.)

The Keywords tool helps you see how this will work in practice. Enter some words, click Get Keyword Ideas and Google will present a list. Add those that seem appropriate to your list by clicking Add. The bar under "Advertiser Competition" shows how competitive each keyword phrase is. You needn't eliminate those where the bar is full or nearly full, but make sure you add any where the bar is empty or nearly empty, since you're likely to be able to advertise using those keywords for very little money.

Also bear in mind the estimates of search volume (local or global, depending on your target market). In very round terms, you want between 15,000 and 30,000 searches across your keywords if you're advertising in the UK, and 50,000 to 75,000 if you're advertising in the UK and US. Clearly, this depends on your specific product and its price level, but you're unlikely to want to bother with a product that generates 100 searches a month; equally, a market that gets a million searches is probably too big for you.

3 **CHANCES OF SUCCESS** Now click Estimate Search Traffic. The next page shows the expected number of clicks (times that users will click on your ad if you sign up for this keyword), the cost per click, and the position you'll appear in the Sponsored Listings. This is in contrast to the number of searches, which you saw on the previous screen. These figures need to be treated with extreme caution, since the actual percentage of searchers who end up clicking on your ad will depend on the quality of the ad. Increase the cost per click (CPC) value until all the keywords are predicted to appear at positions 1 to 3. This will give you a rough guide to what your competitors are paying to appear in those positions in the search results.

4 **YOU PAYS YOUR MONEY...** Now adjust the value down until you see the ads predicted to

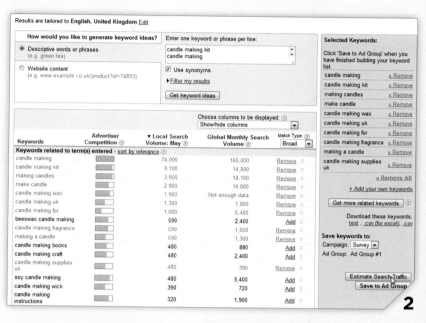

appear at positions 4 to 6. This will indicate what you might pay to appear on the first page of the results.

These figures are very, *very* rough. However, if they suggest, for example, that you'd need to pay £5 per click to achieve a front-page position for your £9.99 product, you might want to think again. Every time a potential customer clicks on your ad, you'll pay Google this amount; the average profit you expect to make out of that customer – taking into account that most people who click the ad won't end up buying anything at all – needs to justify that outlay.

On the other hand, if you can get a front-page position for 10p per click, things are looking rosy: this means competition in your market is not so intense that there's no room for you to start a viable business. In my case, it looks as though I will be able to pay around 10p to achieve a front-page advert for both the keywords "candle making" and "candle-making kit".

I expect a conversion rate for a first sale to any particular customer of around 5%, so I need 20 visitors to make one sale. At 10p, that means my marketing will cost approximately £2 to generate that first sale, and I can now use that figure in working out my costs. Future sales to the same customer will, of course, cost much less.

With www.makingyourowncandles.co.uk, then, Google suggests that I can expect around 100,000 searches per month. I would expect around 5% of those searchers to visit my website, so that's 5,000 visitors. Approximately 5% of these (250) will buy from me as a first-time customer. Clearly, if any of those figures change, the end results could be completely different – but it looks as though there might be a viable market there.

Enter the keywords you think are relevant to your business, and Google will generate more that you may want to investigate. The great benefit here is that everything is based on real search data.

Ask them what they want!

When it comes to running a business, you can't base decisions on gut instinct. You need to find out the triggers that will make prospective customers buy. Too many would-be entrepreneurs tear headlong into business without doing the most basic market research. You've now established that there's a market for your idea, but that doesn't tell you enough about exactly what sort of product or service will do well in that market.

Larry Heiman (pictured left), senior business coach for E-Myth Worldwide (www.e-myth.com), says: "A successful prospective business owner needs to know who their customers are and what they must do to satisfy them as completely as possible, and be able to do so consistently." Fortunately, there's an absurdly simple way of finding out exactly what shape your product should take in order to sell: *Ask your potential customers.*

The classic way of doing this is with the "Three question survey" popularised by Glenn Livingstone (www.glennlivingstone.com). Three questions may not seem a lot but, well chosen, they can ensure you head in the right direction with your product development; and the shorter the survey, the more likely you'll get a good response. For an information product business, the three questions might be:

1 What were you searching for when you found us?
2 What do you want to know?
3 How hard are you finding it to get this information currently?

The most profitable information businesses will be those where survey respondents are finding it very hard to get the information you're going to provide, so question 3 is essential. Question 2 will help you shape exactly what goes into the product and will also help to identify "hyper-responsive" customers. Very broadly speaking, the more words a respondent uses in answer to question 2, the more likely they are to be interested in the product.

"We picked a price we'd feel comfortable paying ourselves."

For a product or service business, you might ask:

1 Are you searching for your own benefit or for someone else?
2 What are you looking for in this product?
3 What would be a reasonable charge for this product?

In the case of a product (as opposed to a service), question 1 might ask if they're buying it as a gift. Whatever questions you choose, the end result needs to be that you have a clear idea of what form the product or service needs to take and how much you can charge for it. Bear in mind, however, that if you're developing a novel product, your customers may not know what a reasonable price would be.

I asked Jason Fried (left), Founder and CEO of 37Signals, how he came up with his initial pricing for the web-based collaboration tool Basecamp. "We guessed. We guessed pretty well. We've made a few minor tweaks since then, but for the most part our prices have been stable for the past few years. At the end of the day we had to pick prices that we'd feel comfortable paying ourselves."

CoffeeCup

CoffeeCup Web Form Builder is an alternative to SurveyMonkey for creating and hosting online surveys, customer feedback and contact forms. It's a paid for service, but you can download a trial from www.coffeecup. com/web-form-builder.

STEP BY STEP Use SurveyMonkey to create your own online survey

1 **CREATE AN ACCOUNT** Go to www.surveymonkey.com and create a free account. This allows you to create surveys with up to 100 respondents. If you find you need more, you can upgrade to a paid account. Click Create Survey and give your survey a name.

2 **ADD A DESCRIPTION** Click Add Question Here and select "Descriptive Text" as the question type. This isn't a question at all, but allows us to add informative text: in this case I'm reminding the respondent what they're going to get for completing the survey. Click Save Question.

If you want to get a good response, you'll need to offer something in return. With an information product, standard form is to give away a copy to all survey respondents (after all, this costs you next to nothing). With an online service, you would give away free access for a period of time. If you're selling a physical product, either give away a sample or, at the very least, offer a substantial discount.

3 **CHANGE QUESTION TYPE** Add another question to your survey. This time select "Multiple Choice (Only One Answer)". Add one option per line, and make sure you click Add Comment Field

if you're not certain that you can anticipate all possible answers: this gives users the option of responding in their own words. Click "Require Answer to Question" to prevent them finishing before picking an answer.

Repeat this process with the remaining questions choosing Comment/Essay Box if you want to ask an open question. Finally, add two additional text fields: one for the user's name and the other for their email address.

4 **START YOUR SURVEY** Click Collect Responses to generate an HTML link that you can embed in your website or send out in an email.

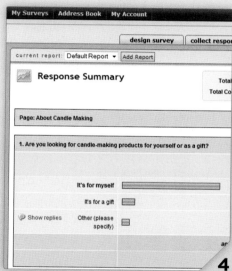

The simplest way to get survey respondents is to set up a minimal website, embed the survey link into it and advertise on Google. I describe how to create a WordPress website in Part 2; you could even use a free WordPress.com account, but I'd recommend installing it on your own domain name. This is because Google rewards sites that have been around for a while with lower advertising costs, making it cheaper when you eventually launch your site.

Find some free articles relating to your product at www.articlesbase.com to populate your home page so that Google sees your site as relevant – again reducing ad costs. Then create a Google Ad that will appear against your main keywords. Invite people to complete the survey and ensure you include the inducement in the ad.

Set a low daily budget and end the survey when you get enough responses. I ran the www.makingyourowncandles.co.uk survey until I had just under 100. As shown in step 4, above, 86% of respondents were buying for themselves – a figure that was unlikely to change much, however many responses I waited for. In the free-format responses to the question "What is the appeal of candle making?" the word "creative" came up a lot, and that will strongly influence the make-up of my product and its marketing. Finally, the most popular price was £15.

This demonstrates the power of surveys. I would have guessed that most people looking for candle-making kits would be buying them as a gift and would expect a lower price. And I'd have been wrong on both counts.

Planning your website

Your online business not only needs a website, it needs the right type of website. Before you think about design, it's essential to find a basic structure that suits your business.

Your website has a single purpose: to sell. In order to do that, however, it needs to achieve the following:

- **Capture the attention of your visitors**
- **Retain that attention**
- **Enable you to begin a long-term relationship with your visitors**
- **Convert visitors into buyers through an efficient checkout process**
- **Establish credibility**
- **Reassure potential purchasers with good contact and support features**
- **Provide best practice and legally required information**

Much of this will be achieved through the specific content of the pages in your site: good copy and reliable technology, for example. However, the structure of the site needs to be planned in advance so you can be sure you've included everything necessary. Most websites include these pages:

- **A home page** This is your front door, so get it right
- **Landing pages** The pages visitors see when they respond to your Google AdWords or email campaigns
- **About us** A page describing the company and your team. This is an opportunity to humanise your business. If you're a limited company, it's a legal requirement to include your registered address
- **Contact us** Visitors need a place to ask questions, and to see that you'll support them if they buy from you
- **Privacy policy** Visitors need to know that you will treat their details with respect. Here's the place to tell them
- **Products/services** A list or catalogue of your products and/or services. Unless there is a *very* good reason not to, you should always include prices
- **Delivery policy** Potential purchasers will want to know when they can expect their products to be delivered, whether they're physical or electronic. Same-day despatch is becoming expected for physical goods, and next-day is the bare minimum. For electronic goods, users expect instant delivery

"The core of your site will probably remain the same, but you need to be able to add and remove pages to respond to needs that arise."

Tip

Take a look at rival websites. What do you like about how they're organised? What don't you like? Also look at http://mybusiness.1and1.co.uk. This is a service that creates tailored websites for different types of business, and 1&1 (a hosting company) has researched the most popular site structure for each business type. There's nothing to lose if you sign up for a free trial – no credit card is required – and see what site structure is suggested.

USING MEDIA Typically, video and audio are used to show a product or service in use. Video is often in the form of a screencast showing software being operated; increasingly, physical products are also demonstrated. The closer you can bring the visitor to the experience of turning the product over in their hands, as in a shop, the better your chance of making a sale. Don't forget, many people are still nervous of buying online, and the more you can do to allay those fears, the better your chance of making a sale.

ORGANIC STRUCTURES Having said all this, the structure of your website shouldn't be set in stone. The core will probably remain the same, but you need to be able to add and remove pages to respond to the needs of your visitors and marketing campaigns as they arise. By creating your site in a content management system such as WordPress, you retain this flexibility.

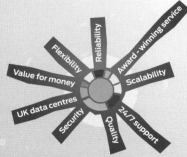

Getting ready for business

You now know what you want to sell and how much the market will pay for it. But how much will it cost to provide? Clearly, if you can't develop the product or service for significantly less than you sell it for, you don't have a viable business. It's time to work out the details and put them together into a business plan that shows how you can make money – both for your own benefit, and to convince your bank or investors.

Your costs will depend on the type of business you're setting up. For an information product, production costs can be negligible: all it costs you is the time it takes. In most cases an information product is downloadable, but even a physical book can be published by services such as www.lulu.com at no cost to you.

For a physical product, on the other hand, costs are likely to be significant. It may be that you're buying in complete products (most likely from a wholesaler) and selling them on. In this case, the production cost is the price you pay to your supplier. If you're assembling a product from component parts, it's the cost of those parts plus any packaging. This is what we're doing with www.makingyourowncandles.co.uk (see opposite). If you've invented a product, it's the production cost plus packaging.

Now, compare the price your customers are willing to pay with the cost of production. This will give you your gross margin. What is a good margin? That depends very much on the market, but I aim for at least a 100% gross margin. While that may sound a lot, out of it needs to come the cost of doing business and, particularly, marketing.

Finally, a software service is the hardest of all to price. As with inventing a new product, the bulk of the cost in this case comes up front in development. If this is going to be expensive, you need to be very sure of your market before going ahead, since it may take some time to get that money back. Our site www.passyourtheory.org.uk was an example of this: it cost a lot to develop up front, but has remained, at its core, largely unchanged since 2005, repaying that investment many times over. Of course, had it not found a market, we would have faced a loss. The more

Expert eye

To dig underneath why people set up in business – or at least why they should – I spoke again to Larry Heiman, Senior Business Coach for E-Myth Worldwide (www.e-myth.com).

"TO TRULY CREATE A WORLD-CLASS COMPANY, IT IS essential that you have a clear business vision, or Strategic Objective, as we call it at E-Myth. Your Strategic Objective is a picture of your business when it is complete. Whether you plan on selling your business or working behind your desk every day for the rest of your life, it is imperative you know where you're going so you can guide the development of the essential processes and systems to get you there.

"Your Strategic Objective is a detailed picture of your vision of what your business will be when fully developed. It helps guide your employees, what areas of the business you focus on, your strategic goals and planning, and the overall leadership of the company.

"Your job as a business owner is to be an entrepreneurial leader. To do that, you must not only understand who you are and what you stand for, but also what it is you want to create. What is the legacy you want to leave behind? What result do you want for your employees, clients, family and community?"

Some businesses are simpler than others. Lulu lets you sell books both through your site and through Amazon with no upfront costs.

it's going to cost to bring your product to market, the more thorough your market research needs to be before you start.

BUSINESS PLAN Every business needs a business plan. Exactly what form it will take depends on whether...

1 ...you're going to need to get finance
2 ...it's a full- or part-time business
3 ...you're forming a separate company

I certainly don't believe in creating documents for their own sake and, as a rule, I suggest spending only as long as is necessary on your business plan. If you're approaching a bank for finance (or even for a bank account), you will need more detail in your plan than if it's purely for your own use. BusinessLink (www.pcpro.co.uk/links/businesslink) has a thorough guide to creating your own business plan.

By now, you should know a lot of what will go into your business plan, and creating the plan itself is simply a process of structuring that information. By going through the sections in the BusinessLink guide, you can be sure you've covered everything.

Above all else, keep your vision front and centre. Why are you setting up in business?

ACCOUNTING AND ADMIN I recommend getting your accounting sorted out before you get going. FreeAgent (www.freeagentcentral.com) is my favourite online book-keeping service and, in fact, one of my all-time favourite web applications. It makes the process of keeping the books up to date as simple as it could possibly be, and ensures that you're always aware of tax deadlines and amounts.

For organisation, I recommend Backpack (www.backpackit.com) from 37Signals. It's a flexible organisational tool that you can use in any number of ways to ensure you keep track of what you need to do, as well as forming a repository of contacts and data.

Case study
3: Defining the product

For MakingYourOwnCandles, our research indicated that we needed to aim at around £15 for our core product. We knew we had to include all the components necessary to create a batch of candles (ten in our case). We also felt it was important to use good-quality components, since our aim is to sell repeatedly to our buyers, and one aspect that differentiates us from the competition will be quality. Of course, quality is likely to cost more, so it's a challenge to get the balance right.

We began by working out what we should include. We did that by trying other kits; by looking online at what was available; and, most importantly, by making candles ourselves. We experimented with materials until we came up with the ideal combination. I then spent many hours researching suppliers until I worked out the minimum costs I'd need to pay.

We kept our core range limited: a series of kits differentiated only by their scent/dye combination, plus a refill kit and a few accessories. This means our customers will have more choice than with standard kits, but without facing the bewildering array of options offered by specialist retailers. It also means we can hope for follow-up sales of refills, accessories, oils and dyes.

A 100% margin would mean the most we could pay for the contents of our kit would be £6.50 (the retail price includes VAT, so the net price is lower). This includes the cost of packaging; in this case, a white box purchased on eBay with a home-printed sticker.

I can't emphasise enough how important it is to get the product exactly right both in terms of features and presentation. Don't short-cut the process of researching and sourcing, or you'll regret it later.

"Good quality would differentiate us from the competition. Of course, quality costs more."

Finding the money

However efficient you are, no business can be launched on a budget of zero, so you need to establish what money you need to get off the ground – and how you're going to raise it.

Your first job is to find out how much money your business needs to generate. This breaks down into finding the money to do four things, which we'll look at in turn:

1 Develop your product or service
2 Market it
3 Run your business
4 Live!

1 **DEVELOPMENT** The cost of developing your product or service will vary greatly depending on what you're selling. If you intend to go freelance in your day job, for example, there's no cost unless you'll be investing in training to polish up or widen your skills.

Information products tend to be relatively cheap to develop; usually the main cost is time, plus, if there's a physical vehicle such as a book, the production cost. For physical products, the figure you're looking for is the cost to establish a sufficient stock to get started. If you're selling a range of products, an essential part of your market research is to establish which are likely to sell best. Remember, internet shoppers have no patience: they expect delivery

There's more to internet advertising than Google AdWords, but you should get AdWords right before moving on to Microsoft's Bing.

have to pay per click and what your conversion rate (the proportion of the users who click your ad who go on to buy something from you) is likely to be.

If you're paying 10p per click and expect a conversion rate of 2%, each conversion is going to cost £5. It's then a matter of deciding how many customers your marketing is likely to send to your site. If 50,000 people search on your keywords every month and you achieve a

> **"Many would-be entrepreneurs believe the best way to fund their business is through investors. As a rule, this should be a last resort."**

within a couple of days, so you need to prepare for demand. Aim to have at least a week's stock in place.

Software development is tricky to estimate. Notoriously, it takes far longer to put together fully working software than you expect. It also suffers from the disadvantage that your costs are largely up front: you can't find out for certain whether the market is big enough to support your software until it has been developed.

2 **MARKETING** Most online businesses market themselves largely online. The beauty of systems such as Google AdWords, and Microsoft adCenter is that you can control very closely how much you spend and get almost instant performance feedback. When it comes to setting your budget, look at how much you're likely to

clickthrough (the percentage of people seeing your ad who click it) of 5%, you'll have 2,500 visitors. At a 2% conversion rate, those 2,500 visitors will produce 50 sales. These sales will have cost you £250 – so, if you wanted maximum sales in that month, this would be your advertising budget. In most cases, however, you'll want to limit your marketing spend to begin with because you'll need to optimise your campaign and can expect to improve its effectiveness by an order of magnitude within weeks. So you won't want to spend as much early on, when your campaign is less efficient.

You also need to take into account the likely cost of developing your website, and any offline marketing.

3 **RUNNING YOUR BUSINESS** You must budget for the day-to-day cost of running the business. This includes any office expenses, staff costs, stationery, hosting, software, equipment, insurance and any accountancy or other professional advice.

4 **MONEY TO LIVE ON** If this is a sideline business or you have another income, it may not be necessary to draw money out at the beginning, which will help you get started and profitable more quickly. Try to draw the absolute minimum out of the company until it's standing on its own two feet and making a steady profit.

WHERE TO GET THE MONEY Many would-be entrepreneurs believe the best way to fund their business is by attracting investors. This could range from six-figure sums from venture capitalists (a rare breed these days) right down to a few hundred quid lent by your parents.

As a rule, however, borrowing from investors of any sort should be a last resort. Commercial investors will expect part ownership – and thus partial control – as part of the deal. This is your business, and *you* should control it.

Another downside of external investment is that it can lead to long-term resentment. The business world is littered with examples of entrepreneurs giving away equity (ownership) in return for money to help start up, only for the investor to continue to have control and receive dividends years later when their input is in the distant past. This happened to me, and I know how hard it can be.

Borrowing from family is, depending on your family, usually a better idea, since they will care about your success as a person too. My recommendation is to borrow in the form of a loan that you repay at a fixed rate (including interest) over a fixed period. That way, your relative gets a good return but doesn't end up owning part of the company.

You might also consider borrowing from a bank. In the current economic climate this might be easier said than done, and will depend on a good business plan. If you're setting up a limited company, you will be asked for a personal guarantee covering the overdraft or loan if your business fails. At the other end of the scale, if you have a good credit rating you may be able to obtain an unsecured loan for a few thousand pounds with little paperwork.

The very best option is to borrow from yourself. If you're lucky enough to have savings, think about whether you can afford to ring-fence part of those to fund your business's early days. Keep a record of your investment and pay yourself back at a reasonable rate. Alternatively, many business owners make use of overdrafts and credit cards.

In the case of MakingYourOwnCandles, we estimated the cost of starting and running the business for three months (by which time we'd know if it was going to be a success or not) at £750, and this manageable amount was funded from another business we were operating.

There are many sources of funding for a new business, but if you can fund it yourself you'll avoid the need to give up part ownership or spend years tied to your initial investors.

Less is more: 37Signals

37Signals, creator of the Basecamp project-management service, has made a business out of "building less" to get its software out there earning money and gaining customers. Its book *Getting Real* (you can read it free at http://gettingreal.37signals.com/toc.php) covers this principle in depth, but here's the company's explanation in a nutshell.

"Conventional wisdom says that to beat your competitors you need to one-up them. If they have four features, you need five (or 15, or 25). If they're spending x, you need to spend xx. If they have 20, you need 30.

"This sort of one-upping Cold War mentality is a dead end. It's an expensive, defensive and paranoid way of building products. Defensive, paranoid companies can't think ahead, they can only think behind. They don't lead, they follow.

"So what to do then? The answer is less. Do less than your competitors to beat them. Solve the simple problems and leave the hairy, difficult, nasty problems to everyone else. Instead of one-upping, try one-downing. Instead of outdoing, try underdoing."

This might seem counter-intuitive, but by focusing on the central problem your software is solving, rather than simply competing on the features your competitors include, you will be able to develop it more quickly, and the end result will be simpler, more focused and, crucially, different to the competition.

37Signals has developed a range of successful online applications, all of which remain closely wedded to its original core principles.

2 Building
Create the right website

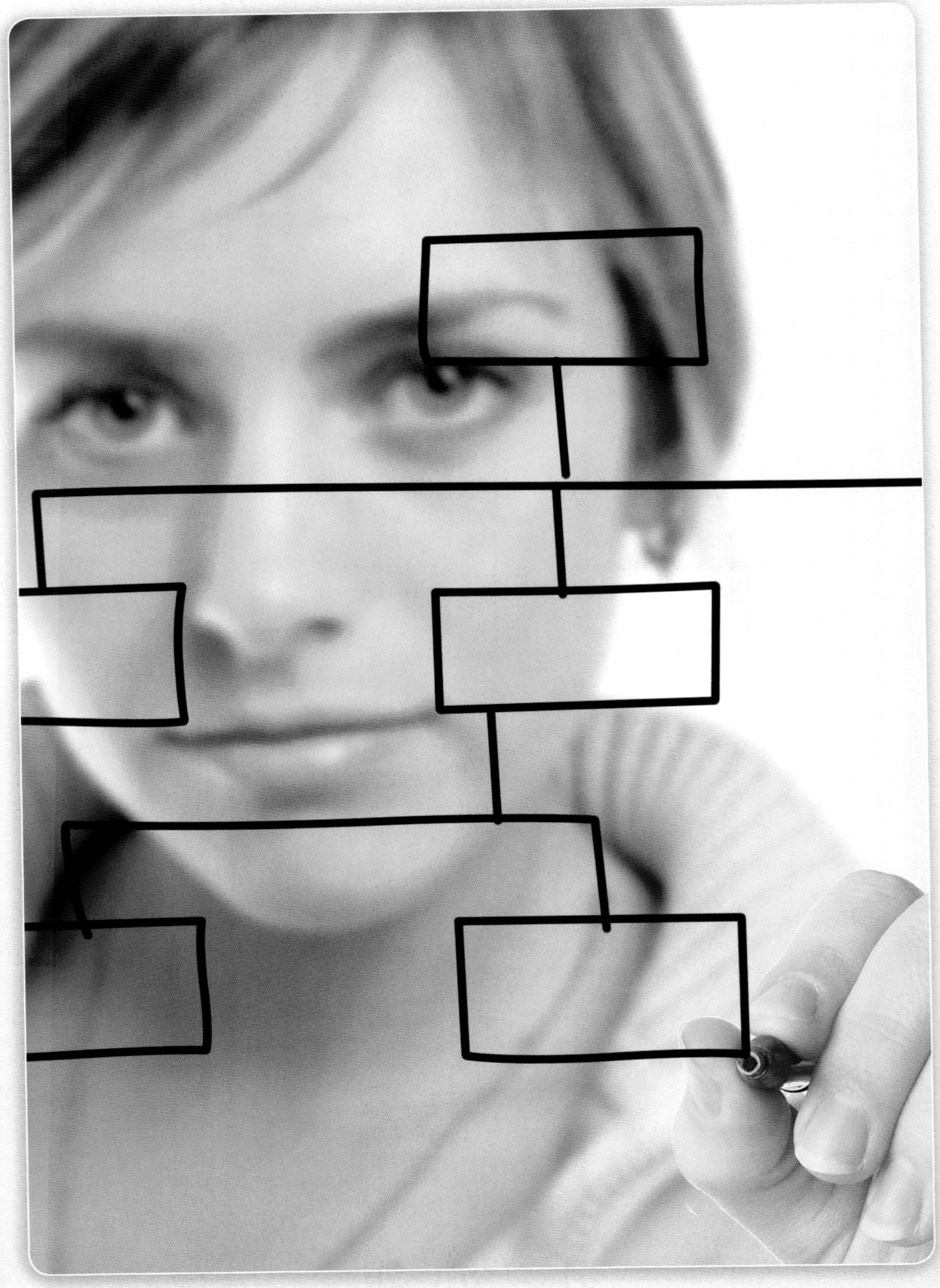

PART 2 Building

Create the right website

Finding a home for your business

Choosing a base for your business used to mean selecting a shop or office. An online business interacts with its customers via the internet, so the choice now is what form of online presence you need. This will serve two main purposes: to persuade the customer to buy and to act as a shopping cart.

Most businesses will also include support and background information, but the main purpose of the website is to get people to buy. A site is made up of HTML pages, along with images, sounds, videos and scripts. Broadly, you have a couple of choices when it comes to where these files are stored and served from.

The simpler option is to have your site hosted on a server owned and operated by someone else. This often means you can use your host's framework to build your internet presence very quickly with little technical knowledge. eBay is a good example of a system that not only hosts your site but also provides the tools to build it.

A number of hosts provide site-creation tools that offer a template-driven approach to site building. This has inevitable limitations, but modern templates offer sites with a professional sheen that can be produced in minutes. Examples include Volusion and 1and1's MyBusiness Site.

DO IT YOURSELF The second option is to rent a web server, or space on a shared server. Generally this means your development process takes longer, but you get full control. As well as being able to construct your site exactly the way you want, you can move from one host to another if you're dissatisfied with their service or, more positively, if your business grows to the extent that you need a dedicated server with higher performance.

So which option should you choose? If you sell physical goods, the quickest way to get started is to use a provider such as eBay to build a shop. You can then test the size of the market for your goods quickly and at low cost before, perhaps, upgrading to your own independent shop.

If you sell services, information products or software then, in most cases, you will be better off renting your own space and building a site of your own, even if your shopping cart is handled by a third party.

Ultimately, most online businesses will benefit from being self-hosted and self-developed. A template-derived site might be fine for a plumber, but it doesn't offer the range of services and control that a more ambitious business will require.

Web hosts' packages are becoming increasingly innovative, with one.com's Cloud Drive service providing online backup, automatic synchronisation and access to all of your data using any internet-enabled device as part of the deal. Naturally, its web-hosting packages have also been created with all the tools you need to get your website online, including a domain name, web space and unlimited email.

Content management systems

When it comes to setting up your own website, on your own domain, just as you want it, you'll need somewhere to start. A content management system (CMS) offers an alternative to doing it all from scratch. For our purposes, a CMS is a ready-made system that enables you to create and edit a website without needing to code it by hand. Once installed on your web server, a CMS can be used to set up and edit the appearance, content and capabilities of your site through a browser-based user interface.

In short, content management systems are:

- **Quick to get up and running,** so you can create a fully working customised site in a few hours
- **Extendable through plug-ins**, making it possible to incorporate additional functionality, often free
- **Reliable and continually updated,** if you choose one of the big players

On the other hand, CMSes are not without their disadvantages. If your site is likely to be *very* simple, the benefits of using a CMS may be outweighed by the bother of installing one. If you're more ambitious, bear in mind that you're limited to the CMS's functionality (albeit extended through plug-ins), and if you

need something specific you might find it doesn't exist. You could create a new plug-in yourself, or hire someone to do so, but this isn't a process for the faint-hearted.

There is one further option, which is to create your site from scratch (or hire a web developer to do it) and incorporate one of the plethora of "micro-CMSes" into it. In this case, the web developer incorporates special fields into the editable pages and the micro-CMS provides an interface for you to update and add content to without needing to edit the HTML itself. A good example is Perch (www.grabaperch.com) from UK design agency edgeofmyseat.com.

TAKE YOUR PICK The three leading players in affordable content management are

WordPress, Joomla and Drupal. All three are open source, free and written in PHP, which means they'll work with most web hosts. If you're looking for the most fully featured CMS with the best support for multiple authors and detailed user management, choose between Drupal and Joomla (with Drupal edging it for most purposes in my view), but as our task is to create an everyday business website, WordPress is by far the best choice.

WordPress is simpler to install and, especially, to get working. It has a wide range of plugins available that extend its functionality (such as shopping carts), and there are thousands of themes from various developers, many free, to change its look and feel. As these are essentially CSS, they can be amended to give you exactly the front end you want.

Joomla is ideal for small company websites where collaboration is part of the functionality on offer. For our example project, however, it's slightly more complex than necessary.

Content management systems are the basis of all kinds of websites, from simple blogs to fully featured commercial sites, enabling them to be set up quickly and at low cost and maintained easily.

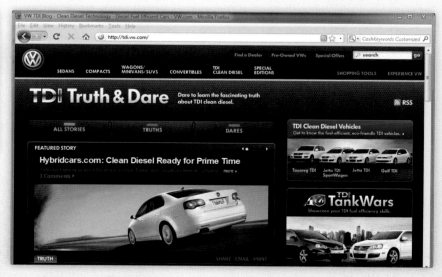

Principles of good web design

The likes of WordPress and Joomla can take much of the hard work out of creating a website, but whether you're using a content management system, a more basic template or building your site from scratch, you need to understand the basics of design if you want to make a good impression.

Design students will have heard of the "Golden Ratio". This number (1.61803399 or thereabouts) describes how the size of the elements of a building, a work of art or, in our case, a web page should relate to each other to give a pleasing effect. If I decide the area of my web page that will be occupied by my copy (text) is going to be the biggest – as it usually should be – then I should make it 1.62 times wider than the smaller column containing my navigation and logo.

There are various theories to support the Golden Ratio, but why not just get on and use it? In fact, I recommend an even simpler approach, which in turn will be familiar to photographers: the Rule of Thirds. If you have one column 1.62 times wider than the other, the smaller column occupies roughly one third of the overall width and the bigger one two thirds. So you can get almost exactly the same effect by dividing your page into three.

Whichever way you achieve it, balance is one of the key aspects of design that separates the professional site from the amateur.

WHITE SPACE One of the other defining elements of a professional design is the active use of white space. White space is any area that doesn't contain text or graphics. It doesn't have to be white, just empty. Amateurs cram their websites full of text and images, all jostling together. Designers use white space to separate elements and, in designer-speak, "give them room to breathe". Take a look at just about any professional website, even the notoriously information-rich Amazon, and you'll see how white space is used. It makes a page look more pleasing and, if you want a more mercenary justification, helps draw the user's eye to the parts you want them to pay attention to.

"Whichever way you achieve it, balance is one of the key aspects of design that separates the professional from the amateur."

Windows fonts / Mac fonts / *Font family*	
Normal style	**Bold style**
Arial, Arial, Helvetica, *sans-serif*	**Arial, Arial, Helvetica, *sans-serif***
Arial Black, Arial Black, Gadget, *sans-serif*	**Arial Black, Arial Black, Gadget, *sans-serif***
Comic Sans MS, Comic Sans MS[5], *cursive*	**Comic Sans MS, Comic Sans MS[5], *cursive***
Courier New, Courier New, Courier[6], *monospace*	**Courier New, Courier New, Courier[6], *monospace***
Georgia[1], Georgia, *serif*	**Georgia[1], Georgia, *serif***
Impact, Impact[5], Charcoal[6], *sans-serif*	**Impact, Impact[5], Charcoal[6], *sans-serif***
Lucida Console, Monaco[5], *monospace*	**Lucida Console, Monaco[5], *monospace***

Only certain fonts are normally used for text on web pages, since others aren't likely to exist on the majority of computers.

The BBC's website is a perfect example of the Rule of Thirds. Each page is divided into three vertical columns, with some elements spanning two columns to give an approximate Golden Ratio of two-thirds to one-third. The colour scheme is basically analogous (using tints of one colour for a calm feel), but some elements are colour-coded with other hues; a consistent medium level of saturation (how vivid the colours are) helps to tie everything together.

An immediate way to add white space to a typical web page is to increase the line height to at least 1.5 times its standard setting (150%); I prefer a setting of 175%.

COLOUR The key to coming up with a colour scheme is to begin with a base colour. If you have a logo, the base colour can be taken from the dominant colour in it. If you need inspiration, I suggest browsing the web for colours you like. Bear in mind that each colour invokes a different emotion in the user, so take care before making your final choice. You can find out more about this at www.color-wheel-pro. com/color-meaning.html. If you aim to sell globally, you may need to consider the cultural implications of your colours.

Once you've picked a base colour, find out its colour value. This is usually given in hexadecimal notation, where the numbers 0 to 9 have their usual meaning and the letters "a" to "f" then take you up to 15. You don't need to worry about this as long as you remember that the first two figures represent red, the second pair green, and the final pair blue. The higher the number (00 being the lowest, ff the highest and 88 somewhere in between), the more red, green or blue is in the final colour. By mixing these, you can create any colour visible to the human eye; in fact, that's exactly how your computer screen displays its range of colours.

COLOUR SCHEMES One way of representing the full gamut of colours is in the form of a colour wheel. Whether two colours work together can be seen from their positions: opposite colours are "complementary", so they create maximum contrast and balance when used together, while colours close to each other are "analogous", giving a more laid-back feel.

You can use Adobe's free online tool, kuler (http://kuler.adobe.com), to generate a colour scheme, as seen overleaf. All you need to use this is an Adobe account, which is free to create if you don't already have one. Once you've signed in, select Mykuler and create a new scheme. The middle colour in the row is defined as the Base Color. Below, the numbers represent colour values described in various ways. If you have a colour in mind, enter its values into one of the spaces provided, then click Set as Base.

Kuler allows you to apply any one of a series of rules to generate a fresh colour palette. If you're following along in Kuler right now, the range you're probably seeing is Analogous, which picks a series of colours all next to each other on the wheel. The effect is of a subtle change from left to right. Experiment by switching rules until you get a palette you like: it saves you the hassle of working out which colours go together. ➜

Building on the traditional colour wheel method, Adobe's Kuler leaves you no excuse for creating a colour scheme that doesn't work.

→ While these are called "rules", they're just a guide. If you're a non-designer, I suggest you base your design on a "monochromatic" or "shades" colour scheme, then add a complementary colour to brighten it up. One rule of thumb is that the more photographs (or other colourful images) you use, the fewer colours you should have in your design.

Most sites use white for their main content area and black for their body text, so the colours you've chosen will most often be used for the space outside the content area (the canvas or background) and for graphical elements. Some sites swap this and use black for content with white text (like kuler) and that's fine: the key is to get legible contrast between the content and the background.

FONTS Rule number one: don't use Comic Sans. Ever. No, really. Back when desktop publishing began, suddenly the local vicar had access to, oh, tens of fonts, and felt the need to use them all. On every page. Far too many websites adopt the same approach and end up as an amateurish mess. Things can only get worse if you choose fonts such as Comic Sans that aren't designed according to any conventional principles, and therefore convey no sense of authority or professionalism and, in large amounts, are painful to read.

So, rule number two: limit the number of fonts you use. I suggest between no more than three per page. You can get away with one, but most well-designed sites use two or three. Generally speaking, you'll use one font for all your headings and one for your body copy (paragraphs). Any additional fonts will be for specific purposes.

Fonts – or, strictly speaking, the typefaces that they embody – come in three kinds: serif, sans serif and decorative. Decorative fonts, such as THIS and *this*, should be used very sparingly, if at all. Serifs are the little hooks on the ends of letters such as these; typefaces that lack them, like this, are sans serif. Serif faces include **Times New Roman** and **Georgia**, the latter being rightly popular on the web because it's easy to read and looks good at a range of sizes. Sans serifs include **Arial** and **Verdana**.

Print designers can choose from thousands of typefaces, but when a user visits your web page they'll only see the fonts you've specified if those fonts are already installed on their computer. A list of the ones you can rely on is at www.ampsoft.net/webdesign-l/WindowsMacFonts.html. A few of these are decorative, one is Comic Sans (no!) and some are unusable system fonts, leaving a small number that are safe and either good or at least tolerable.

"Rule number one: don't use Comic Sans. No, really. Decorative fonts should be used very sparingly, if at all."

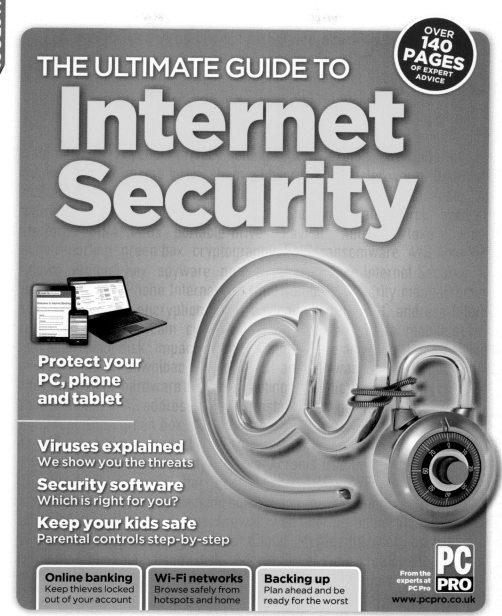

Choosing how to host your site

Web pages are made up of text, image and media files that are stored on a server and viewed through a browser. In effect, your site is a document that the user opens, and it needs to be stored somewhere anyone can access. There are three choices: shared servers, dedicated servers and virtual private servers.

With all types of hosting, you're paying a company to store your website on a server, on their premises, connected to the internet. You produce the necessary files using whatever web design software you prefer (or pay someone else to do this) and upload them to the server, where other users can access them by entering your web address into their browser. Factors that affect what you can and can't achieve with your site include the speed and reliability of the server and what types of content it supports.

The differences between the three basic types of hosting arrangement are as follows.

Shared As the name suggests, this is where you share a server with dozens, hundreds or even thousands of other websites.

With shared hosting, your site is stored on the same computer as many others, in much the same way you might run several programs at once on your PC. This limits performance, but reduces the price.

Shared hosting is the cheapest option and, usually, the easiest to set up, because you're not taking control of a computer, just adding your files to one that's already set up. On the other hand, the fact that you're sharing the web server means your site's performance can be compromised by the sheer weight of traffic the server has to cope with. Even if only a few people are trying to view your pages, you're also affected by the number accessing the other sites that may be on the same server.

Having said that, a good-quality shared hosting plan is a perfectly sensible choice for many online businesses, including those selling products online or simply using the internet to publicise themselves. You don't have the level of control over your hosting that either VPSs or dedicated servers offer, but in many cases, you simply don't need it, and you might not have enough technical knowledge to take advantage of it if you did.

As you would expect, the quality of shared hosting varies hugely between providers and across their product ranges. A package costing £2.99 per month is likely to be aimed at "home" use. At that level, you could expect to be squashed on to a server with many hundreds of other sites and to have a very limited range of features. Most hosts also offer "business" packages, and these will include greater bandwidth allowances (so more people can access your site before you start incurring extra costs), more sophisticated management features and promises of better performance. Performance essentially is the difference between visitors seeing your website straight away or being left waiting while pages struggle to load.

Dedicated A dedicated server is a physical machine leased in its entirety by you. You get complete control

over your machine through a browser-based control panel and root/admin-level access. These computers usually run either Linux or Windows Server.

Dedicated servers are much more expensive than shared hosting, with prices beginning at around £100 per month, but they're almost always the right choice if you're developing a web application. In other words, if your core product is delivered to the customer via the internet, rather than being a physical product that is merely ordered online, a dedicated server is likely to be the best choice. It's also worth considering for any kind of online store that aims to attract large numbers of customers, as a shared service is unlikely to cope with high demand, even in short bursts.

Virtual Virtual private servers (VPSs) sit between shared and dedicated hosting in their cost and features.

To you, they offer all the functionality of a dedicated server for a fraction of the price: indeed, what you get appears to be a dedicated server in every detail. In reality, a single computer is running several "virtual servers". Each copy of the server software thinks it's running on its own computer, but in fact the machine's processor is handling them all at the same time, while each has its own hard disk partition. Since the physical resources of the server are shared between the virtual servers, you can expect to get less hard disk space, lower memory and some competition for processor time, reducing performance.

However, VPSs are an excellent halfway house between shared hosting and dedicated servers. For around £30 a month you get most of the benefits of dedicated hosting for a price closer to business class-shared hosting.

OPERATING SYSTEMS Now that you've decided which type of hosting to plump for, your next decision is which operating system your web server should run. In everyday computing, the vast majority of users choose Windows. The choice is far less clear-cut with web hosting. Linux has long been the dominant web server operating system; it's reliable, lightweight, free and, crucially, the native environment of many of the web's core technologies, including PHP and MySQL. You can get Windows versions of these, but my preference is to run them under their intended operating system. (Incidentally, while Apple's Mac OS X operating system – available only on Macs – accounts for a respectable minority of desktops, it's not very ➜

The great thing about a good hosting service is that this chap, or someone like him, looks after the server that runs your website, so you don't have to.

→ widely used for commercial web hosting; Mac fans are likely to pick Linux.) For myself, I always begin with the assumption that my web server will run Linux, and will only consider Windows if there is a compelling reason to do so. For example, if a web application needs Microsoft's .NET Framework to run, Windows is the only choice.

Bear in mind that your familiarity with desktop Windows is of precious little use when it comes to configuring a Windows-based web server. With both Windows and Linux, you're shielded from the complexities of the operating system by browser-based control panels, which allow you to handle most tasks through a clear, icon-based interface. I don't pretend to be a Linux expert, and I could count the number of times I've needed to resort to the command-line interface on the fingers of one hand in the four years we've had a dedicated server.

All things considered, if you intend to create a website to sell products or publicise your business, a Linux-based hosting product is almost always going to be appropriate – and indeed the vast majority of shared hosting plans feature Linux. If you're creating a web application, on the other hand, your choice will depend on the technology you plan to use: .NET applications require a Windows server, while most other commonly used technologies are more at home on a Linux box.

SPACE AND BANDWIDTH Hosting packages will include a predefined amount of hard disk space. Generally speaking, as you might guess, the more expensive the package, the more space you'll get. However, the majority

of websites require very little space, so don't imagine that you need to pay for the kind of hard disk space on your web server that you might have in your desktop PC. Most sites will easily fit into a few hundred megabytes – even a media-heavy site such as PassYourTheory.co.uk needs less than 3GB in total – so disk space is not likely to be a deciding factor in choosing a host. Treat "unlimited space" offers, therefore, with the disdain they deserve: it's not something you need to pay extra for.

Hosting packages usually specify a maximum bandwidth. This is the total amount of traffic that your site is allowed to handle before excess charges apply. If you have a web page that contains 80KB of data, for example, then each time one person views that page they're using 80KB of your bandwidth allowance. As with hard disk size, you may be surprised by how little you need. You would need hundreds of gigabytes of bandwidth only if you were running a media-streaming service. As a very rough rule of thumb, you should typically be allowed ten times your hard disk space in bandwidth per month. Again, in practice the bandwidth allowance is likely to be so high that it's irrelevant when it comes to selecting a host.

TECHNOLOGY As a bare minimum, your shared hosting package should include PHP 5 (the programming language that adds dynamic functionality to web pages) and MySQL 5 (the most commonly used database), with permission to create one database. You might not know yet that you're going to need these technologies, but they cost nothing, offer the possibility to add functionality to your site without

"Most websites require very little space – don't imagine you need the kind of hard disk space on your web server that you have in your PC."

There are good reasons to go with a UK-based web host such as Tsohost, including customer support and prices starting at just £2.99.

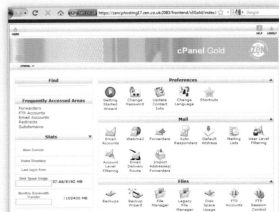

cPanel, installed on many servers, allows you to control the setup of your space and domain through an easy-to-use graphical interface.

needing to change packages later and, crucially, are required if you want to install WordPress and many other web applications that can make creating your site easier.

You also need a control panel to configure your web space. The most popular one for shared hosting is cPanel, and I recommend also ensuring that Fantastico De Luxe is included in your package. This is a bolt-on that offers one-click installation of a number of web applications, including WordPress, various other content management systems, photo galleries and discussion boards. Find out more at www.netenberg.com/fantastico.php.

For dedicated servers, cPanel is joined by Plesk. You get far greater functionality than with a shared host, allowing you to make low-level changes to your system configuration. Just remember that with great power comes great responsibility...

SERVICE-LEVEL AGREEMENTS

For dedicated hosting or VPS, only consider providers who offer a guaranteed "service level". The most important component of this is the percentage of time over any particular month that you can expect your server to be working. While 99% might sound excellent, bear in mind that a 1% downtime is over seven hours per month. You should be looking for at least 99.9% guaranteed uptime for a dedicated or virtual private server.

With shared hosting, you're much less likely to find a quoted figure. I suggest contacting the host's helpdesk (which in itself will tell you something about their responsiveness) and ask if they have a guaranteed uptime, or failing that if they can tell you what their uptime has been in, say, the past year. You can't expect quite such a high level with shared hosting, since you're paying so much less.

CONTRACT LENGTH There's no reason to sign up for more than a month-by-month commitment if you're intending to use shared hosting or a VPS. Avoid any host that doesn't at least offer the option of a monthly contract. With dedicated servers, it's more common to have an initial commitment of 12 months followed by an agreement to give one month's notice to terminate. Be very wary of signing up for longer to get a bigger discount – you don't know if this host is going to suit you yet.

EMAIL HANDLING Make sure, before you select a shared hosting package, that it includes enough email addresses. To have any credibility, you need to be able to send and receive emails from an address that includes your domain name. The days of being able to get away with an AOL or Hotmail email address are now long gone.

Case study
4: Buying a hosting package

With MakingYourOwnCandles.co.uk, we ruled out a dedicated server (at least initially) on cost grounds. At this early point, despite all our research, we can't guarantee that the income from the site and the traffic that comes with it will make a dedicated server worthwhile in the reasonably foreseeable future.

This does mean storing up a potential problem for later: if the site is a massive success, we might need to move across to a dedicated server, and this is not an easy process.

That left us with a choice between a VPS and shared hosting. Memset's "Miniserver" VPS started at around £16.50 (£19 inc VAT) per month including cPanel, while Zen's nearest equivalent shared hosting plan was £12 (£14 inc VAT). We finally decided on the cheaper option, because we don't anticipate needing administrator access to our server and because we're not going to be hosting our shop on the site. Had our product been a web application, we would certainly have gone for a virtual server, which I think offers the ideal compromise between performance, features, control and cost.

MAKING THE DECISION The best way to choose a host is through experience – either your own or that of people you respect. The PC Pro Excellence Awards (www.pcpro.co.uk/links/awards) bring together the experience of thousands of readers, so that's a good place to start.

For the past six years, Memset (www.memset.com) has won the PC Pro Web Host award, while in 2011 Fast2host (www.fast2host.co.uk) won Highly Commended. In 2010, Zen Internet (www.zen.co.uk) took this prize.

Based on these results, if you want shared hosting your first port of call should be Zen or Fast2host (since Memset doesn't offer shared hosting plans). Along with Zen Internet (www.zen.co.uk), I use www.heartinternet.co.uk for my shared hosting and have found it to be pretty good.

Or perhaps you're motivated by environmental concerns. If so, consider companies that power their datacentres using 100% renewable energy, such as Kualo (www.kualo.co.uk).

If you take the VPS or dedicated hosting route, I recommend you make sure that cPanel is included (or Plesk). Not only does this enable you to manage every aspect of your web space without needing to resort to Linux commands, it's also a sign of quality shared hosting by a provider that has thought about how the space will be used.

For dedicated servers, I suggest you begin by looking at Memset and Fast2host's options, which start at lower prices than Zen Internet's. You can see for yourself which providers rank poorly on the PC Pro Awards page, and I would avoid taking any risks: your web presence is too important.

Choosing and registering a domain name

Selecting a domain name is one of the most important decisions you'll make in setting up your business. Your web address is a crucial part of your brand, and might appear on everything from T-shirts to press releases. Most crucially, it plays an important role in your internet marketing.

If you've been following from the beginning, you'll know that your domain name should include your most important keywords, if possible. This is because of the way Google matches the text of ads (sponsored keywords) and indexed websites against the search terms that users type in.

Even though Google indexes the entire content of millions of websites, and can find words buried deep in their pages, the domain name of a site – much like the title of a book – is still the clearest guide to relevance. If a user searches for 'candle making', and the domain includes those words, that's a strong indication that it's relevant to this user, so Google will tend to place it higher up.

Not only that, but on Google results pages the terms that the user typed in will be highlighted in bold wherever they appear. If that means at least part of your domain name ends up in bold, it will make your ad or listing entry more likely to be spotted by the searcher.

TOP-LEVEL DOMAIN The top-level domain (TLD) is the final part of the web address, such as ".co.uk", ".com", ".net" or ".org". If you're aiming primarily at the UK market, it makes sense to choose .co.uk. For an international audience you might consider .com, but it depends on your intended identity. In your market, do you believe that being perceived to be a UK company will result in more sales? If you don't know, buy both .com and .co.uk and split-test them. You may want to use both anyway, if they're available.

The .net TLD was originally intended for ISPs and other networking companies, but there's no formal regulation on this, so it's a viable alternative if the .com address you want is unavailable. Personally, I'd only use .net if my product was tech-related. Not-for-profit organisations tend to be the main users of .org, another popular TLD. Again, there's no policing of this, but I'd avoid it unless you are a charity or public sector organisation.

SECOND CHOICES What if the domain name you want has already been taken? There are plenty of other TLD extensions you could use, including .me.uk, .net.uk, .biz, .mobi and .eu. Each name exists separately within each TLD, so if someone else already has mywidgetcompany.com, you can still register mywidgetcompany.co.uk, and so on.

However, unless you have a compelling reason to use these alternative TLDs, they should be avoided. There's

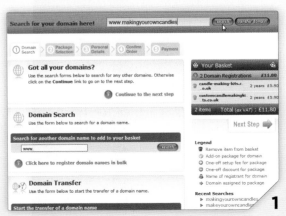

little point in spending money marketing the name 'Kevin's Candles' if users who go to kevinscandles.com (the most obvious domain) will find a completely different company – particularly since this domain is also likely to rank highly in the Google results when people search for 'Kevin's Candles'.

For a business targeting users of mobile devices, .mobi might be justified; if you're a pan-European company or you sell into Europe, .eu is a valid choice. The TLD .biz was invented to provide an alternative to .com, but I know which one I'd consider had higher credibility.

If the exact domain name you wanted has gone, try putting the keywords in a different order or turning nouns into verbs. Also check whether the existing domain name owners are actually using it for anything: they might be persuaded to sell for a reasonable price.

Try to buy as many combinations of your keywords as possible, as well as covering the main TLDs. Domain names are cheap, so don't scrimp and regret it later.

I used Daily.co.uk for my domain name registration, as I found it competitively priced, reliable and easy to use. Once registered, your domains can be transferred into the care of your preferred web host. Alternatively, ask whether your host can register domains and how much it charges for this. Always check whether there'll be a fee if you later want to transfer the domain to a different host.

1 **SEARCH THE WEB** Begin by searching for your chosen domain name at www.one.com or another registration service to see if it's available. At this point you should be looking for all reasonable combinations, so that if your research leads you to a different name later, there's a chance you've already bagged it. Notice here that one of the two domains I've already added to my shopping basket includes hyphens. This is because the unhyphenated version had already been taken. There's also an argument that it might actually be easier to read.

Nominet is the controller of the .co.uk top level domain, and its website has lots of useful information about how domain registration works.

Making a mark

Whether a domain is available is not the only consideration. You should also ensure your business name doesn't infringe an existing trademark, or you could face legal action. You can check UK trademarks at www.ipo.gov.uk/tm/t-find/t-find-text, and US ones at http://tess2.uspto.gov. The catch is that these lists aren't comprehensive. Searching the web for all combinations and variations of your intended name is also sensible. If the .com or .co.uk address is already in use, think about whether that company might object if you start up in business at the .net or .biz equivalent. As a rule, a name that's unique in its market, such as Amazon, will be protected, while a descriptive name, such as Lots of Cheap Books, may not be.

2 **UK OR US?** There are many TLDs. I avoid all but the most common for commercial sites. I'm looking for .co.uk where it's a UK business selling to a regional audience (as with www.makingyourowncandles.co.uk), or .com for an international business. While most .com domains are registered by US companies, .com doesn't necessarily imply a US base.

3 **DEVIL IN THE DETAIL** Make certain you get the registration details correct. If the domain is to be owned by your limited company, that should be reflected here, but otherwise register it to yourself. Bear in mind that domain names can have a value, sometimes quite unexpectedly, so make sure you stand to get the benefit.

4 **GET YOUR WALLET OUT** Time to pay up! Fortunately, domain names are cheaper than they've ever been. Those ending in .co.uk cost only a few pounds per year, which makes it worth registering as many as possible. These domains are registered for two years, after which you can renew them. Others can be registered for longer, but I tend to stick to two years; after that, you might not want the domain any more.

How to set up your web space

So you've registered your domain name and chosen a host for your website. Here's how to get your web space ready.

I'm using shared hosting with Zen Internet (www.zen.co.uk). A shared hosting plan will generally have a default web address something like yourusername.webhost.co.uk. So, having registered your own domain, you need to arrange things so that typing this into a browser points to your web space.

1 DNS First go to your domain name registrar (in my case www.daily.co.uk) and change the DNS records for your domain to point to the IP address you've been given by your host. The "MX records" section handles email routing, so you should usually enter your default web address here. This done, click Update DNS. Bear in mind DNS changes can take many hours to take effect.

2 POINT AND CLICK Now go to cPanel in your shared hosting plan. Click Parked Domains, type your domain name and click Add Domain. Your domain name will now point to your shared hosting space.

To copy files to this space you'll need an FTP account. If you're only hosting one domain in your web space, you might as well use the default FTP account details that your host will have provided you with. If you don't

have any FTP software, head over to filezilla-project.org and download the free FileZilla FTP client, which we'll use now.

3 CONNECT Click File, Site Manager, New Site. Enter the default domain provided by your web host, then the FTP user name and password. Click Connect and your site should open in the file browser interface. Now open Notepad and type the following:

```
<h1>Any heading you like</h1>
<p>This proves that my site works</p>
```

and save it as index.html. Copy this to your website's root folder – usually /public_html or /httpdocs – via FTP.

4 HEAD HOME Now type your domain name into a web browser. You should see your simple home page. It may not look exciting, but it's proved your setup has worked. If you get a DNS error, try typing in your default web address instead. If the page appears here, either you've messed up your DNS settings or you need to wait a few minutes. If it doesn't appear, go to FileZilla and make sure you've copied the file into the right folder.

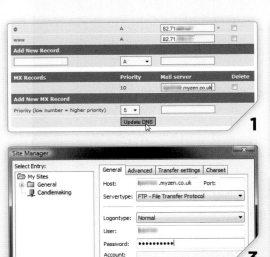

Get your business online the easy way.

Create your website easily in a matter of minutes with Website Builder.

from £4.99 per month

1. Choose a template

All our templates have been professionally designed and help you get your website up and running fast.

2. Add your content

Insert your own images and content including dynamic items such as Twitter updates, video clips and picture galleries with the click of a button.

3. Publish your site

In just a few clicks you can publish your brand new website to the internet. Plus you can make changes anywhere, anytime.

Whether you're an expert, novice or somewhere in between, Website Builder is the easy way to build your website.

Try the free demo and see for yourself!
Visit 123-reg.co.uk/website-builder

123-reg.co.uk

Creating a site using WordPress

WordPress is becoming an increasingly popular tool for creating a website quickly without needing specialist knowledge. And best of all, it costs nothing. Here we'll show you how to get it installed and working, and on the following pages we'll cover the basics of editing your site's look and feel.

Start by downloading the WordPress code, free of charge, from www.wordpress.org. (Don't confuse this with www.wordpress.com, where you can use the same technology to create a more limited site on WordPress's own server.) Download the Zip file version to a temporary folder on your PC, then extract the file into its own folder. If you don't have a Zip tool, the excellent 7-Zip can be downloaded free from www.7-zip.org.

1 **CREATE YOUR DATABASE** As we've mentioned, WordPress is a content management system (CMS). With a CMS, you store your content in a database from which it's retrieved, and displayed within a web page template, when visitors access your site. Your first step is to set up this database: specifically, a MySQL database on your web server.

To do this (assuming, again, that your web space includes the cPanel user interface; others may vary), go to www.yourdomainname.co.uk/cpanel – replacing "yourdomainname" with the domain you've now set up and pointed to your web space – and type in your cPanel username and password. Click the MySQL databases

icon and enter a name for your new database, such as "wordpress". Click Create Database. You also need to create a user account to access the database. Yet another login to remember? Yes, but you'll only ever need this to enter into WordPress when you first set it up; as long as you note the details somewhere in case of emergencies, you can then forget them. Enter a username, such as "wpuser", and a password, then click Create User. Bear in mind that cPanel may add your cPanel login name to the front of the username and database name. For example, if your login was jsmith, your username – assuming you'd typed "wpuser" – would be jsmith_wpuser.

2 **ADD USERS** Further down the same page, assign this user to your database. Select the user from the left-hand drop-down and the database from the right-hand list, and click Add User To Database.

We now need to enter these details into WordPress. Open up the folder on your computer containing the WordPress source files you downloaded. Find a file called "wp-config-sample.php" and rename it to wp-config.php. Open it in Notepad or another text editor (such as PSPad).

MySQL Account Maintenance

Current Databases:

admin_cardmakerdb Delete Check **Repair**

Users in cardmakerdb
admin_dbuser (Privileges: ALL PRIVILEGES) Delete

Connection Strings

Perl `$dbh = DBI->connect("DBI:mysql:admin_cardmakerdb:localhost", "admin_dbuser", "<PASSWORD HERE>");`

PHP `$dbh=mysql_connect ("localhost", "admin_dbuser", "<PASSWORD HERE>") or die('Cannot connect to the database because: ' . mysql_error());`
`mysql_select_db ("admin_cardmakerdb");`

New Database: wordpress [Create Database] **1**

Add Users To Your Databases:

User: admin_wpuser ▼ Database: admin_wordpress ▼

Privileges:

☑ ALL   or

☐ SELECT   ☐ CREATE
☐ INSERT   ☐ ALTER
☐ UPDATE   ☐ DROP
☐ DELETE   ☐ LOCK TABLES
☐ INDEX   ☐ REFERENCES
☐ CREATE TEMPORARY TABLES

[Add User To Database] **2**

Find the following line:

define('DB_NAME', 'putyourdbnamehere');

Now replace "putyourdbnamehere" with the name of the database you just created, such as "wordpress". Note that you need the single quotation marks shown. On the following lines, replace "usernamehere" with your MySQL username (such as "wpuser") and "yourpasswordhere" with your MySQL password. Save the file.

In FileZilla, copy all the files in the /wordpress folder via FTP to the root of your website; or, if you want to set up a blog within a site, create a subfolder.

Run the installer by opening the file /wp-admin/install.php within your website root folder. (Note that if you haven't put the WordPress files in the root folder, you'll need to add the subfolder to this address, for example yourwebsiteaddress/blog/wp-admin/install.php.) On the install screen, give your blog a title, enter your email address and click the Install button. If you don't see this screen, pay attention to any error messages and fix them first.

Within a few moments you'll see the Success message. You'll be given the username "admin" and a randomly generated password. Make a note of it and copy it to the clipboard (highlight it and press <Ctrl-C>). Click Log In. Type "admin" in the Username box and the password in the other field (press <Ctrl-V> to do this). Click Log In again.

You should see a message at the top prompting you to change your password to something easier to remember. If not, this can be done on your Profile page.

3 **APPLY A THEME** On your WordPress Dashboard, click Visit Site at the top and you'll see a plain, boring, standard WordPress web page. Before we go any further, we'll find a theme to give our site a more appropriate and engaging look and feel. WordPress has thousands of themes available, but if you want a bespoke

site, I recommend the Thesis theme (www.diythemes.com) as it's built with extensive customisaton in mind.

Click Site Admin to go back to the Dashboard. Click Appearance, Add New Themes. Use the "feature filter" to reduce the number of themes to choose from: tick some boxes and click Find Themes. For most purposes a two-column layout is ideal; you could also choose an appropriate colour. Having found a theme, click Preview to see how it looks, then Install. You'll be asked for your FTP information (the same as you used to connect in FileZilla). Click Proceed.

If this doesn't work – it might say it can't find wp-content, for example – you can do it manually. Go to http://wordpress.org/extend/themes and type the name of the theme you wanted. Click Download and save the Zip file. Unzip it and copy the entire folder (including its containing folder) via FTP into the wp-content/themes folder.

Either way, back at your Dashboard, click Appearance/Themes and you should see your new theme.

4 **THE END RESULT** Click Activate and then Visit Site and you should see your new website in all its glory. Unless you're astonishingly lucky, though, this site won't yet be absolutely right for you. You'll need to spend a little time tweaking its settings and appearance. Fortunately, as we'll see on the next page, this is surprisingly easy for non-experts to do.

So many WordPress themes are available that you should be able to find one on which to base your site. More can be found via Google, including sophisticated and professional paid-for themes that cost only a few dozen dollars.

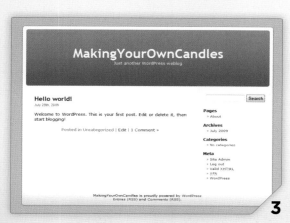

3

4

Editing your WordPress site design

One of the joys of WordPress is that you can edit your theme to get the look you want. Your site is made up of PHP for the functionality and MySQL for the content, while CSS defines the appearance. Because these are all separate, you can change the look completely without any knowledge of MySQL or PHP.

Most WordPress themes are designed for blogs, so you may want to edit your theme to make it more like a shopping site. This will involve turning off features and services such as the RSS feed and comments. Each function is controlled by one CSS rule, so you can change the whole site just by deleting one line of code.

The Web Developer toolbar for Firefox provides all sorts of extra data about a web page, including detailed CSS information. You can find it at http://addons.mozilla.org.

In WordPress, go to the Dashboard and create your home page: remember it must be a page, not a post.

1 **EDIT YOUR WIDGETS** Widgets are plugins available with the standard WordPress installation. They typically appear in sidebars on your site and allow you, for example, to list pages and posts.

For a website, you're likely to need a list of pages plus the "Meta" widget, which allows you to log in and edit the site.

Under Appearance in your WordPress Dashboard, you can see a list of Widgets on the left and where they can appear on the right. In this example there are four possible locations, but this will depend on your theme. To add a Widget, drag and drop it from the left-hand panel to one of the locations on the right. To remove it, reverse the process.

Because of the way WordPress themes work, you may find some Widgets appear by default although they're not listed here. If you want to remove all Widgets from a location, the only way may be to add a blank Widget to override the default. The best choice is the Text Widget. Drag and drop this into any locations you want to be blank; as long as you don't enter any text into the Widget, nothing will be visible. It's a bit cack-handed, but it works.

Widgets provide an easy way to add functionality to your website, but for a straightforward sales site you may not need them. Fortunately, like most other things in WordPress, they're simple to manage.

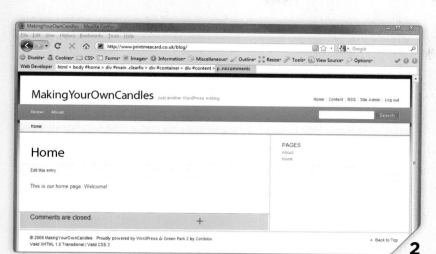

2

3 NO COMMENT Use the "Find in page" function in Firefox to find the CSS rule name; I searched for ".nocomments". We're looking for a rule that applies only to .nocomments. If it's a combined rule, with other elements alongside it, we won't modify it because that would change all those elements. Modify the line to match the following text, or if there's no rule just for .nocomments, create one by adding the text:

.nocomments { display:none; }

4 HEY PRESTO Click Update File. Reload your home page and you should find the comment message has disappeared. In my experience, this technique of hiding unwanted elements using CSS is the one you'll use most often. You can edit the main CSS file in the same way to make other changes to the style rules.

2 EDIT THE CSS WordPress makes it possible to edit the CSS for your site through the Dashboard. If you're going to be making major changes you might prefer to use an editor such as PSPad, but the built-in editor is sufficient for most purposes.

Take a look at your site as it stands by clicking Visit Site. I suggest opening it in a separate window or tab for convenience; you can do this by clicking the link with the right mouse button and choosing the relevant option.

By default, WordPress allows visitors to add comments on any page or blog entry. This isn't appropriate to a sales website, so go to Settings > Discussion and make sure "Allow people to post comments on new articles" is deselected. Now, though, "Comments are closed" will appear on your page, so you'll need to delve into CSS to remove it.

On the Web Developer toolbar in Firefox, click the CSS button and choose View Style Information. An info bar appears under the toolbar, and when you move your mouse pointer over the web page, the Web Developer toolbar shows the CSS style name of the area under your pointer. Clicking brings up the specific CSS rules that apply to it.

In the screenshot (above right), we've highlighted the location of the mouse pointer and the CSS rule name: p .nocomments. To make the "Comments are closed" message invisible, we just need to change the rule. Go to Appearance > Editor in the Dashboard; the main stylesheet (style.css) will be loaded by default, and is usually the file you want. You may see a message at the bottom of this page telling you to make the file writable if you want to edit it. If so, run FileZilla, go to the /wp-content folder of your site, find the /theme subfolder and, within it, right-click the style.css file. Select File Permissions, and in the Numeric Value field type "666" (I kid you not!) and click OK. Then reload the editor page in WordPress – just click Firefox's Refresh button – and you should find an Update File button has appeared.

3

4

Getting your site written

Ask any freelance web designer and they'll tell you that, while their clients are happy to lavish plenty of time and effort on the look and feel of their shiny new site, they'll pay almost no attention to getting the words right. This is partly because design is sexier; partly because the bulk of the design work is done by the designer, while the writing needs input from the business owner; and partly because writing is hard.

I can't tell you how important it is to get the words right, particularly on your home page and sales landing pages. No matter how impressive the design of your website or how effective it is from a usability point of view, poorly chosen or badly written copy is the fastest way to encourage your potential customer to click the Back button rather than take the action you want.

To make sure your words are working for you, here are my top seven tips for successful copywriting.

1 It's your job

While it's fine to hire an external copywriter, the responsibility for getting the copy *right* is yours alone. One test of a good copywriter is that they will ask to spend a lot of time with you to understand your business and

process as you can yourself. That's not to say you can't or shouldn't hire a copywriter to help polish the wording, but the bulk of the work needs to be done by you.

2 Know your customer

Probably the biggest mistake you'll see in web copy is that writers have written it for themselves rather than for their target audience. Clearly, your audience isn't you: after all, you don't need to buy your product.

If you've been following the advice so far, you will have carried out a survey to help with your product development. The results of this survey will help you understand the characteristics of your audience. Not only

"We aimed our driving test site at 17-19s. It turns out that this group are already confident of passing and expect to get everything free."

customers before they write a single line. Either way, the process will involve a lot of your time and effort: this isn't something you can abdicate responsibility for.

Why? First, because it's your business and – just as you'll be heavily involved in selecting or building the product or service you sell, and you'll be making dozens of key decisions as you develop your business – your intimate knowledge is essential to defining the message you're presenting to your potential customers.

And second, because the quality of your copy could make the difference between profit and loss, between success and failure. This means that when you're deciding on your priorities, copywriting should be right at the top. Because it's so critical, you can't expect someone else to bring the same level of commitment and knowledge to the

will you learn what they're looking for in their purchase but, if you included any open-ended questions, you'll also be familiar with the sort of language they use – and, indeed, how many of them don't have English as a first language, which will affect the way you write your copy.

My company launched the subscription-based driving theory test website PassYourTheory.co.uk in 2005. At the time, we didn't conduct a pre-launch survey, although we've run many surveys subsequently to learn how to improve the product. We thought we already knew who our target audience was.

After all, isn't it obvious? You might well assume, for example, that a driving theory test website should be aimed at 17- to 19-year-olds, so we designed the site – and wrote our copy – to appeal to this age range.

However, subsequent surveys have shown us that while we might get a lot of traffic from this age group, the people who actually buy from us tend to be older, and our most profitable customers are in their late twenties and disproportionately female.

Some of the things we discovered were that 17- to 19-year-olds expect to get everything for free and that they're supremely confident about passing their tests with a minimum of effort. So they don't see the need for tuition products and have no inclination to pay for them. In retrospect this may seem unsurprising, but our choice to aim our product at them seemed logical, if uninformed, at the time. As it happens, many competitors have come and gone over the years, and in each case they've been aimed at teenagers. We know what they were doing wrong.

Learning this about our target audience changed everything when it came to presentation and, critically, copy. Our surveys and other analysis have also discovered what specific needs our customers have when it comes to theory test training, and this now informs both our product offering and our copy.

If a potential customer has a need in mind when they type their search term into Google, and they see that need reflected in the Google Ad that comes up and then reflected again in the page they arrive at when they click it, they're much more likely to buy.

To demonstrate this, I conducted a test (you'll see how to do this in part 4 of this book) comparing the effectiveness of a specialised landing page with the standard "one size fits all" home page. Within a day, Google had produced enough data for me to be certain that I had a winner: the landing page outperformed the home page by more than 65%. And the only significant difference between the two was the copywriting.

The moral of the story is that you should learn as much about your customers as you can. Write directly for them. Anticipate what's likely to be on their mind when they reach your site, and reflect that. Relevance is everything. ➜

Copywriting is one of the hardest and most critical jobs in putting together your web presence. Even if you hire a professional to polish your words, it's up to you to figure out how best to address your visitors and turn as many as possible into buyers.

3 What's in it for them?

When visitors to your site read your copy and evaluate your offer, the question they'll be asking themselves is: "What's in it for me?" While a website is designed to be visited by many thousands of people, for each visitor the experience is a personal one. Just as with a book, the conversation is essentially one-to-one: you are talking directly to the reader.

Having learned something about your target audience, you need to write your copy so that this audience sees the benefits in your products compared to those of your competitors. You must present your products in terms of *benefits*, as opposed to its features and their advantages.

Here's an example. Let's imagine you go to a PC superstore to buy a new laptop. The clichéd portrayal (also sadly realistic) of the computer salesperson is that they'll bombard you with facts – usually read direct from the point-of-sale labels – without any explanation.

"It has a 160 gigabyte hard disk" is a feature. "Which means there's enough space to store around 80,000 photos or 30,000 music tracks" is an advantage. But what's the benefit? Perhaps: "So it has plenty of space for normal purposes and won't need to be upgraded in the near future." (OK, for the pedantic, that's two benefits).

All the user cares about is that the hard disk is big enough. By putting the feature in context with the advantage, and explaining what the consequence of the feature is (with the benefit), not only is the user's concern allayed but the reason to buy the product is comprehensibly and plausibly explained.

A useful way to present your Feature-Advantage-Benefit information is to use the linking words: "Has

[feature]. Which [advantage]. So [benefit]." Remembering the "so" is critical, as it ensures you are explaining what the benefit means, not assuming your customers can work it out for themselves.

Some more examples:

PassYourTheory.org.uk **has** a unique hazard perception walkthrough **which** guides you through a typical clip pointing out when to click, **so** you can approach your test with complete understanding and confidence.

This book **has** a section on copywriting **which** explains the key principles of good copy **so** you can avoid typical beginner's mistakes and save money.

4 What do you want them to do?

You should know what you want your customer to do, whether that's buy a product immediately, ask for more information or sign up for a mailing list. But does your customer know? Never assume that this is obvious: make it crystal clear what action you expect them to take, as many times as possible.

It's essential that you have this action "above the fold". This means it will appear on your web page without the viewer needing to scroll down, because some may not get as far as scrolling. The problem, of course, is that there's a huge range of resolutions on PC screens. Gone are the days when almost everyone was using 1,024 x 768; most new monitors are widescreen, some are as big as 30 inches, and at the other end of the scale there are mobile devices and netbooks with various formats and resolutions.

For most purposes, your "buy" button or signup area can be placed at around 500 pixels down the page and you'll know that the vast majority of your audience will see it without scrolling. However, if you're targeting mobile users you would need to think about placing the button higher and testing the site on multiple devices.

5 Keep it simple

There's no avoiding the importance of simple, clear, grammatically correct English. Irritating though it may be to many entrepreneurs, getting this right will have a direct impact on your conversion rate (how many visitors go on to buy something). Remember you are communicating more than just a message in your copy; your words also represent your product. If your copy contains grammatical

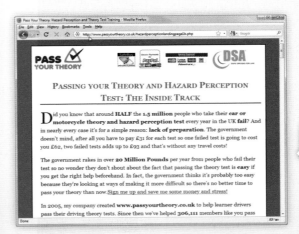

65% more people responded to this landing page than to our home page. Note the call to action "above the fold" (in blue).

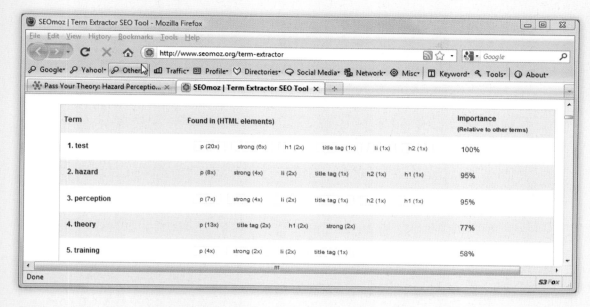

Term	Found in (HTML elements)						Importance (Relative to other terms)
1. test	p (20x)	strong (6x)	h1 (2x)	title tag (1x)	li (1x)	h2 (1x)	100%
2. hazard	p (8x)	strong (4x)	li (2x)	title tag (1x)	h2 (1x)	h1 (1x)	95%
3. perception	p (7x)	strong (4x)	li (2x)	title tag (1x)	h2 (1x)	h1 (1x)	95%
4. theory	p (13x)	title tag (2x)	h1 (2x)	strong (2x)			77%
5. training	p (4x)	strong (2x)	li (2x)	title tag (1x)			58%

The Foxy SEO Tool plugin for Firefox includes a range of tools that can help you check your copy for relevance to your target market. This one links to the SEOmoz tool and shows the relative importance (as seen by Google) of the words on your page.

"In the past, marketers crammed their web pages with search terms, often invisibly. If you try this now you will end up blacklisted."

errors and spelling mistakes, that suggests to many buyers that you're careless, so they're unlikely to buy from you.

Follow a ruthless and rigorous editing process. Begin by getting all your thoughts written down. Apply all the tips given here through a series of drafts until you get to your final version. This version will almost always end up much shorter than the first. Every paragraph, every sentence, every word must serve the purpose of making it more likely that your audience will buy your product or service. Any words that aren't relevant are not only wasted, they make it more likely that you'll lose the reader's attention before they decide to buy something.

Re-read your copy, asking yourself whether your visitors really need to know everything you've included.

 ## Be friends with Google

Google rewards relevance. Why? Because it's what searchers want. The more relevant Google believes your web pages to be, the better they will rank and the cheaper your advertising will be.

Google determines relevance primarily from the websites that link to you (and those that you link to) and from the content on the page. At the most elementary level, it will compare the copy on the page with the search phrase

that the user typed in. In the dim and distant past of the early 2000s, this led to internet marketers cramming their pages with search terms, often invisibly. Google is far too sophisticated to tolerate this sort of behaviour now, and if you try these dated techniques you will end up blacklisted.

The secret to a good ranking is to write copy that your target audience will appreciate. That's pretty much it: no black hat techniques are required. A well-structured site will result in landing pages that are naturally closely matched to the keywords visitors have typed in. Google will see these pages as relevant and reward you accordingly.

7 Get your headline right

The most important line of your copy is the first one visitors see. Headlines fall into several types, including questions ("How much is peace of mind worth to you?"), calls to action ("Sign up now for free peace of mind") and direct headlines ("Free peace of mind here"). One of the most popular is the "how to" ("How to get free peace of mind in seconds").

The best headlines grab the user's attention with something either interesting or too good to pass over. If you need some inspiration, have a look through Jay Abraham's "100 Greatest Headlines Ever Written" at http://ypcommando.com/tips/17.html.

Make your site more attractive with rich typography

If you're fed up of being forced to select from the handful of web-safe fonts to ensure your site design is consistent across operating systems and devices, you'll be relieved to hear that Typekit and Google might just have the answer.

Just for once, Internet Explorer was the pioneer of rich typography with its adoption of the @font-face CSS rule in, believe it or not, Internet Explorer 4. The @font-face style allows the browser to download and use fonts stored remotely – as opposed to any fonts preloaded on your computer or smartphone – and is now supported by Internet Explorer (6+), Firefox (3.5+), Chrome (4+), Opera (10+) and Safari (3.1+).

The problem has been that very few fonts are licensed for distribution this way and, where they are, the high-quality fonts can be expensive. That's precisely why so many websites use such boring and plain fonts.

Typekit (www.typekit.com) is an easy to use system that seeks to address this issue. Typekit serves fonts "on-the-fly", thus protecting the intellectual property of the font designer. From small beginnings, the Typekit font library now includes hundreds of fonts including, most recently, a range of excellent-quality Adobe typefaces.

Google Font Directory (http://code.google.com/webfonts) aims to offer a similar service, but it has a much smaller range. Moreover, Typekit offers a free membership option, so I would recommend starting with that.

Having lots of choice comes with its own dangers. I covered this in "Principles of

High-quality fonts can be expensive, which is why so many websites use such boring and plain fonts

good web design" (see p46), but it's even more important when you have hundreds of fonts to choose from rather than the small set of web-safe typefaces. The purpose of your website is to help market your business, and part of this is to create and reinforce its image.

In almost all cases, this will mean using professional, mainly conservative fonts – but don't be dismayed, as this still leaves a huge range available to you. The free account at Typekit, for example, includes the lovely Adobe Garamond Pro, which can be used for either headings or body text.

The end result to look for is typography that's different enough to be distinctive but without drawing undue attention to itself: it's possible for your choice of fonts to "try too hard" and undermine your professional image. (For an example of this, see screenshot 4.)

1 **CREATE YOUR FIRST KIT** Begin by signing up for the free trial account at www.typekit.com and creating your first kit. The next step is to select a font. For the purposes of this example, we're going to replace the header font in the default WordPress 3 installation with a new font, so I selected Decorative. Once you find the font you want, click "Add to kit".

2 **PUBLISH YOUR FONT KIT** The kit editor will now open with your chosen font loaded. To get the CSS code, click the Advanced link and then select the code that appears between the braces in the lower example of the two. In my case, it said, "font-family: 'rosewood-std-1', 'rosewood-std-2', sans-serif"; copy this text into Notepad for use later.

Click the Publish button to make your kit live. Now click "Embed Code" to obtain the JavaScript you need, and copy it into Notepad.

3 **INSTALL THE TYPEKIT PLUGIN** We now need to get the WordPress site set up to work with Typekit. To do this, you'll need to install the Typekit Fonts plugin for WordPress (see p73 for more on adding WordPress plugins). Once you've done this, select it from the Setup panel in the WordPress dashboard.

Paste the embed code into the top field. This will be placed into the header of every page and is required for Typekit to work. In the bottom field, create a CSS rule. In this example, I want to change all headings by using the h1 rule (the other headings are derived from this one). I've pasted the Typekit CSS code into the h1 rule. This will use the custom font in supported browsers; if the browser doesn't support it, the default sans serif font will be substituted.

You can add multiple lines here to modify other CSS rules (for example, the p rule for paragraphs) and, in that way, completely alter the typography of the site.

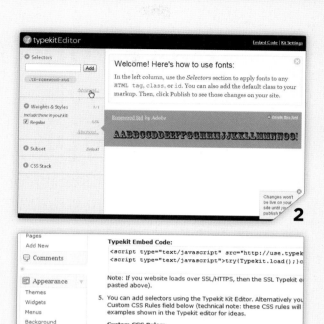

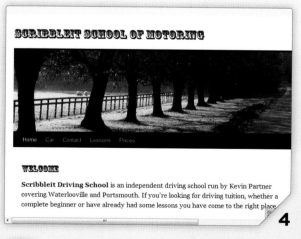

4 **VIEW THE RESULTS** Click Save Settings and view the site. All being well, you'll see the new fonts in use. In my case, the results are pretty repulsive and serve to illustrate my point that an increase in choice means you need to take care in making the right choice for the right situation.

Images and graphics

No web page is complete without at least one image. Can you remember the last site you visited that had none? But they need to be used with care, and you need to be clear why you're using them. To help you choose wisely, bear in mind that images fall into three types: branding, illustrative and decorative.

Branding Your logo is an essential part of your brand, and you need it to work well and look professional.

Trying to get a logo developed on the cheap is a false economy. MakingYourOwnCandles.co.uk needed a logo, and I made the mistake of using an online logo company that charges only £25. The results were absolutely diabolical. After eight rounds of amendments it was still diabolical. The only aspect I liked was the typeface, which turned out to be available as a free font, so I paid the money, took the design, deleted everything but the text and added the graphical element myself.

On a later project, I used 99designs.com. With this service, and others like it, you set up a competition and designers from around the world compete to come up with a winning design. There's a minimum prize fund of around £175, which, believe me, is very reasonable. So reasonable, in fact, that it may not attract experienced professional designers, but you do have the benefit of opening up your job to people from countries with lower wage expectations. I had a very successful experience on this occasion and was delighted with the results. It's also possible to set up contests for the design of entire websites, but I don't recommend this, because web design involves a lot more interaction between you and the designer than a logo does.

If you're prepared to invest a little more money in your "corporate identity", there are plenty of UK-based graphic designers who can oblige. Ask around locally for recommendations or search the web; the best approach is to find existing work that you like, then find out who designed it (if the graphics aren't credited, the site owner may not mind telling you who did them) and ask them to quote for what you need. Professional designers will expect a clear brief and will not usually be prepared to work "on spec"; if you commission work from professionals, you will have to

"Trying to get a logo developed on the cheap is a false economy. I paid only £25 and the results were diabolical."

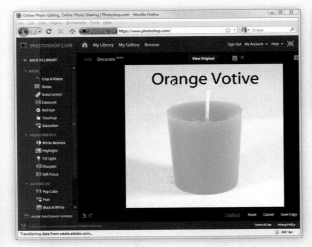

Photoshop.com offers a sophisticated image editor free of charge. It works entirely online, via your web browser, and is especially suitable for editing photos for websites because you won't need to work with high-resolution files that take ages to upload and download.

You can use free space on sites such as Photoshop.com to store photos and insert them into your web pages using links (above) without having to host them on your own web server.

pay for it, though you can ask for changes, within reason. Be wary of agencies, as opposed to invidual designers. They can help guide you through the process, but will cost a lot more and may pressurise you to spend more than you need to.

Other graphics on your site should also reflect your branding, at least in their colours and ideally in style.

Illustrative

Illustrative graphics are photographs and other images depicting the product itself.

They might be photos of a physical product or screenshots of software. For a service, you might include photos of customers alongside their testimonials. If your product needs explaining or demonstrating, you might need to get diagrams drawn.

When taking photos of your product, I recommend investing in proper lighting and a light cube. These can be bought at low cost from eBay and, along with a tripod and a reasonable camera (I use a Sony Alpha a200 entry-level DSLR, but a digital compact will do fine) you can achieve impressive results. Good-quality product shots increase your customers' perception of your professionalism, which means you will make more sales for higher prices.

For screenshots, you can't beat the low-cost Snagit from Techsmith (www.techsmith.com/snagit) which also includes an editor that offers batch image processing.

Decorative

Any graphic that doesn't either enhance your brand or illustrate your product or service needs to be treated with caution.

Images with no purpose serve only to distract visitors from the parts of the page you want them to concentrate on. If it doesn't have a reason to be there, get rid of it.

SOURCING IMAGES If you need photos of your specific product, you'll have to get them from your supplier or take them yourself. Generic photos and graphics can come from other sources. Don't steal them from other people's websites: quality may be compromised and you could get sued for copyright infringement. (This really does happen, and the costs are far higher than buying the images in the first place.) There are plenty of free or low-cost "stock" and clip-art libraries. A good source is www.clipart.com, which includes illustrations, photos and photo objects (pictures of things on a transparent background). Of the stock

Moving images

I'm struggling to think of an animation that actually enhanced the website it was on. Some sites are created entirely in Flash, but as well as requiring more design skills this makes it harder to achieve high search-engine rankings. Dropping animation into an HTML page is rarely a good idea, because most web users now equate animation with adverts and will ignore it. Don't use animation just to show off, and *never* as a lead-in to your site. The dreaded "skip intro" link was never a good idea.

If you have a good reason for including animation, the only format to use is Flash SWF. You don't need to buy Adobe's Flash application to create animations; the best tools I've seen are SWiSH Max and miniMax (www. swishzone.com), as used for the spinning globe above, which offer much of the functionality of the Flash authoring tool at a lower cost.

image libraries, my favourite is www.fotolia.com; an image suitable for web use costs either 75p or £1.50 depending on its size, so it's hardly going to break the bank. Another popular choice is www.istockphoto.com. You can buy images individually or by subscription; the latter is intended for people who regularly need more content, but you could spend time selecting a set of images and then sign up for a short period and download them all.

My favourite photo editor is Adobe Photoshop Elements. If you're going to be creating your own videos, it makes sense to buy it in a bundle with Premiere Elements. Having said that, if you're only likely to edit a limited number of images, you might be able to make do with the online version of Photoshop Elements (www.photoshop. com), which is free. This allows you to perform basic edits and then either link to the image on Adobe's servers or download it for uploading via WordPress. Alternatively, there's Google Picasa (http://picasa.google.co.uk), a free editing program with a growing number of useful functions.

You should always save images at the exact size you want them to appear on your site, in pixels, rather than relying on setting their width and height properties in HTML. This ensures the image files are no larger than necessary and quality isn't lost when browsers downsize them. Most images should be saved in JPEG format, and you'll need to adjust the compression settings so that the image still looks good but is as small in file size as possible.

FILE FORMATS There are three file formats widely used on websites – JPEG, PNG and GIF – and it's usually pretty easy to work out which would be the best for your purposes. For an icon or diagram with relatively few colours, or a simple design with no gradient fills, consider GIF. These files support only 256 colours (including one transparent colour) and compress to small sizes. GIF is a good choice if your image is black and white, even if it's a photo.

If you have a full-colour picture that needs to support transparency, PNG is your only choice. For example, although most photos include backgrounds and are inserted into the site as a rectangle, some – described as "photo objects" or "isolated" – are designed to have a transparent background. This may be supplied as a "clipping path" or "alpha channel", but you'll need to load the image into a photo editor and save it as a PNG to make the transparency work when the image is included in a web page.

In just about every other case, JPEG is the right format. It tends to offer better compression than PNG while supporting more colours than GIF. However, JPEG doesn't support transparency. It's completely supported in all browsers, whereas older versions didn't handle PNGs well. So your default choice should be JPEG, with the others only being selected for specific purposes.

Video and sound

Used appropriately, sound and video can enhance your site's message. Used poorly, they can drive away visitors in an instant. Here we'll find out what are the top irritations and what really works, and see how to add audio and video to a WordPress site.

The most important thing to remember when adding "rich media" to your site is to make sure playback is under the control of your visitor. There are few things more annoying, or more likely to lead to the visitor clicking the Back button, than a sound file or video that auto-plays as soon as the user arrives at your page.

Having said that, well-produced video and audio can be excellent attention-grabbers for your most important messages. As a rule, video or audio is used on a landing page to reinforce the main purpose of that page, which is usually to get a visitor's email address or initiate a sale. Rich media is likely to be less welcome on your home page or other information-rich pages within your site, since when a visitor is viewing those pages they're likely to be looking for something specific, and it's much quicker to do so in text and graphics, which are all visible immediately, than in a video, where you have to wait and see what appears.

SOUND: THE VOICEOVER Please don't use sound as a musical backdrop to your site: this breaks our first rule. Even if the site is promoting a band, samples of your music should be controllable by the visitor – and by that I do *not* mean you start the music automatically and offer a Stop button. While this might be mildly acceptable the first time someone arrives at your site, can you imagine how irritating it will be a dozen visits later? Assuming they ever come back, which of course they won't.

A better use of sound is for speech. No matter how short your message, always write a script. This is the only way to make sure you say everything that needs saying without the otherwise inevitable "ums" and "ahs".

Sound can be deployed as a widget built into your site, with a playback bar giving the visitor control. More often than not, this widget will be Flash or JavaScript-based and the sound will be in MP3 format.

Recording speech requires minimal equipment and software. I strongly recommend investing in a decent microphone. Samson produces a range of USB microphones, available from audio stores such as www.dolphinmusic.co.uk from around £60, that dispense with the need for a mixing deck or pre-amp and plug straight into your PC. Avoid services that let you phone in your audio and receive it as an MP3 file: this is convenient for business tasks, but the quality is too low for recordings that you want to present to an audience.

The best choice among free audio-editing software is Audacity (http://audacity.sourceforge.net). Despite an interface out of the 1990s, it does a good job, and recording spoken audio isn't, after all, rocket science.

Having output your audio to MP3, you then need a way of embedding it in your page. For a self-coded site, my tool of choice is SWiSH Jukebox (www.swishzone.com), which takes an MP3 – or a series of MP3s – and outputs a Flash SWF file incorporating a customisable control bar.

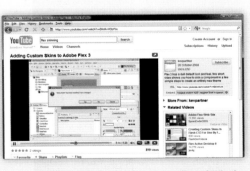

Software and product demonstrations are an ideal use for video, whether on your own site or YouTube.

Here's the editor of *Wired* magazine popping up as a talking head to get his message across.

For a WordPress site, a number of plugins exist to host MP3s; my favourite, for its sheer simplicity, is WPaudio (http://wpaudio.com).

VIDEO: THE TALKING HEAD Generally speaking, video on sales websites takes two forms. First, there's the "talking head" beloved of internet marketing gurus. Typically this involves the site-owner talking directly into the camera, seeking to persuade visitors to sign up or buy a product. This can be effective since, done well, it can inject enthusiasm and dynamism into what otherwise might have been dry copy. It works especially well where there's no physical product that you can show off.

Second, and more rarely, you'll come across a video that shows a product being used. I expect this to become more common, especially on high-price items. Imagine, for example, how much more likely you'd be to buy an item you'd just seen opened and used in a video than one that's shown only as a box shot.

> ## "Video on your website can take one of two forms: the talking head and the product demonstration or presentation."

To make your video look professional, you need to pay attention to two things above all else: sound and light. Unless you're going for an "urban guerrilla" look, set up your camcorder on a tripod in a well-lit location. Natural sunlight is often best, and certainly cheapest, but otherwise you can get good results from a bright halogen uplighter, which creates a good lighting level without obvious shadows.

Recording sound on video can be tricky. If your camcorder has a mic input socket, a lapel microphone will work fine. If not, I recommend recording the sound separately using a digital dictaphone. Place it just out of view (or tape it to a broom handle and get someone to dangle it out of view, like in the movies) and you can then combine it with the video in an editing program such as Premiere Elements. It's a bit of extra work to get it synced, but the quality will be far better than with the internal mic.

Pocket camcorders such as the Sony Bloggie (www.sony.co.uk) are increasingly popular and cost around £100. Almost all such camcorders offer "Full HD" video, but this is overkill for most sites; shoot in 720p and you'll require less bandwidth. The only downside to pocket camcorders is that, if you're filming yourself, there's no flip-out LCD panel to watch while you record. A budget full-size digital camcorder is another option, with today's tapeless models making it easy to import your footage.

DEMOS AND PRESOS Computer-generated or presentational video is known in some quarters as "poor man's video", but can be extremely effective. For example, if you're selling a software product, you might create a screen-capture video showing the product in use, with accompanying narration.

While this is simpler to set up than a live "talking head" video, getting it right takes preparation and a script, since you don't want to record any mistakes. Camtasia Studio (www.techsmith.com/camtasia.asp) is my favourite tool for the job, as it's very simple to use and produces high-quality results. It's available on a fully functional 30-day trial.

You can also use Camtasia to capture a PowerPoint slideshow, add a voiceover and output the result as a video. This can work well, but remember that most presentations are boring even when given live, let alone on the web. I'm a firm believer in Guy Kawasaki's 10/20/30 rule: 10 slides in 20 minutes with no text at less than 30-point size (http://blog.guykawasaki.com/2005/12/the_102030_rule.html).

Don't use PowerPoint's built-in clip art – buy low-cost stock images, as described on p69 – and try to avoid the built-in templates. Take the time to create your own and your video won't look like just another PowerPoint.

HOSTING VIDEO Once it's created, you'll need to decide whether you're going to host your own video content. If it's purely for use on your website, it makes sense to store it in your web space. However, if you've created a marketing video that would make sense independently of the site, hosting it elsewhere might be a way to drive traffic to your pages.

For example, a product or software demonstration video should be hosted on YouTube, so that people searching the site will find it. Having uploaded it to YouTube, you can also embed it in your site using the link that YouTube provides. Don't embed your own controller in the video, as YouTube adds its own. Just upload the movie to YouTube, and once it's live you can copy and paste the "Embed" code from its YouTube page into your HTML.

Pocket camcorders such as the Sony Bloggie offer a cheap and simple way to capture video for your website. Just make sure you pay as much attention to lighting and audio quality as you would when shooting in a professional format.

Adding plugins to your WordPress site

WordPress allows you to add functionality to your site with a huge range of plugins. There are currently over 7,000 available, covering everything from polls to searchengine optimisation and even simple online shops. Most are free, although some have paid-for "premium" versions, and they can usually be installed at the click of a button.

Exactly which plugins you'll need will depend on the type of business you're setting up. If you're selling a physical product range, you might decide the plugins supplied with WordPress provide everything you need to get started. If you're setting up an information business, you might need a plugin that allows you to sell memberships that give access to restricted parts of the site. Even if you're only using your website to support either an offline business or an eBay business, you'll almost certainly find plugins that will make your site more effective.

PLUGINS EVERY SITE SHOULD HAVE All the following plugins can be downloaded via Plugins >Add New in your WordPress Dashboard. Enter a search term and select the plugin you want, then click Install. This will bring up a dialog box giving more information on the plugin.

Most plugins can be installed automatically by WordPress, but if not, in most cases all you have to do is download a Zip file, unzip it, then upload it via FTP, complete with its containing folder, to your /wp-content/plugins folder.

Once this is done, you'll find the plugin listed under Plugins > Installed. Click Activate and it will begin working. In most cases you'll need to configure it, and this is done under Settings in the Dashboard.

All in One SEO

We'll be covering search engine optimisation in the final part of this book. For now, suffice to say that when it comes to getting your site ranked highly by Google, and therefore noticed by customers, SEO is essential. As the leading plugin for this purpose, All in One SEO should be installed on any site you create in WordPress. It gives you the same control over SEO as you'd have if you created your own site from scratch.

Install the plugin, enable it and set the Home Title, Home Description and Home Keywords. As in our example (left), as a first pass you should simply ensure that your main keywords are included in all three fields while using natural language.

You've probably seen websites with text at either the beginning or end of the page containing the same keywords repeated endlessly. This is a very old-fashioned technique aimed at fooling search engine "spiders" into believing that the site is very relevant because the main keywords represent a high percentage of the total words on the page. However, Google and the other search engines have long since got wise to this, and now penalise such ham-fisted attempts to fool them.

The All in One SEO plugin makes it easy for you to ensure that your website is search-engine friendly.

Register Plus allows you to create customised user registration schemes, adding whatever items of personal data you want to collect.

Akismet

If you enable comments on your site, you'll soon realise that blog comment spam is as big a nuisance as email spam. "Comments" full of advertising or nonsense will quickly swamp your pages. Fortunately, WordPress makes it simple to tackle them through the Akismet plugin. This is normally installed when you set up WordPress, so all you need to do is activate and configure it. You'll need a WordPress.com API key; if you have an account with WordPress.com (remember this is different from WordPress.org, which you're using),

Pick a plugin

When it comes to selecting a plugin, the key questions to ask (and all the answers should be in the plugin's page within the WordPress Plugin Directory) are:

- **Have lots of other people used it?**
- **Does it have a good rating?**
- **Is it being actively developed?**

You also need to check whether it's compatible with your installed version of WordPress. Be aware that WordPress issues updates to the core system very regularly, so I wouldn't worry if the plugin doesn't say it's compatible with the very latest version. For example, if you're using version 2.8.6, as long as the plugin states it's compatible up to, say, 2.8.4 then I wouldn't worry too much. You can, after all, uninstall a plugin at any time.

you'll find it in your Profile: if you don't, just follow the link to set one up – it's free. Once you have your API key, go to Plugins/Akismet Configuration, enter it and click Update. Akismet will then work on your behalf, eliminating the vast majority of spam comments so you don't have to.

Register Plus

In most cases you'll want visitors to register with your site. This is the simplest way to build a list of people interested in you and your products. In the next part of this book we'll look at setting up an email list, but the Register Plus plugin means you can immediately keep track of interested visitors from the moment you launch your site.

WordPress has a built-in registration function, but it's very basic. Register Plus allows you to add custom fields to the registration form so you can learn more about your visitors when they sign up. You can also let them set their own password up front (rather than having to use an auto-generated one and change it through their profile later), and you can replace the WordPress logo with your own.

Under Settings > Register Plus Settings you'll see a whole list of options. For now, make sure you tick "Allow New Registrations to set their own Password" and "Enable Password Strength Meter". If you have a logo, upload it here. Make sure you tick "Prevent fake email address registrations". The alternative is to enable Captcha image verification, where users have to type in words shown in a box, but I've found this confuses some people, and anything that puts off potential customers is to be avoided.

Use the User Defined Fields section to add any extra data you want to ask for. You might want to know the user's gender or age range, or what led them to your site. Don't ask superfluous questions; every question will reduce the number of people who bother to complete the process.

Exclude Pages

You'll also be creating pages that you don't want to be included in the standard site navigation. These will include "thank you" pages for purchasers and those that sign up to your mailing list along with landing pages. The "Exclude Pages from Navigation" plugin adds an "Exclude Pages" group to the "Edit Pages" screen. To make a page invisible to the navigation system, simply deselect "Include this page in user menus".

Custom Meta

The default Widget that contains the "log in/register" link isn't customisable and contains options that aren't appropriate to a standard website. Install the Custom Meta

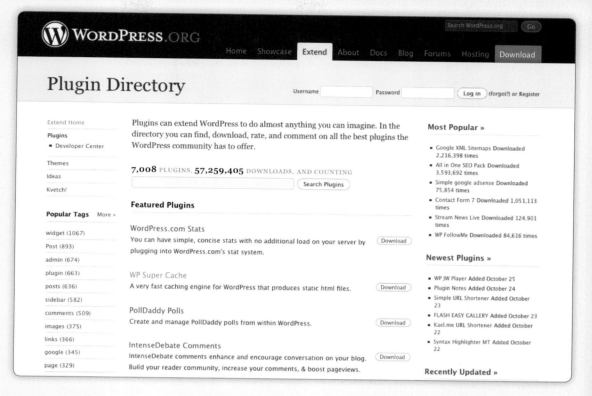

plugin and, unlike the others listed here, it will appear in your Dashboard under Appearence/Widgets. Find the Meta Widget and remove it, replacing it with the new Custom Meta widget. Give it a title such as "Log in" and select "Show 'Register/Site Admin'" and "Show 'Log in/Log out'" since these are the only relevant options.

OTHER USEFUL PLUGINS Given that there are over 7,000 plugins, you're likely to find something that meets your needs. The more specialised plugins tend to cost money, but it will be a fraction of the cost of creating an equivalent function from scratch.

MemberWing

As its name suggests, MemberWing is a membership manager. It allows you to protect parts of your site from non-members, and even put preview content in place which is then replaced with the real content when the user pays.

MemberWing is extremely sophisticated and includes integration with payment processors such as PayPal and Google Checkout, automatically adding new paid subscribers to the list of premium members and removing them when their payment expires. It also includes "drip feeding" of content, where pages are opened up over a period of time to each member. This is ideal for training sites where the course is delivered one week at a time.

If you don't need drip feeding, the Webmaster One version of the software ($99.99) is likely to fit the bill; otherwise, Professional One ($149.95) is the right choice.

WP Shopping Cart

This provides a shopping cart that integrates with your WordPress site and various payment gateways. It works well for a limited product range, but you may find it too limited if your business revolves around selling a range of products; on the following pages we'll look at more sophisticated shopping cart options.

WP Shopping Cart provides a straightforward way to take payment for products as long as your e-commerce requirements are fairly basic.

Create an app for your business

Smartphone and tablet apps can be an excellent marketing tool. There are hundreds of millions of active devices in circulation, which means your customers are likely to use them, so having your own app gives you extra exposure to people who hardly ever use a desktop browser.

It's expensive to have a custom app developed but, if you're willing to make a few compromises, it's possible to create your own app using one of the many services available online. The general quality of these services is poor, especially if you eliminate those that charge a monthly subscription for allowing you to continue distributing your app. I used iBuildApp.com because it not only offers a free, ad-supported version of its service, but also because it's the most fully featured.

Not every business should have an app. If you're an online shop, for example, there's little point trying to sell your products using an app since none of the online builders offers ecommerce functionality – the time would be better spent making the main site mobile-friendly. An enterprise that's aimed primarily at desktop/laptop users should concentrate on them first, although in that case you need to take care because the number of mobile internet users is increasing rapidly.

TO APP OR NOT TO APP So, who should have an app? If you're a local business – for example if you sell products online for local collection or offer an online service

with a local aspect – then having an app can be very useful. However, the best use for an app is often as another channel for your existing marketing efforts. For example, if you have a blog, a YouTube channel or a Facebook page, all of these will be generating data that can be easily incorporated, live, into your app and updated automatically.

MakingYourOwnCandles has its own blog (www.makingyourowncandlesblog.co.uk) which attracts several thousand visitors a month and around half of all mailing list signups – plus it helps boost the search engine rankings of the main site by linking to it. We also have our own YouTube channels, so an app that brings these to a smartphone is ideal.

One final thing – if you want your app to be widely used (and you do) then it needs to be submitted to the Apple App Store or Google Play. Since it's much easier, and cheaper, to submit to Google's service, we're using that, and targeting the hundreds of millions of Android smartphones and tablets.

 FIRST STEPS Start by heading to iBuildApp.com and clicking the Create Your App NOW!

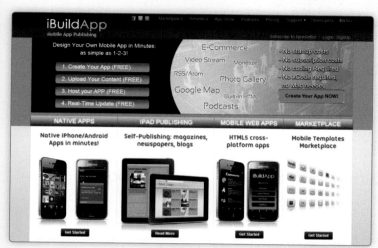

This simple, ad-supported app displays a YouTube feed.

button. You can sign in using your Facebook account or register an account on the site. Click the Create App button and, on the following screen, select a template for your app. You can change just about anything so, in most cases, Custom is the right choice here. If you prefer, you can click the View More Templates button to see a big gallery of premium templates – most of which available for a few pounds. Click the Use It button to select your template.

2 **THINK KEYWORDS** You'll now be asked to select a name for your app – make sure your keywords are included! Click Create and you'll be taken to the "Customize your app" screen. This is where you'll spend the majority of your time. You can edit the background (I used a plain white colour), upload your logo and edit the text to appear on the front screen. In the Manage Navigation section, you can add and delete sections for your app. For example, we added the RSS feed from our WordPress blog as a "Tips" section and our YouTube feed as a "Video" section. We also added contact icons, a Facebook

icon and even a photo icon that allows customers to take snaps of their candles and send them to us. Click Save & Complete when you've finished.

3 **ADD DETAILS** You can now fill in the information that will appear when your app is uploaded to your chosen app store. Again, make sure you get your keywords in! Bear in mind that you'll have the opportunity to edit this when you actually upload the app. You need to provide a 1,024 x 1,024 size version of your app icon so that iBuildApp.com can generate all the required icon sizes for your platform. Click Continue. On the next screen you'll generate a certificate for the app and a Google Maps API (even though we're not using Maps in our app). Click Continue and iBuildApp will build your app.

4 **YOU HAVE AN APP!** After a few minutes, the app should appear in your control panel. You can now download it. To submit it to Google Play, you need an Android Developers Account, which costs $25 per year. Go to https://play.google.com/apps/publish/signup and use your Google account. The process is painless, fast and cheap – three words that don't necessarily apply to Apple Developer registration. Once you've registered, you'll be able to log in to your Developer Dashboard and submit your app to Google Play. This should take a few minutes (again, the Apple process takes at least a week as they manually review all apps) and, within hours, your app will be available in each country you choose. Congratulations, you're an app publisher!

"The best use for an app is often as another channel for your existing marketing efforts."

PART 3 Selling

Maximise your sales

How to set up an eBay shop

eBay is a quick and effective way to begin selling physical products. You don't even need to market your shop – eBay does it for you. A basic eBay shop costs £14.99 per month and can be set up in minutes. But spending a little time configuring it and getting your listings right can have a huge impact on your success. Remember, you pay a listing fee whether or not your product sells, so you need all your listings to result in sales.

Here we'll walk through the process of opening up a shop with eBay. Before you start this process, there are two important hurdles to overcome. To open a Basic shop, you must have an existing eBay membership with a minimum feedback score of 10. In other words, you must have received ten feedback ratings from purchases you've made on eBay. Alternatively, you must be PayPal Verified.

Frankly, you need to be PayPal Verified in any case to be able to run any sort of business online, so I would suggest that if you're not already, you go through the process of getting verified. This is just a matter of connecting your PayPal identity to a bank account. These requirements are there to make it harder for scam artists and other undesirables to set up eBay shops and, inconvenient though it can be, it does makes sense.

YOUR PRODUCT Don't start building your shop until you have your product ready. When we set up the MakingYourOwnCandles eBay shop, we had our first sale within two hours. Online buyers expect next-day despatch at the latest, so if you haven't got an initial stock you're risking embarrassment and, worse, negative feedback.

1

2

3

4

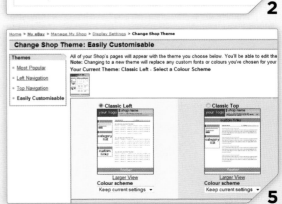

5

Feedback – the ratings you're given by those who buy from you – is an incredibly important element of eBay trading.

    Make sure you're very clear about the cost of making your product. Keep this in mind as you add your product listings, because eBay presents you with all sorts of opportunities to "enhance" your listings. These may help sales, but they cost money and therefore reduce your profit margin. On the plus side, listing fees are per *listing*, not per *product*: if you're selling ten products in the same listing then – assuming you sell all ten – the actual cost per product is a tenth of the total fee. Selling fees, however, accrue on top of this and are paid on each individual sale.

    Follow these steps to create your eBay shop.

1 **STEP INSIDE** Go to www.ebay.co.uk and sign in, then point your browser to www.ebay.co.uk/shops and click "Open a Shop". (There may also be a link to this on the eBay home page, but it tends to move around quite frequently.)

2 **START WITH THE BASICS** You'll almost certainly want to begin with a Basic shop. "Featured" shops have lower fees to compensate for their higher monthly fee, but you need to sell a lot of products to make it worthwhile. Note, though, that Featured shops seem to appear higher than Basic shops in the product listings for any given search, all things being equal.

    You also need to enter your shop name. In most cases you should be using a name that includes your search keywords, and if you intend to set up your own website, the shop name should be very similar to your domain name. In our case we've gone for MakingYourOwnCandles, which is exactly the same as our planned domain. Click Continue.

    The next screen may offer you some free subscriptions to eBay products (in my case Selling Manager and Sales Reports Plus). Decide whether you want to take them up – check for small print first – and click Continue.

3 **TUNE-UP TIME** You'll then be asked if you want to perform a "Quick Shop Tune-up" of your nascent emporium. I suggest you take a look and decide for yourself which of the options makes sense to you. Personally, I prefer to specify the settings for my shop from the ground up. To do this, go to My eBay and select Selling. Under Shortcuts, click Manage my shop. This should bring up the "Manage my Shop" summary screen.

4 **FIRST IMPRESSIONS** Click Display Settings to edit the appearance of your shop. If you have a logo, make sure you include it in your design (to find out how I got my logo, and why I don't recommend you take the same route, check out www.scribbleit.co.uk/

blog/?p=229). The aim is to have your eBay shop and your future website share a similar design, even if that only really amounts to the colour scheme. For professional logo design at a low price, check out http://99designs.com

    We look at colour choices on p46, so take a look at that when coming up with a palette. In my case, orange and yellow are considered "creative" colours, and are also reminiscent of fire, so they fitted in well with candle making.

5 **SAME DIFFERENCE** Click "Change to another theme" to browse through the available shop structures. Although there's a reasonable range of themes, they all tend to be much of a muchness. This is a weakness of selling on eBay, but at least everyone's in the same boat! Personally, I prefer the "classic" themes, which you can access by clicking the Easily Customisable link. I think they result in cleaner, more appealing designs which you can more easily mould to your liking. Click Save when you're done.

    Choose "Edit current theme" to modify the colour scheme, some fonts, and that's about it. Choose colours from your palette and pick plain fonts (Verdana is a good choice from the limited options). Click Save Settings and then go through the other links under Shop Design to customise your shop. The most important one to sort out at this point is Product Categories. When you've finished tweaking, click the Shop Summary link to go back to the "Manage my Shop" screen.

6 **OPEN FOR BUSINESS** Finally, click the View My Shop link to see your shop in all its glory.

An eBay shop can never be truly "yours" in the same way as a website you design from scratch, but it's the quickest way to create a working ecommerce site. By adding your own colour scheme and logo,s you can make it look reasonably well branded.

Selling your first items on eBay

As a new eBay seller, you start at a disadvantage. eBay rewards established sellers, with high volumes and good feedback, by making it easier for their items to appear higher in the search results. At first, you're likely to be listed near the bottom of the results for any category. So what can you do about it?

Any user who searches a popular eBay category will find hundreds of results competing for attention, and the higher up the listing you are, the more views your product will have. It's therefore absolutely essential that your products appear as high as possible, but it's not obvious how you can influence that, given that you won't be a PowerSeller for some time.

Exactly how eBay ranks results is a bit of a mystery, but my observations are:

- It gives a significant boost to items that offer **free postage**. The cynical might conclude that this is because if you include postage in the price of your product, eBay makes more money, since listing fees increase according to the price of the product.

- The more you pay for your listing in terms of eBay's **optional extras**, the higher it is likely to appear relative to your other listings.

- When you're selling multiple items, **items that are already selling best** will appear above the others.

- Counterintuitively, **items with longer to go** until their listing ends will appear above those with shorter end dates. Again, it may not be a coincidence that the fees will also be higher on these items.

The 80/20 rule applies to eBay selling, just as it does to Google AdWords and many other aspects of running an online business. If you're one of the 20% of businesses that systematically analyse the impact on profitability of each of their options, you have an instant edge on your rivals – an edge that might make the difference between a viable business and a failure.

My advice is to "split-test" your listings. Wherever possible, create two listings for identical products (this works best if you're also selling in quantities). Make the listings the same except for one feature. For example, you might pay the extra fee for a subtitle on one of the listings. Run the two items simultaneously until they finish and compare the results.

First, look to see which of the two comes up higher in the rankings (you should find the subtitle gives a slight boost), then compare sales. Also compare the number

1

2

of views of each product. If one of the two listings is a clear winner, your next should be based on that one, testing a new feature each time.

This may seem long-winded, but expecting instant results on eBay is a fantasy. It's only by following an analytical approach that you will develop an understanding of how to market your product effectively. Here's how to get started with your listings.

1 **BEYOND THE BASICS** Click Sell at the top of the eBay home page, then select Advanced Sell. There's a principle with systems such as eBay, Amazon and Google AdWords that you should never allow the service provider to pick your settings for you, because they're unlikely to suit your product exactly.

Type a descriptive phrase into the text box: this will help eBay find a product category. Click "Start selling", and select from the categories you're presented with. If you can't find the right category, click Browse to look through the entire category list. Click Continue.

2 **TITLES WITH IMPACT** As with a Google Ad, your title is critical. Use your research from p26 to give you a head start, and make certain your keywords are in the title. It's worth experimenting with adding "new" to the title (if your product is new) because many people still assume that all items on eBay are used.

3 **PICTURE PERFECT** Now add some pictures. The first is currently free of charge, so there's no excuse for not having a photo, and it's usually worth adding at least one more. Don't use generic shots that just convey the type of item; buyers want to see the actual product they're buying.

Make the effort to take a good photo, as it makes you look more professional. You can get perfectly acceptable results with a bog-standard digital camera: the essential part

to get right is the lighting. Natural light is often best, but you need to minimise shadows, and that often requires a couple of lamps (with "natural light" bulbs) and preferably a light tent; a small pop-up white tent used to diffuse light. If you do have a digital SLR, this is where it will pay for itself. Take all your photos in RAW mode and you can adjust the exposure and other settings without digital noise (grain) and image compression artefacts becoming visible.

4 **CLINCH THE SALE** Spend time on your descriptions. Always repeat the title of the listing at the top of the description box. You need to list, briefly, what you're offering and, if you have a unique selling point, say what that is. eBay buyers have very short attention spans, so you must clinch the sale early – in this respect, less is more. ➜

Attractive photos of your product are well worth the effort, as they'll make all the difference when buyers are choosing between numerous listings. If any objects appear in the photo that are not part of what you're selling, make sure this is clearly stated in the description, even if you think it's obvious.

| Basic | Self Hosting |

Select pictures for upload   Try th

(First picture is free. Each additional picture is £0.12.)Add up to 12 pictures.

Browse..   Recommended size: Between 1000 and 1600 pixels on the longer side

	Pictures	Status
1	teacup.jpg	Pending
2	candlemakingsamplekit.jpg	Pending

Copied 0 / Pending 2 / Available 10

Select optional picture upgrades

ℹ Good news! Gallery Picture is free. Add a picture and we will show your item to buyers in se

3

Add pictures   Remove all pictures

ℹ Good news! Gallery Picture is free. Add a picture and we'll show your item to buyers in search re

✱ **Describe the item you're selling**   Add or remove options | Get help

| Standard | HTML |

Arial ▾   10 ▾   A▾   B I U   ≡ ≡ ≡ ≡   ≔ ≔   ⇥ ⇥   ✎ Check spel

candle. This is the ideal way to have a go at candle making at very low expens

Candle making offers you the enjoyment both of making the candles and

4

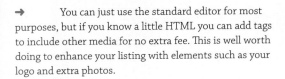

→ You can just use the standard editor for most purposes, but if you know a little HTML you can add tags to include other media for no extra fee. This is well worth doing to enhance your listing with elements such as your logo and extra photos.

5 **PRICING OPTIONS** In most cases you'll want to list your items as "Buy it Now" purchases. The advantage of this to the buyer is that they don't have to wait until the end of the auction to know they've secured the item – it's more like buying from a shop. You can experiment with the auction option once you make a success of "Buy it Now". Also enter how many you want to sell: if you have multiples of the same product, entering the

item with additional postage. That's an amazing result given that there were only 98 items in the list overall, and it put the free p&p version of my item on the front page.

At the bottom of the page you'll see "Your fees so far": remember these eat into your profit. Click Continue.

6 **FEATURE PRESENTATION** You'll see a number of options under the section "Make your listing stand out". Most of these will have a positive impact on sales, although it may be minor. This is an area you should test, beginning with the cheapest option. Featured Plus is expensive and guarantees only that you'll appear at the top of the search page *that you'd normally appear on*. In other words, if you would otherwise appear

---

"Expecting instant results is a fantasy. With an analytical approach, you will develop an understanding of how to market your product."

---

quantity here cuts down on your listing fees and adds to your credibility as a retailer rather than a private seller.

As a new eBay shop-owner you may be limited to accepting only PayPal, but in any case PayPal should always be an option. If you have the ability to accept cheques as well, you need to decide whether the hassle of doing so outweighs the extra sales you might generate; few retailers accept cheques these days, but some eBayers prefer them to PayPal.

Now for the important question of postage. eBay likes items with free post and packing, so your first split test should be to see if you can make more money increasing the price to include it (thus making p&p "free") or selling at a lower price plus p&p (and coming further down the results).

As an example, my first split test resulted in the item with free p&p appearing 34 places above the identical

halfway down page 3 of the results, paying for Featured Plus would make you appear at the top of page 3.

If you select Featured First, you stand a chance of appearing at the top of the first page – depending, presumably, on how many others are also paying for this. These very expensive options should be experimented with only once you've nailed down your pricing and presentation.

Check out the listing preview to ensure it looks how you want it to. Make sure you review your fees and, crucially, note the Final Value Fee. The Listing Fee is paid once, no matter how many items you're selling within the same listing; the Final Value Fee is paid per sale. Be certain you can make a profit after these are taken into account.

Once finished, don't forget to click "Save this listing as a template" so that you can base other product listings on it. Click "List your item". Give it a few minutes and see where it appears when you search for it.

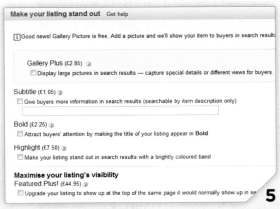

5

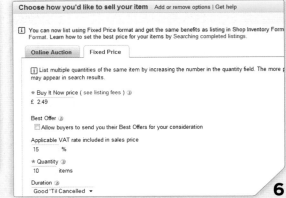

6

Sell like a pro on Amazon

Selling on Amazon is the online equivalent of having Tesco stock your blueberry jam. Not only does this give you a huge potential audience within a trusted environment, but Amazon will also take care of payment processing and, for an additional fee, it will even store and ship your goods from its warehouses.

Amazon has a clear plan to be the world's primary online shopping destination across a wide range of products and, as a small businessperson, you can fight it or use its megalomania for your own purposes.

For some businesses, using Amazon as your primary e-commerce platform makes sense. A dealer in antique books would be crazy to ignore the world's dominant bookseller. For other businesses, it isn't so clear. There are some product types Amazon doesn't sell and others that aren't its prime business. For many online businesses, Amazon offers an additional sales channel to pick up customers who wouldn't find you through Google.

Case study 1: The independent web shop

We could have sold all the MakingYourOwnCandles range of candle-making kits from within Amazon, but we chose not to. Firstly because Amazon isn't strongly associated with craft products. While customers searching on Google for "beeswax candle making kits" would see our product in their search results even if it was hosted by Amazon, our efforts to promote the business would benefit Amazon as much as us. You lose control over search engine optimisation and, crucially, the entire sales funnel.

However, the most important reason we chose to have our own shop was that, once the customer arrives on an Amazon page, Amazon prompts them to consider the products of competitors via the "What other items…" and "Customers who bought this item also bought…" sections of the listing page. It's all too easy for the customer to get distracted and click away from your page.

But it's possible to use this customer behaviour to your advantage by maintaining your own online shop as well as selling selected products on Amazon. That means customers using Amazon to search for candle-making kits are likely to see our products either as a direct result of searching or having visited the page of a competitor.

Amazon's Webstore service makes it possible to have the best of both worlds. Webstore is Amazon's own e-commerce platform for creating independent online shops. It combines well with the systems for selling on Amazon, which means you could have a single back-end providing order, inventory and customer management

By listing your products on Amazon, you get a simple store front to which you can direct customers.

whether the customer purchases on your site or Amazon. And by using Webstore, you don't have to worry about payment processing as it's built in.

However, we chose BigCommerce for two key reasons. The first is that Webstore doesn't offer the customisation or depth of features we get from BigCommerce. As we saw our own shop as providing the majority of sales, it was essential to get the very best product we could.

The second reason is that I don't like all my eggs in one basket. What if Amazon changes its terms of service in a way that, for whatever reason, could exclude us and cut off our only source of income?

Amazon has an ever increasing range of e-commerce services but, broadly speaking, they fall into three related groups: Amazon Webstore, Sell On Amazon (aka Amazon Marketplace) and Amazon Payments. Whatever your situation, if you sell products that are compatible with Amazon, you can probably generate extra business by cosying up to them.

MOVE IT ON, SHIP IT OUT The more items you have in your inventory, the more useful Amazon's packing and distribution service could be. Indeed, Fulfilment by Amazon may make it possible to sell a far wider range of products than you otherwise could. Let's say you were doing nicely selling a limited range of phone accessories but wanted to increase turnover. One option would be to expand your range, but to do that you'd need more storage space and it would take longer for you to find each item.

Amazon, on the other hand, is a company well used to handling millions of items efficiently. By signing up

to the Fulfilment by Amazon service, you send them batches of your products which it stores and ships when ordered. Your only involvement in this side of the business is to send new supplies in bulk to Amazon as required – a much less onerous task.

This service costs money, naturally, so your income from each sale drops, but so does the time you need to devote to fulfilment. For businesses with lots of products and limited resources, it's often a trade worth making. One added benefit is that your products can then be delivered to the usual Amazon timescales and costs, including free delivery. This is certain to increase your conversion rate.We signed up our candle kit business to FBA in early 2012 and doing so has resulted in a net increase in our business with very few problems. It also means we are able to sell our products in the EU without the hassle of having to ship them abroad ourselves.

Choose the Fulfilment by Amazon service and it will stock and ship your products for you – at a price.

The editing functions available to Amazon Webstore users are less sophisticated than the best e-commerce packages.

Britishwatchcompany.com is a fully functioning online shop built using Amazon's Webstore technology.

Case study
2: The reseller

Let's imagine you've started up an online business reselling smartphone cases. You buy 100 for each of the best-selling phones (perhaps 500 in the case of the iPhone) at around £1 each using www.alibaba.com to find suppliers and you intend to sell them for £3 each.

With this sort of business, it may not be sensible to set up an independent shop but rather to sell your products where your customers are already looking: in this case primarily Amazon and eBay. It's likely that the products you're selling are already being sold on Amazon by someone else (you'd have found this out during your research phase and worked out how to undercut them or offer something they don't)

and this makes integrating into Amazon simple.

By becoming a Pro Merchant, you can add products by simply searching for them within your merchant control panel. If they exist on Amazon's database, you are asked to add information about your price, service and stock availability. It really is as easy as that. But the simplicity of the process means that lots of suppliers use this approach so differentiating yourself is critical.

You might offer lower prices, lightning-fast delivery or perfect customer service and Amazon makes each of these easy to achieve. Although it takes time to build up a reputation since only a tiny minority of buyers leave feedback, prospective customers believe these comments are impartial and they trust Amazon, which makes the rating all the more valuable.

Setting up shop on Amazon

You've decided you want to sell through Amazon; now it's time to actually do it. The good news is that, once set up as a merchant, it can take just a few minutes from sitting down in front of the Seller Central control panel to having your new product uploaded and ready to be sold.

If you're a business, it almost always pays to select the "Sell a Lot" option here to become a Pro Merchant.

Before setting up your shop, you need to decide whether you want to "go pro". Go to http://services.amazon.co.uk, click "Sell on Amazon" and you'll be asked whether you expect to "sell a little" or "sell a lot". If you expect to sell more than 33 items per month then the choice is simple: opt for the latter and sign up for a Pro Merchant account. But what if you sell fewer?

The standard merchant account charges 75p per item on top of the normal seller fees (see p15) whereas the Pro account charges a flat rate of £25 per month (plus VAT) so once 33 items have been sold it becomes cheaper to pay the flat rate. However, there are other benefits to the Pro account that mean it's probably the best choice for you.

For example, there are some product categories that Amazon limits to Pro Merchants only; for example, if you're selling PC software you'd need to go Pro. Pro Merchants also have a vastly better set of web-based tools they can use to add and edit their products, manage their inventory and interact with customers. Finally, only Pro Merchants can add products not already listed in Amazon's database, so for our candle-making kit business we were left with no choice. If you don't feel you can make enough profit to pay the £25-per-month fee then you'd be better off waiting until your business has grown a little before becoming an Amazon merchant.

SIGNING UP You can base your merchant login on your existing Amazon account but it's usually best to keep the business separate by setting up an entirely new account using a business email address and details. The process is pretty straightforward, although it includes various verification procedures that might take some days so it's worth getting started as early as possible.

Once you've signed up, you'll arrive at your new home: the Seller Central control panel (above right). You'll spend most of your time in the first two sections on the left-hand side: Inventory and Orders. But before you start adding products, go through the links under Settings to make sure the information there is accurate and complete.

It's particularly important that you ensure the Shipping Settings are correct. If you're selling books, CDs or DVDs then Amazon takes care of this by imposing its standard postal costs, but for other items it's up to you. It's usually best to choose a weight-based model for shipping rather than a price-based model since that's how most postal systems work. Amazon allows you to charge a base price per shipment plus an additional cost per kilogramme weight. Exactly what you charge will depend on the delivery methods you choose but don't shirk the calculation: guesswork is likely to result in losing money on post or, if you've set it too high, missing out on sales.

ADDING PRODUCTS To add the first new product, go to Inventory/Add a Product. If you're selling a product that's already in the Amazon catalogue, enter its name and click the Search button. Select it from the list and click the "Sell yours" button.

If you're adding a new product, click "Create a new product". You'll then be asked to choose the appropriate category for your listing. Your starting point should be the category chosen by your competitors or those of the products most similar to yours.

Warning! Amazon places restrictions on the Toys and Games category in the lead up to Christmas. Presumably to reduce the number of returns and refunds, it will only allow established sellers who've sold a minimum number of products in the preceding period to have their products appear in this category. In 2012, sellers needed to have sold 25 units in the 60 days leading up to the start of November or their listings would be suspended. They also need to meet certain minimum defect, delivery and returns standards. If you're concerned that you might not meet those levels then check to see if there's another category your products might qualify for.

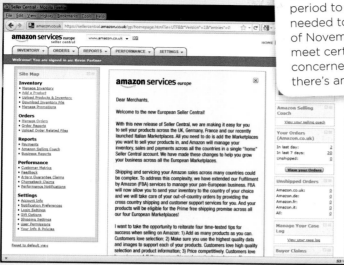

The Seller Central control panel lets you create products, manage orders and feedback, as well as generate performance reports.

On the Vital Info page, complete all the mandatory fields and as many of the optional fields as possible. The more information you provide the more credible you are. And, of course, the better your customer will understand the product. Many categories include a mandatory "EAN or UPC" field – this is the barcode for your product. Don't panic if you don't have one at this point, as obtaining a barcode is pretty simple (see below right).

The rest of the pages apply both to products that exist in Amazon's catalogue and new products. In this case, click Next to move to the Offer page. Again, complete as much information as you can in addition to the mandatory information. You can also enter a Sale price for a fixed period: I always like to discount new products as it makes them stand out in the Amazon search listings (reduced prices are shown in red) and, naturally, increases the conversion rate.

If you have a separate shop, the price on Amazon should be similar but not necessarily identical since the cost of sale is different. For example, on your own shop you'll have the cost of your e-commerce software and hosting plus the cost of marketing (usually via Google AdWords) whereas on Amazon these are replaced by the monthly Pro Merchant fee and commission.

The next step is to add product images. Add as many as needed to make sure the customer understands both what your product will look like when they receive it (a box shot, for example) and how it will look in use. Err on the side of adding too many rather than too few pictures.

The "Key Product Features" you list in the Description section will appear as bullet points under Technical Details on the product listing page so it's essential you get these right. Make sure you give enough information

here for the customer to be able to decide whether they're interested in your product.

Spend time on the "Product Description" field; I still find it shocking how many sellers can't be bothered to describe their products fully. Again, this appears on the product listing page and it's probably the section most people scroll to first. This field supports basic HTML tags (although this is undocumented) so you can bold text and use italics as well as using the <p> and <br /> tags to split the content into paragraphs and lists. If you don't use these tags, the text gets condensed into an offputting single paragraph.

The "Search Terms" on the Keywords page might seem self-explanatory but Amazon automatically indexes the product title and manufacturer so there's no point repeating those keywords here. Amazon doesn't index your product description or bullet points so check whether there are keywords in those fields that need carrying across.

Finally, on the More Details page, although it isn't marked as a mandatory field, you must insert an accurate shipping weight if you've chosen weight-based shipping. Once done, click "Save and Finish". At this point Amazon will check you've provided all the information needed and upload your photos. New listings and amendments to existing products take a few minutes to propagate through Amazon's systems so don't panic if changes don't appear instantly. Once the listing has appeared, check the product detail page. Make sure the photos have successfully uploaded and that the bullet points and description are correctly formatted.

Here's our final product, now available to the millions of Amazon customers.

How to obtain barcodes

EAN is Europe's product numbering format. Obtaining a new EAN is expensive as it involves joining the regulatory body for a hefty yearly fee. The good news is that you can obtain EANs cheaply from companies that have bought them in bulk and most will render the EAN as a barcode for you. I use www.barcode1.co.uk at around £25 for a single barcode. Important: your code does NOT need to be registered with the regulatory body unless you intend to sell it with multiple retailers.

Making money from your Amazon shop

Setting up an Amazon shop and putting products on the digital shelves is just the start. To have a successful Amazon business means finding customers, persuading them to buy and then fulfilling their orders efficiently – in that order.

We moved from 60th in a general search to third for a longer tail phrase by adding the right keywords.

HOW DO CUSTOMERS FIND YOU?

Assuming you've added your products and chosen good categories and keywords, determined customers will be able to find them. Most products are sold as the result of a search either within Google or on Amazon itself, and it goes without saying that the higher up the results you are, the more sales you'll make.

So, how does Amazon decide how to rank the search results? Well, if you thought Google was secretive about its algorithms, it can't hold a candle (ahem) to Amazon. However, based on my research, there are four main factors that influence where a product ranks.

1 SEARCH TERMS

Amazon compares the user's search query against the product name, the brand/manufacturer and the keywords you've included manually when adding the product in the first place.

This is yet another example of why it's so important to know your main keywords. These keywords must be in the product title but you can include subtle variations and additions in the "Search Terms" section of the product details.

Amazon appears to use keywords to assemble a list of matching products and then works out their relevance to the search terms to begin ranking them. So, without a product title and details that match the search query, your product won't even appear on the list. Once this list has

been generated, keywords become the main ranking factor.

As with Google, it's easier to compete for "long tail" keywords and this is where the "Search Terms" field can really pay off. For example if a searcher types "candle making kit" into the Amazon product search box, they'll see over 100 results. While it's important that you rank as highly as possible, it may prove impossible to get a front page listing.

For example, if the searcher types "candle making kit with dye", they see a handful of results, the top one being our Pink Rose candle making kit. Why? Because "dye" is one of the extra search terms I added when I created the product. Given that the other products in the list are all books, it looks to the customer as if there is only one candle-making kit available.

The best way to generate your long tail keywords is to look at your Google AdWords campaign. Select one of your main broad match keywords and click the "See search terms…" button followed by Selected to limit the results to just the keyword you chose.

This will show you all the search terms Google's algorithm exposed your ad to – in other words it's a list of phrases customers used to find you. Since they're likely to use similar phrases when searching on Amazon, it's worth harvesting the best and transferring them to your Amazon products.

In our case, I've found that people often add the words "make", "scent", "craft" and "easy" to their search so

Google AdWords can provide a helpful pointer to the keywords you should be choosing.

Amazon's new Reports interface helps you focus on how your products are performing.

I've added those search terms to the Keywords tab on the product details pages for all the products they apply to.

Just as it's still possible to achieve a position on the front page of Google for a long but highly profitable keyphrase, by using this technique you can laser-target your Amazon products. Indeed, in my experience there's much less competition in the product search so it's possible to dominate a valuable category simply by picking the right keywords.

As an example, when I added the word "easy" to the search keywords for a kit that languished in 60th position for a search on "candle making kit", it appeared in third place for a search on "easy candle making kit". Fewer people will search on that keyphrase but they'll all see our kit, whereas they're extremely unlikely to find it when searching more generally.

2 SALES PERFORMANCE

Once Amazon has used keywords to select the appropriate products and assign a "relevance" weighting, it further refines the positioning based on a range of other factors. Broadly speaking, the greater a product's sales, the higher it will appear compared with identical products that have sold less well.

Looking at our range, there's a clear correlation between sales of a product and its position relative to our other products. Being higher up the listings also results in more sales, of course, which further boosts a product's position. This sounds like a classic case of chicken and egg so it pays to think creatively about how you could get sales without relying on search position, at least for long enough to get it on the front page.

Nothing is more important to your position in the Amazon product search listing than the product title and the keywords you select.

For example, you could promote the product to your email list, along with a direct link to encourage the first sales. We've provided a link directly to our Amazon store in our shop's main menu. Some customers prefer to buy through Amazon so they can use their existing account and it suits us because these sales will help boost new products.

3 NUMBER OF SELLERS

I've seen definite evidence that keywords and sales performance are key factors Amazon takes into account but it also seems that they reward products being sold by multiple sellers. The truly diabolical candle-making kits sold by retailers, therefore, tend to rank higher because more people resell them. MakingYourOwnCandles kits are only sold by us so we're always going to be at a disadvantage

4 SELLER PERFORMANCE

You might be surprised to learn that I can find no evidence that the quantity or quality of user reviews plays any part in ranking. I find this surprising and I suspect Amazon will work it into its algorithm at some point. I suspect that it factors in the seller feedback, returns rate and other metrics but I can't prove this as I can only look at the figures for my business. I also suspect Amazon favours sellers that use its fulfilment service, but maybe that's just my cynical mind.

Running a profitable shop

Amazon keeps a close eye on what it calls "Customer Metrics", including returns rates, cancellation rates, how often you're late despatching the goods and whether you've been caught violating policies.

Imagine you're selling a popular digital watch. Amazon will only show one product page but one of the sellers will be chosen as the default – in other words it will be that merchant who will get the sale when the customer clicks "Add to Basket". If Amazon stocks the item, it will be the default; but if not, it uses customer metrics, price and, no doubt, sales performance to choose the lucky seller. The number of times you are the default divided into the number of times the page has been viewed is the "Buy Box Percentage". This is a key performance metric – it also has a huge impact on your conversion rate.

So it pays to provide Amazon-level, or better, customer service. Make certain all goods are as described, despatch quickly and on time, respond to queries promptly and stick within all policies.

Finally, make sure you have a system in place for customer feedback. New customers are much more likely to buy from a seller with several positive ratings – even having just a few can make a big difference. And, after all, you should be interested in what your customers have to say about your service and products.

Amazon offers a powerful platform for selling products but making a success of it requires time, attention and care. You must pick the right products, create good listings, get systems in place to fulfil orders efficiently and, above all, get your keywords right. Choosing appropriate search terms can be the difference between bang and bust.

Running a stockless store using Fulfilled By Amazon

Once you've established a profitable business selling products, you'll probably find the growth of your new online enterprise being limited by two factors – manpower and physical space.

Traditionally, the answer to running out of hours in the day was to hire someone, but most online businesses are now turning to outsourcing in all its various forms to help them achieve more without the huge commitment of taking on employees.

As your product line expands, you'll find that the proportion of your time spent finding, packaging and despatching orders also grows – as does the space needed to keep stock. Every successful small business experiences that slightly terrifying moment when it threatens to expand beyond the capabilities of the founders to handle everything, as well as the space they have available in their homes. Fulfilled by Amazon (FBA) is one way to stave off this moment, perhaps permanently.

For MakingYourOwnCandles, FBA has been a huge success since we joined the scheme in early 2012. By offloading the picking, packing and delivery of some of our products to one of the most efficient order management systems in the world, we've been able to increase our turnover without needing to take on extra staff or hire an additional warehouse of our own.

GETTING STARTED Begin by listing your products on Amazon as described in "Setting up shop on Amazon" (*see p80*). If you have existing inventory you've been despatching yourself, as we did, it's a simple matter of selecting each product you want to hand over to Amazon and choosing "Convert to 'Fulfilled by Amazon'" in the dropdown. And that's all there is to joining the scheme – you can leave just as easily.

Timing is everything here. As soon as you switch to Amazon fulfilment, these products become unavailable for customers to buy – and will remain so until you've shipped them to Amazon. So, if you have a large range, it might be worth converting them a few at a time so that the immediate cashflow hit is minimised.

SENDING YOUR PRODUCTS TO AMAZON
Once you've identified the stock you want to go to Amazon, you can book a shipment. The shipping process is fairly straightforward, the main choice being whether you want to use stickerless or labelled inventory. If your products have barcodes, choose stickerless. If not, Amazon will generate stickers for you to affix to your products. You then set the quantities of each product you want to send and select an approved carrier from the list of options.

Judging the amount of stock to send is one of the key decisions you need to make. Bear in mind that you must have at least enough to cover the time it takes to restock. To work this out, estimate your daily sales and then multiply that by the time it will take to get your product on Amazon's shelves. At MakingYourOwnCandles, our experience has

By signing up to Fulfilled By Amazon, you become part of its world-class inventory management system.

been that it can take up to five working days from the moment Amazon receives the product to it being available for sale. We'd foolishly assumed that, given they're capable of despatching purchased products same-day, they'd have a similarly efficient stocking system. The end result was that our best-selling Amazon product was out of stock for well over a week, despite having been sent on a next-day courier.

You should also bear in mind that you pay for the courier, and this must be factored into the calculations you make about whether FBA is worth it. In our case, we charge slightly more for our Amazon products, partly to make up for this extra cost and partly because we believe our shop customers deserve the best deal. To further muddy the waters, Amazon has many distribution centres and it often requires you to split a shipment, thus doubling the cost.

MANAGING YOUR FBA PRODUCTS

Amazon will let you know when you make a sale – in our case we manually enter all these sales into BigCommerce so we can keep a single set of figures. Your main task is to keep an eye on the inventory level and prepare new shipments in plenty of time. On the one hand, you don't want your products to be unavailable when customers attempt to buy them; on the other, it's expensive to leave stock sitting unsold on Amazon's shelves. Remember, lack of cashflow kills more small businesses than any other cause.

This is especially challenging if you have a seasonal business. In the case of MakingYourOwnCandles, during our peak months of November and December our turnover is around four times that of our quietest periods, so an error either way could be very expensive.

IS IT WORTH IT? Despite these caveats, a well
managed FBA programme can be well worth it for many businesses. By handing over at least some of your product range to Amazon to fulfil, you outsource not only delivery but warehousing and, crucially, customer service. If the product gets lost or damaged on its way to the customer,

they contact Amazon and not you. Whilst the customer is refunded out of your balance, this is almost always recovered from the carrier with no effort on your part.

Amazon also handles all payment processing and automatically remits your credit balance every two weeks. As long as you keep on top of the inventory levels, there's nothing else for you to do but leave them to sell your product. This means you can take time off from the business, perhaps even enjoy a holiday, without sacrificing cashflow or inconveniencing your eager customers.

Overall, FBA offers a tempting, partially automated, fulfilment system for online businesses experiencing growing pains as well as newer businesses with a large range of Amazon-friendly products. Indeed, it's possible to create a profitable enterprise that deliberately uses the sophistication and capacity of Amazon's fulfilment system to stock a far wider range of products than it could handle itself, thus punching well above its weight.

FBA: how much does it cost?

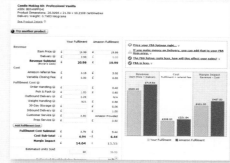

Amazon provides a handy online calculator (type "FBA calculator" into Google). If your product is already stocked on Amazon, you can use its Unique Product Code or barcode number to find it. Down the left-hand column, enter the cost details of your product at present. Don't forget to enter estimates of the time spent per item on packing and customer service as well as the postal cost.

Most of the right-hand side is pre-filled but you should add in the per-item cost of sending the product to Amazon's warehouse, along with the cost of preparing it for shipment

The FBA calculator allows you to work out what the overall cost of switching is likely to be.

and the number of units you sold using your own fulfilment in a month.

Finally, estimate the percentage increase in your sales by switching to FBA. In our experience, this isn't mere fantasy – customers are more likely to buy if they know Amazon is delivering the product, not least because it almost always means they can choose a free delivery option. 20% is a reasonable estimate of the sort of boost you can hope for.

The calculator will now work out whether you're likely to make more or less money using FBA. Bear in mind that, even if the two forms work out roughly equal, you have benefited from freeing up time to work on other aspects of the business, or to process orders placed through your online shop. Usually, however, FBA represents either a break-even or a profit.

How to take payment

Your online shop is built, your virtual shelves are filled but how are you going to take payment? You need a reliable, secure and affordable method that's as convenient as possible for your customers or you risk losing sales at the last hurdle.

In practice, this means accepting debit and credit cards as well as PayPal. It isn't usually worth the effort to accept cheques or cash so you should avoid these unless you have a specific reason for doing otherwise.

DO YOU WANT TO BE A MERCHANT?

To accept credit and debit cards two services are needed: a merchant account and a payment gateway. A merchant account is needed irrespective of whether you intend to sell online, over the phone or in a physical shop. It's a specialised type of bank account used for handling credit card transactions. A payment gateway is used to capture the card details when the customer buys a product so that the funds are transferred to the seller.

As a seller, you'll normally be charged two fees for each transaction – one by your bank and the other by your payment gateway. For example, CardNet is LloydsTSB's merchant account provider and SagePay is its recommended payment gateway. CardNet might charge, say, a 2.5% fee for each credit card payment (depending on your business type and how long you've been trading) and SagePay £20 per month for up to 1,000 transactions per quarter.

How do you, as a new online business, get a merchant account? The answer is, almost certainly, that you don't. Even in normal economic conditions, major banks would baulk at providing the ability to process credit cards to new businesses – including those that can prove themselves to be kosher. This is largely because of consumer protection legislation which means that the buck stops with the processing banks if a card is used fraudulently or processed incompetently. For example, if someone were to steal your credit card and use it to buy a laptop from an online shop, you would expect your money back. Mastercard or Visa will then request a "chargeback" from your bank which it will pass onto you. If your company doesn't have the means to pay then the bank foots the bill.

PayPal Website Payments Pro allows you to accept credit and debit cards from within your shopping cart.

Google Checkout offers similar features to PayPal Website Payments Standard but requires your customers to have a Checkout account.

PAYMENT PROCESSORS

PAYMENT PROCESSORS Fortunately, this huge gap in the market is filled by a number of services that, effectively, combine a merchant account with payment processing. These services are easier and quicker to set up and most accept applications from startups. However, they will almost certainly work out to be more expensive than merchant accounts for all but the smallest online retailers.

How much do they charge? That's easy: the four main services all charge 3.4% of the value of the transaction plus 20p (as of October 2011).

PAYPAL WEB PAYMENTS STANDARD

For most new online businesses, PayPal is likely to be your best (and perhaps only) choice. Once you have a verified business account you'll be able to accept both instant payments and, for selling products, standard payments. Every shopping cart I've ever seen can integrate with PayPal Web Payments Standard (PWPS) and it's often the default choice when starting up.

In most shopping carts, PWPS offers a "checkout with PayPal button". When the customer clicks the button, they are taken to PayPal's site to make their payment. If they don't have a PayPal account, they can pay via credit or debit card.

Once payment has been made, they're prompted to return to the shop for the order confirmation screen. PayPal lets your e-commerce software know that payment has been successfully taken so you can ship the order.

You're then free to initiate a funds transfer from PayPal to your linked bank account.

Identifying the nature of your business is a crucial step in putting together your plan.

> "For most new online businesses, PayPal is likely to be your best choice."

Plucky British competitor to PayPal, Nochex is an interesting alternative for new businesses looking for a payment processing service.

PAYPAL WEB PAYMENTS PRO

PAYPAL WEB PAYMENTS PRO Web Payments Standard provides a good, basic service but it suffers from an important limitation: your customer is taken off-site to pay. The page they're taken to is heavily PayPal branded, which not only undermines your credibility (have you ever seen a major retailer use this approach?) but can also confuse customers who don't have PayPal accounts, damaging your conversion rate.

Web Payments Pro, on the other hand, integrates directly into your shopping cart payment page. The customer pays by plastic, not PayPal, and they're presented with the familiar card fields. It feels more professional, it involves fewer steps and they stay on your site throughout. Web Payments Pro also includes "Virtual Terminal", which allows you to take payments via phone, fax and post, something that will be more appealing to some businesses than others.

Unlike Standard, Pro charges a £20-per-month fee as well as the same 3.4% + 20p charge per transaction, so you won't be saving any money by upgrading. However, on MakingYourOwnCandles.co.uk, we got a sizeable bump in business when we implemented it that more than made up for the monthly cost.

PayPal suggests that if you take more than £1,000 in online payments per month, Pro is a good choice – and I think that's just about right. In fact, we run Standard and Pro alongside each other. Customers who want to pay by PayPal click the button provided by Standard, those that want to use their card type it straight in. We find that approximately 60% choose the latter option.

Signing up for Web Payments Pro, however, is not as simple as Standard. Because customers use credit and debit cards with this service, PayPal becomes exposed to possible chargebacks to a much greater extent. The main factors PayPal takes into account seem to be the trading time and history of the applicant, putting a startup at a major disadvantage. In this case, PayPal will probably insist on keeping a "reserve" for 90 days. Typically, it will hold back 20% of each day's takings, making them available to you 90 days later. This will limit your cashflow during the initial 90 days but, once the reserve amounts start being paid daily, it'll free up. A company with a longer trading history may well have no reserve applied.

GOOGLE WALLET

Google Wallet works very similarly to PWPS. To use this method to make a payment, the customer must have a Google Wallet account. If they do, then it's just a matter of signing in and authorising the payment. If not, the customer can create a Wallet account – as long as they have a Google account.

All of this rigmarole means that you can't rely ➡

Step 6: Payment Details

Complete the form below and then click the "Pay for Order" button to pay for your order using our secure server.

* Credit Card Type: Visa

* Cardholder's Name:

* Credit Card Number:

Numbers only, no spaces or dashes.

* Expiration Date:

* CVV2:   What's This?

Total Amount: £7.90

[Pay for Order]

Ideally, you should opt for a payment system that means your customers can pay without leaving your site.

solely on Google Wallet or you'll lose a lot of customers who simply can't be bothered to register an account. This situation is rapidly changing as more and more people buy Android phones and sign up with Google Wallet to pay for apps, but it will never be more than an additional convenience method.

Unlike PWPS, Wallet holds onto your money after the customer has paid. For the first 60 days after you become a Google Merchant (that is, someone who accepts Wallet), you are paid ten business days after the customer completes the transaction. After this probationary period your payments will be sent automatically within a couple of days.

AMAZON PAYMENTS

By signing up with Amazon Payments, you can integrate the Amazon checkout system into your online shop. This can either mean having the user complete the process on your site, or using a pop-up window to allow them to log into Amazon. The biggest benefit of Amazon Payments is it means your customers can use their existing Amazon accounts and stored card details to pay.

The first step is to check that your e-commerce package supports Amazon Payments; BigCommerce, for example, doesn't. Signing up is, on the face of it, a simple process, but it can take some time to go through the various checks.

Once set up, Amazon makes payments every 14 days; you can't manually transfer the money across to your bank account. Furthermore, Amazon keeps a sum in reserve to "secure the performance of your payment obligations", which, in plain English, means "in case too many customers ask for refunds".

For at least the first six months, the reserve amount is the total of all unresolved transaction disputes plus the last 14 days of sales. For example, let's say you started trading on January 1 and sold £250 of goods in the first 14 days. On the 14th you'd be due absolutely nothing

because Amazon is now holding that back in reserve. If you went on to sell £350 from 15 to 28 January, your balance would be £600 and on the 28th you'd be paid £250 because Amazon is holding back the last 14 days' sales in reserve.

After six months, or 100 transactions, Amazon will consider replacing this reserve with one based on your refund rate (which should be very low).

NOCHEX

The chances are you've never heard of Nochex, but it's a viable alternative to the better known services we've talked about so far. Nochex is a UK-based payment processor that works similarly to PayPal and Google Wallet in that it supports customers setting up accounts but, unlike its competitors, it's happy to accept credit or debit card payment. My site PassYourTheory. org.uk used Nochex for a number of years and we noticed a big improvement in our conversion rate when we added it alongside PayPal.

Again, check that your e-commerce provider integrates with Nochex before applying. Nochex protects itself from excessive chargebacks by keeping an agreed amount in reserve. The amount will depend on your business history and the industry you're operating in but, once you've built up that amount in your Nochex account, you're free to transfer the excess to your bank account at will. If and when you close your Nochex account, the reserve will be returned to you after 180 days, just to be sure there aren't any late chargebacks in the system.

MAKING YOUR CHOICE

For a new online business, your choices will be limited. You shouldn't have any problem getting a PayPal Web Payments Standard account set up and integrated into your shopping cart. However, PWPS, on its own, is usually only a short-term solution. Broadly speaking, the more payment options you offer, the higher your conversion rate will be because fewer customers will

amazonpayments

VISA   MasterCard   SOLO   Maestro

There are obvious advantages to Amazon Payments, but note its reserve system when calculating your cashflow.

abandon the process at the payment stage. However, this needs to be balanced with the administrative burden of handling several payment processors as well as the cashflow implications of having money tied up in reserve accounts.

For MakingYourOwnCandles, we used PWPS for the first nine months or so and then upgraded to PayPal Web Payments Pro. Whilst we haven't used Virtual Terminal yet, we know that most of our customers prefer to pay by plastic rather than by logging into, or creating, a PayPal account. Your target audience might feel differently, of course, and the only way to find out is to ask them before you consider changing your processing arrangements.

So, for new businesses, the best approach is usually to use PWPS to build up a history and to prove the viability of the business. It might well be worth approaching Nochex early on to see whether you can sign up without having a punitive reserve imposed, but the aim is to keep things simple at this stage and only use payment processors who give you instant access to your cash.

Once you've been trading successfully for six months, you can look around at other options. Which you choose depends on your target audience, e-commerce package and cashflow requirements. For a younger, tech-savvy, audience Google Wallet is a good choice but if you want to be able to accept debit or credit cards directly within your shopping cart, PayPal Website Payments Pro is likely to be the only option at this point (see the boxout below for more on this tricky decision).

Your choice of payment processor in the early months should be seen as part of a long-term strategy with

the ultimate aim of having a merchant account. To get a decent rate, you'll usually need to show that you've been trading successfully for a couple of years. In the meantime, you should be periodically checking that you have the best payment system in place at that time. Don't simply install PWPS and forget it or you'll be turning away potential sales. After all, your customer's hand is in their wallet – it's your job to make sure you can handle whatever comes out.

PayPal Web Payments Standard allows you to integrate the "Pay with PayPal" button into your store.

Payment processing: Why cashflow is king

Running out of the cash needed to meet bills is the main reason businesses go bust. This is just as much a problem for "lean" startups with server and marketing costs to pay as it is for the bigger company struggling to afford their payroll and office costs. So it's essential you work out the impact your choice of payment processor will have on your cashflow.

The only way to do this accurately is to use several months' trading data. You can then project forward the effect of, for example, Amazon's policy of holding back the sales of the previous 14 days. With PayPal's Web Payments Pro, it will depend on what terms they offer. For a newish business, the cost of losing access to 20% of your turnover for 90 days is likely to outweigh the benefits of the service, particularly since if you applied after a period of successful trading you should get less punitive terms.

In fact, the cashflow implications of your choice of payment processor are likely to trump other considerations. When you do feel ready to upgrade to a better processing system, think about running it alongside PWPS so it only handles a comfortable proportion of your turnover. Remember that any good shopping cart service will allow you to turn payment methods on and off so you can manage the proportion of funds that get tied up.

In my experience, 60% of online customers choose to pay by card which, for newer businesses, would then be partially kept in reserve. The remaining 40% pay by PayPal, which is instantly accessible. Balancing cashflow is a key business skill made more difficult by the varying policies of the payment processors: make sure you understand the effect of each choice before you decide.

Adding a shopping cart

You have three choices when it comes to shopping carts: you can build your own from scratch, buy or download a pre-built system and adapt it to your purposes, or sign up for a third-party service. Your decisions will depend primarily on whether you're selling subscriptions (where members buy access to hidden parts of your site), software (which only buyers can download), or a physical product.

SUBSCRIPTIONS If you're selling subscriptions, you may need to build your own cart, since no two sites' requirements will be quite the same. Having said that, if you're simply protecting content from non-subscribers, then Amember (www.amember.com) is a good choice, and the WordPress plugin MemberWing (see p75) offers similar facilities as long as you can bend your site model to fit.

SOFTWARE If you're selling software, your best bet is likely to be one of the many specialist selling platforms such as www.regnow.com. These integrate payment with the emailing of registration details to buyers that enable them to unlock the product they've bought.

PHYSICAL If you're selling physical products, the choice is between hosting a payment system on your server or outsourcing to a third party. osCommerce (www.oscommerce.com) is a PHP-based open-source ecommerce package that you download and install on your own server. It's a great choice if you have a wide range of products and are prepared to spend time configuring it so that it matches the look of your site and integrates with your payment processors.

If you want to get up and running quickly and you have a more limited product range – up to, say, 100 products – then a WordPress plugin should do the job. WP e-Commerce (also known as WP Shopping Cart) is a free plugin with additional modules that can be purchased later.

These solutions give your customers a way to select products. You then need a way of collecting their details and receiving money from them. The simplest choices are Google Checkout (http://checkout.google.co.uk) and PayPal (www.PayPal-business.co.uk). You'll need a Google Checkout Merchant account or a PayPal Business account respectively; both are easy to set up. In each case, a small sum of money is automatically deposited in your nominated bank account. This is used to verify that you own the account: to complete the setup, you're asked to type in the amount of the deposit that was made. You should allow two working weeks to complete the process.

Both Google Checkout and PayPal allow non-members to pay by credit card. However, PayPal traditionally doesn't allow a credit card that has been registered against a PayPal account to be used independently. So if you are a member, you can only pay via PayPal, not directly by

card. This can cause confusion and irritation to customers, particularly if they've forgotten their PayPal details, so I suggest you add another provider besides Google Checkout and/or PayPal. For example, Nochex (www.nochex.co.uk) is a UK provider of secure payment processing. Although it offers customer accounts like PayPal, relatively few people have Nochex accounts, so you can simply use its credit card facility to offer users the option to pay directly by card, without much risk of their accounts clashing.

When we launched PassYourTheory.co.uk in 2005, we offered PayPal and WorldPay as methods of payment. WorldPay turned out to be expensive, so we swapped it for Nochex, reducing our costs while offering similar facilities.

One final note on payment: think very carefully about accepting payment by cheque. It's likely you'll attract extra orders that way, but our experience – through both PassYourTheory and eBay – has been that accepting cheques is more trouble than it's worth. A high percentage of orders are never paid for, and they take longer to process and require more administration work.

SETTING UP YOUR CART Install the WP e-Commerce plugin in the usual way (see pp73-75). You should then hide all the pages created by the plugin. Go to Pages > Edit and you'll find a series of new entries: Products Page, Checkout, Transaction Results and Your Account. For each, click Quick Edit and tick Private Page to ensure that only you, not visitors, can see these pages during development.

You'll see a new section in the Dashboard called Products. Go to Settings and, under General Settings, enter your regional information.

1 **PAYMASTER** Click Payment Options. The easiest payment provider to get started with is PayPal. Anyone with a PayPal Business account can offer PayPal Payments Standard, and to get that working all you need is your PayPal address. Enter this here.

2 **CHECKOUT PROCESS** Under Checkout, ensure you include all the relevant fields. If you need an extra field (for example, to let customers add special requirements) you can add it at the bottom. The most important of the other tabs is Shipping Options. Under Shipping Modules, select one of the Internal Shipping Calculators options, float your mouse over an option until Edit appears and click it. More often than not you'll want to choose Weight, and you can then add Layers, which specify cost bands. Unfortunately, the weight is expressed in pounds (lbs), so you'll need to convert from the grams used by the Royal Mail when working out your postage rates.

3 **ADD PRODUCTS** Now click Categories under Products on the left. You must set up at least one category, and in most case you'll need lots. Categories make it easier for customers to browse your shop; not everyone likes to use search. You want to have multiple products per category, but not too many. It's also a sign of credibility if you have various categories.

It's now time to add your first product. Click Products > Products and complete the form. In the Stock Keeping Unit field, type in the stock code you want to use for the product. Write a complete description using the Rich Text Editor, making sure you include everything your potential buyer needs to know. Select the category it belongs to and add any search tags that make sense.

The remaining fields are obvious. Finally, upload your product images; the more the better. Customers need the online equivalent of picking up and trying the product and that, generally speaking, means plenty of photos.

4 **TESTING** You should add a test product, at a low price, that you can use to make sure it all works. Then see how your shop is shaping up by editing the Products page and clicking Preview. Make sure you thoroughly test the entire process before it goes live.

Nochex is an alternative payment-processing service that makes a useful addition to systems based on Google Checkout and PayPal.

3

4

"Think very carefully about accepting cheques. Many orders are never paid for, and they require more work to process."

Is hosted e-commerce right for you?

We've seen how a WordPress plugin can bring e-commerce to your website, but for more power and features you need a "proper" e-commerce system. You have two choices: install the software on your own server or have it hosted for you.

Having it on your own server gives you complete control, but also complete responsibility for everything. Generally speaking, you also have to pay for the software up front, so the additional control comes at a hefty price.

For MakingYourOwnCandles, we decided to go down the hosted route. This meant we had a lower initial cost, ongoing hosting included in the monthly fee and simpler setup. We wanted a tailor-made system that would handle sophisticated order management, payment processing, discounts and stock levels, as well as the capability to expand with us as our business grew.

After much research, we used the relative newcomer BigCommerce (although fairly new, it's actually a hosted version of InterSpire's much respected e-commerce platform). The beauty of a hosted system such as BigCommerce is that it's possible to get up and running very quickly indeed, helped by the relatively intuitive user interface and good range of built-in design templates. Our site was an immediate hit with customers. Despite my usual preference for installing software on my own server, going down the hosted route has proved a complete success, not least because the software has undergone two major upgrades since then with hardly any action required by me.

The critical factors in deciding whether to opt for a hosted e-commerce solution are:

- **How many products do you have?** I wouldn't want to manage more than a couple of dozen using WordPress.

- **Do you need sophisticated order management?** For example, if you're expecting to make repeat sales to the same customers then an e-commerce platform will provide a complete order history and a record of your interactions with the customer.

- **Do your products vary greatly in weight?** Fully fledged e-commerce systems offer integration with postal systems, so you can offer multiple options to your customers and have the system calculate the cost based on the dimensions and weight of the package.

- **Do you expect to grow substantially?** Changing systems is a pain in the neck. If you're certain you'll stay small, WordPress is a good option. However, if you expect to expand, it makes sense to go for a solution that is overfeatured for your current needs (within reason) and that you can grow into.

The first step is to trial an e-commerce system to see how your online shop looks and works in its potential new home.

Volusion's e-commerce platform offers similar features to BigCommerce, but with UK-based support. Take it for a free 14-day test-drive by signing up at www.volusion.co.uk/free-trial.

Cshop's tagline is "get serious about selling", and they are. Its commerce engine is developed in-house, and it works with clients to meet their individual needs. Take a look at www.cshop.co.uk.

STEP BY STEP Build an online shop in BigCommerce

1 **SET UP A 15-DAY TRIAL**
BigCommerce is a fully featured new e-commerce system that provides everything you're likely to need, whatever the nature of your online shop. For a shop with up to 100 products, it costs $24.95 (around £16) per month with a $49.95 (around £32) setup fee. My experience suggests you can get the setup fee waived if you ask the customer service agent who helpfully emails you on signing up for a trial. Or perhaps I'm just very charming and very lucky.

To get started with the 15-day trial, go to www.bigcommerce.com and click the "Try BigCommerce Free" button. Complete the shop details screen. You'll see the "Shop Address" field at the bottom which, in this case, means our shop will have the address http://southcoastpcs.mybigcommerce.com – not particularly attractive but, once set up, you can integrate an existing domain name so that, as in www.makingyourowncandles.co.uk, you can have a standard URL for your shop.

2 **SET UP YOUR STORE** Click the "Create My Store" button and the BigCommerce control panel will appear. Click on "Setup My Store" and you'll be presented with a step-by-step process to do just that. Once complete, click "Configure Store Settings" to complete the details in the Website tab. Make sure you enter the correct address and that "Search Engine Friendly URLs" is ticked: this will help with your rankings.

Click the Localization tab and set the units you'd like to be used throughout the store: in most cases you'll want to use metric units. Click Save when you've finished.

3 **FIX THE DESIGN** We're now going to give the site an initial design. The task here is to pick the design that's closest to the one you want to end up with – you can radically alter your design later. From the control panel, click the second step, "Design Your Store". At the time of writing, there are 40 templates, all of which are

superbly designed; whichever you pick, your site will look good from the beginning. Click the template thumbnail to take a closer look and, when you've selected the one you want to use, click "Apply this Template".

4 **FIX THE CURRENCY** The last stage in this initial setup process is to specify currency settings. To do this, return to the main control panel screen and click the Settings menu at the top and click "Currency Settings". In most cases you're simply setting the default currency, so leave the name unchanged. Select United Kingdom in the Country/Region list box and change the Currency Code to GBP. Next to Currency Token, replace the dollar sign with the pound sterling symbol. I'm not sure why the "Decimal Places" field is there: leave it at 2! Click Save to return to the control panel summary screen.

It's now time to take a look at our nascent website. From the control panel, click View Store to see it in all its glory.

1

2

3

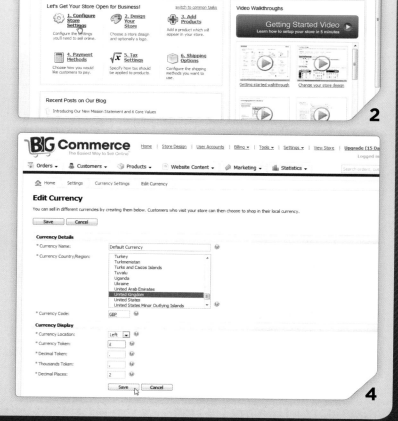

4

Getting ready to sell with BigCommerce

Once the basic site settings have been put in place, it's time to customise the look and feel, integrate your site with one or more payment providers, and connect to the Royal Mail. On the previous page we explained how to integrate BigCommerce into your website. Now you can get down to business.

1 **DESIGN MODE** Use the link in the email sent to you by BigCommerce to log into your shop's control panel. Click Store Design at the top, then the Design Mode tab and the "Open My Store in Design Mode" button. This opens up the store exactly as it will look to your customers, except for a small Design Mode toolbar floating at the top left. This is much more than a Preview mode: this is the actual page, except that you can edit it.

Make sure the Toggle button is depressed to enable design mode. You can now move, edit or delete the various elements of the interface. For example, to remove the Newsletter panel, simply right-click over the panel and select "Remove Panel". To edit the heading text on the page, click it and edit. To edit how the heading looks, or to add panels or other user interface elements, you need to invoke the built-in editor.

2 **EDIT STYLESHEET** Let's say you want to change the appearance of a heading. Your first task is to work out which CSS tag controls its appearance, and the easiest way to do that is to use the Web Developer toolbar, as I explained in "Editing your WordPress site design" (see p68).

From the Web Developer toolbar, select "View Style Information" and click on the heading. In our example, the rule to change is called "TitleHeading". To edit it, right-click over the heading and select "Edit Stylesheet". Scroll down to find the appropriate rule, edit it and click Save. Once you're done, click Close & Refresh.

If you want to make extensive changes to the design, you can download the entire site or edit it via FTP. In practice, however, I've found it's possible to get the design you want with a few hours' work within Design Mode.

1

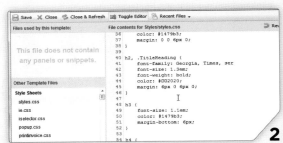

2

3

4

5

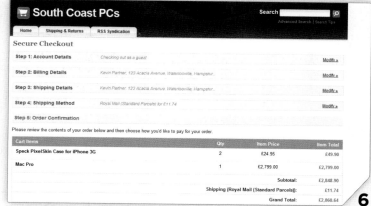

6

3 **TAKING PAYMENT** You now need to make it easy for your customers to pay you. By far the simplest way to begin accepting payments is to use PayPal. Your customers can then pay you either through a PayPal account, if they have one, or by debit or credit card. All you need is a working business PayPal account.

From the control panel, select Settings at the top and click Checkout Settings. BigCommerce allows you to use its parent company Interspire's Secure Payment Gateway, but that service supports only US dollars; select "I already have my own merchant account or payment provider set up". A listbox will appear listing the payment providers BigCommerce supports. Many of them won't be applicable for a UK business, but there are still plenty to choose from. In this case, we'll choose PayPal Website Payments Standard.

There's no need for Test Mode with this form of payment as it's so simple. Click Save when you're done.

4 **GET SHIPPING** One of the most impressive features of BigCommerce is its ability to link directly with postal services around the world, including Royal Mail. Other services require the shop owner to enter their own postal rates and weight bands so that not only are you stuck with the Package rate for just about everything, but every time the Royal Mail raises its charges, you have to implement those changes by hand across the site.

To set up live integration, select Settings at the top right of the control panel and then choose Shipping Settings. Begin by entering your store location settings: this helps determine which providers are available. Click Save, then click the Shipping Zones tab. If you're only shipping to the UK then click Edit Settings in the Default Zone. Each Zone can have multiple shipping methods: for example, in the US you could pick several providers depending on the nature of the product being shipped. In this case, all you need to do on the Edit Zone screen is decide whether you want to apply a handling fee to each order to represent the cost of packaging the item. If you don't, then you must remember to build this cost into the product price.

Next, select Royal Mail in the Shipping Method listbox. This will cause the Royal Mail settings to appear underneath. From here you can select which of the Royal Mail's services you want to use. Bear in mind that if you add Special Delivery or Recorded Delivery, you're going to generate a lot more paperwork. Click Save and your integration is complete.

5 **TESTING TIMES** You can now test the integration by going to your site, clicking "View Store" from the control panel and adding an item to your shopping basket. Now, click the "Estimate Shipping & Tax" link and you'll be prompted to enter some details. BigCommerce will then contact the Royal Mail and, through the miracle of e-communication (rather than the first-class postal system), you'll see the postage options for your products along with prices.

Return to the control panel and complete the final step – specifying tax settings. Essentially, all you do here is indicate whether your prices should include VAT. In most cases, if you're registered for VAT then your prices should include it. However, if you're selling to businesses then you have the option to show the net price. In my view, it's best practice to show the inclusive figure.

6 **CHECK IT OUT** You should now have tested the entire shopping process. If this is your first experience of a BigCommerce shop, you're likely to be impressed by how professional and efficient the process is. I particularly like the one-page checkout screen with built-in support for user accounts.

You can also control whether your customers have to create an account before buying from you. I've tested this and I recommend allowing customers to proceed as guests if they wish, since this increases your conversion rate.

How to stock your shelves in BigCommerce

The final step in getting up and running with BigCommerce – and actually making money from it – is to add a product along with its category, image and pricing information.

1 **DELETE TRIAL PRODUCTS** In the control panel, click Products and then Product Categories. Select all the categories by clicking the checkbox in the header bar and click "Delete Selected".

2 **ADD CATEGORIES** You need to add at least one category to be able to add a product. To do this, click "Create a Category". Complete the Name and Description fields; the description will appear above the products in your category's "home" page and can include embedded images and Flash.

Repeat the process with your other product categories. If you have multiple categories, you can arrange how they will appear in your shop menu.

3 **ADD NEW PRODUCTS** We're now in a position to add a product. Back at the home page, click "3. Add Products". Give your product a descriptive name and select the category it should appear in.

In the Description field, give your product a full description. With a book, for example, it should give a good idea what the book is about. For a more complex product, you need to include everything your customer might need to know to decide whether it's right for them. In the case of our candle-making kits, we include a complete listing of the kit contents plus a description of who the kit is aimed at, what options there are, and what makes it unique.

BigCommerce allows you to specify a range of price options. For example, if you record the "retail price" of your product along with the actual price you're selling it at, then BigCommerce will automatically put a line through the retail price and add your price underneath, along with the amount the customer has saved.

You can also record a "sale price". This has much the same effect, but applies to products you've sold at a higher price and have now reduced.

BigCommerce also offers a sophisticated coupon code system which, on MakingYourOwnCandles, we use to offer customers a 10% discount on their first order. Unfortunately, there's no way to limit each customer to using it only once: a frustrating and pretty basic omission.

For the live connection to Royal Mail to work, you need to enter the product's weight and dimensions. Remember to do this in the packaging you intend to use.

4 **ADD PHOTOS** Click the "Save & Keep Editing" button. You'll notice there are a number of tabs along the top, but the critical one at this point is the Images/Videos tab. A photo is an absolute requirement for all physical products, and the most recent upgrade to BigCommerce has added integration with the online Picnik photo-editing service for minor changes. Although BigCommerce will allow you to link to photos from other sites, in my view you should always upload your

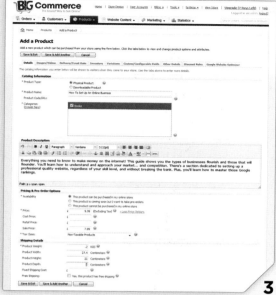

3

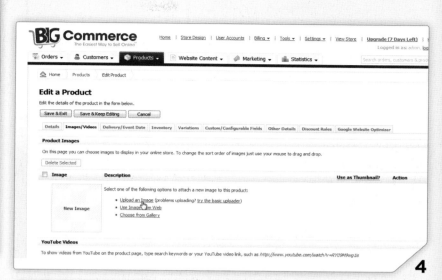

4

5

6

own product shots, since that way you stay in control and not prey to the vagaries of someone else's server availability.

BigCommerce's magnify feature allows visitors to zoom into an image to see more detail. There's no need to resize it precisely, but if you've taken your own product shots you'll need to reduce their original resolution before uploading them. To add a photo, click the "Upload An Image" link and use the dialog to locate your image.

If it's not immediately obvious what the photo is, add a description and click Save & Exit if you're done, or Save & Keep Editing if you want to add extra photos.

5 **STOCK LEVELS** Whether you'll need to use the other tabs under Edit a Product will depend on the nature of your business. In our case, we use the Inventory tab to keep track of stock levels, the Variations tab to allow us to cater for multiple combinations of scent and dye for our candle kits and, occasionally, the Discount Rules tab when we want to offer discounts for multiple purchases.

Once you've added your product, it pays to take a look at it to make sure it looks as good to the customer as

you intended it to be. Back at the control panel click View Store at the top right, then find your product in the shop. Make sure you click on the product to see its full listing and interact with it as you'd want your customer to.

Congratulations: your shop and its first product are now set up! It makes sense to set up your first product by hand, even if you intend to use BigCommerce's Import Products function, which allows you to upload a CSV file from a previous shopping cart.

6 **PREPARE FOR LAUNCH** Once your products are imported, you need to take the final steps in preparing your site for launch. Use the "Website Content" dropdown in the control panel to add pages covering the obligatory "About Us" information, along with contact options and your terms and conditions. A number of companies sell pre-written terms and conditions, including delivery policies, privacy policies and the arrangements for refunds. Once purchased, you simply fill in the blanks and delete any paragraphs that don't apply to you. Nothing beats specialised legal advice, so if you're in any doubt I recommend talking to a commercial lawyer.

Best practice

You should register with the Information Commissioner's Office (http://ico.gov.uk) to ensure you stay on the right side of Data Protection Law. I'd also recommend joining one of the online shopper protection bodies such as SafeBuy (www.safebuy.org.uk) or Internet Shopping Is Safe (www.imrg. org/isis). Both of these bodies will help you make sure you're following best practice, as well as providing reassurance to your customers that you're a reputable and trustworthy company. This will almost certainly result in an improved conversion rate.

Build a shop for free with PrestaShop

One of the key challenges for a new business is cashflow. Every penny you spend on product development, for example, is a penny less for buying stock. That's why it's tempting to build a shop for free rather than opt for a hosted ecommerce service.

While hosted services such as BigCommerce and Volusion represent the simplest and safest way to create a fully functioning online shop, the improving quality of the leading open-source alternatives means that you don't necessarily have to use a paid-for service.

PrestaShop is one such alternative: a well-featured ecommerce package that has built up a respectable following since its launch in 2007. The most immediately obvious difference between this and a hosted package is that you upload it to your own server and run it from there. Fortunately it's been created using coding language PHP and database technology MySQL – two of the most widely used formats – so you'd be hard pushed to find a mainstream hosting company that doesn't support PrestaShop.

However, it's unlikely that the free or very cheap hosting packages will support it. Even if they did, it would be unwise to rely on the bottom-end offerings. You therefore need to factor into your calculations that you'll have to spend, perhaps, £7-£10 per month on hosting.

Setting up the software is also more complicated compared with a Volusion store, for example, which can be up and running in a matter of clicks. The bonus is that this task only needs to be done once and that if you're technically minded it's quite straightforward: essentially all you do is upload the software to your server, create a MySQL database using your host's control panel and go to your website in a browser. The rest is handled via a slick setup process.

WHICH TO CHOOSE? So, how do you decide whether to go for a hosted service or opt for open source? First, if you don't have the technical skills to FTP the files to your server, then a hosted service is your only option. Assuming you do know your FileZilla from your Firefox, the choice is more difficult. In November 2009, we launched a pilot version of MakingYourOwnCandles – one of the priorities was to keep costs to a minimum in case it turned out the market we thought existed didn't. PrestaShop would have been a good choice for that early version of the online shop because we could have both established the viability of the business itself and put PrestaShop through its paces as a possible platform for the full-fat version of the online shop. This is the beauty of free, open source software – it only costs you time, not pounds, to experiment.

The compromise is that none of the open-source alternatives have the sophistication and range of features of the best hosted platforms. BigCommerce and Volusion offer everything from gift vouchers to extremely complex product variation rules. But, for a basic shop, osCommerce or PrestaShop might well fit the bill, without the bill.

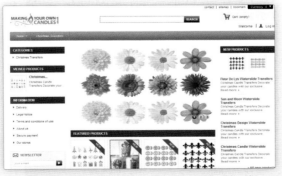

PrestaShop enables you to create a professional online shop for free – but it's not for everyone.

Taking payment is an essential part of any ecommerce package and PrestaShop includes an efficient, well designed shopping cart.

STEP BY STEP How to install PrestaShop

1 **CREATE A DATABASE** Start by going into the control panel of your hosting account, where you need to create a MySQL database. In the case of Heart Internet accounts, this is done by creating a username and password combination – the system then creates a database with that name and password. Make sure you have a note of them. While you're in your control panel, make a note of the FTP username and password for your domain and, if necessary, unlock it so you can connect.

Go to PrestaShop.com and download the latest stable release as a ZIP file. Extract the file into a folder. Use FileZilla and your FTP details to copy the contents of the Prestashop folder into the web folder of your site (usually public_html or similar). You've got it right if you see "address.php" in the public_html folder.

2 **CONFIGURE IT** Once the files have been successfully uploaded, start up a browser and type in the web address of your shop. You'll see the initial setup screen – tick the terms and conditions box and click Next. The next page confirms that you have the required technology and software for PrestaShop to work. Refer to your hosting provider if there are any warnings here, otherwise click Next.

Complete the Database Configuration screen with the username and password you used to create your MySQL database. Note that for many hosts, the database name and login are the same. Click the Verify Now button and, assuming there are no error messages, click Next to move onto the next screen.

3 **CUSTOMISE YOUR SHOP** On the Shop Settings page, give your shop a name. This should, ideally, include your main keywords. Next to "Install demo products" click No to save yourself the bother of having to delete them.

You can upload your logo at this point – it's best to resize it before uploading so you can make sure it looks properly proportioned.

Finally, choose a username and password for your shop account. Make sure the password is a strong one! Click the Next button to complete the configuration process. PrestaShop will now set everything up.

4 **YOUR FIRST VISITOR** Before you can view your shop, for security reasons you must delete the "install" folder. Do this by going to the site in FileZilla and deleting just that folder by right-clicking it and pressing Delete. Finally, you must also rename the "admin" folder. To do this in FileZilla, right-click the folder, select Rename and type in the new name – for example "shop-admin". Doing this makes the site slightly more secure because any hacker attempting to access your control panel would initially have to work out which URL it was on.

Now, type your shop's web address into your browser and you should be taken to your shiny default home page.

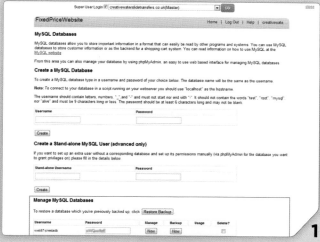

1

2

3

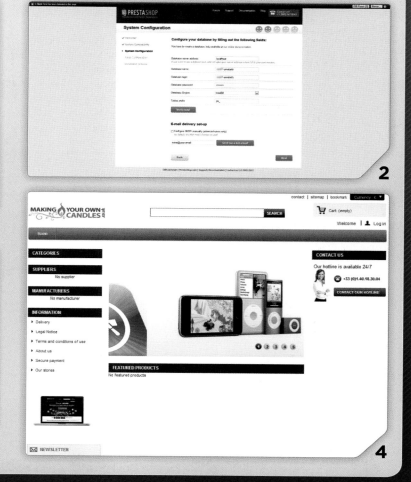

4

STEP BY STEP Preparing for business in PrestaShop

1 **MEET THE DASHBOARD** Take a look at the control panel for your shop. Remember when you renamed your admin folder? You now need to navigate to that folder in a browser – in our case it's www.creativewaterslidetransfers.co.uk/shop-admin. Enter your username and password and you should find yourself at the dashboard. There's an introductory video in the top-left corner, along with a summary of your sales activity and customer service threads at the top right. For now, we're interested in the two items in red on the left-hand side. We're going to ignore the second one because it requires a change to the server configuration that's beyond the scope of this tutorial – it would only affect a store with a lot of traffic. Click the top item in red.

2 **WRITE FRIENDLY URLs** URL rewriting turns URLs like www.myshop.co.uk/?pageid=10298 into URLs like www.myshop.co.uk/christmas-transfers. It makes the addresses of the pages on your site easier for humans to read, but more importantly it means Google can better index the page. If someone Googles "christmas transfers", the presence of those two words in your URL will give you a ranking boost. It's easy to get this working. Clicking the red item takes you to the Preferences/SEO & URLs. Click the Yes option next to "Friendly URL" and click Save. Test this by launching your shop and clicking on any link.

3 **TAKE PAYMENT** A shop is no good without a way of taking payment. You can add functionality to PrestaShop by installing Modules. These cover every aspect of both the shop-front and backend. For now, we want to set up a credit-card-processing module. Begin by clicking the Modules menu and selecting Payments. Make sure the country and currency settings are correct, then click the "See the list of payment modules" button. In this case, we're going to use Google Wallet. Until recently, this was called Google Checkout and the module (at the time of writing) still had that name. So, if you don't see a Wallet module, look for one called Google Checkout. Click the Install button and then, once it's been added to the list of active modules, click the Configure link.

4 **SET UP GOOGLE WALLET** To use this module, you'll need a Google Wallet account. Go to www.google.com/wallet/merchants.html and sign up – it's one of the simplest ways to start taking online payments. You could also install and use the PayPal module if you prefer. Go into your Wallet account and head to Settings/Integration to find your Merchant ID and Key. Back on the PrestaShop module page you'll see, under the heading "Information", the settings Google Wallet needs to be able to link to your store. Copy the API callback URL into the corresponding field in your Google Wallet Integration Settings and make sure the method is set to XML. Finally, make sure the API version number in Wallet is the same as that used by the module. Click Save in PrestaShop and, all being well, you're set up to take payment.

STEP BY STEP Getting stocked up in PrestaShop

1 **ADD CATEGORIES** It's time to put some products on our virtual shelves. The first step is to create categories for the products. Begin at the Dashboard and click Catalog/Categories/Add. Give the category a name, remembering to include likely keywords where possible. Add a description, again including keywords if you can do so naturally. You can optionally add an image to summarise the category but it's much more important to get the Meta title and Meta description right.

The title should include your keywords as this will help boost the ranking of the page. The description doesn't affect the position, but it's what Google displays beneath the URL in the search results so it's essential it encourages customers to click. Finally, add a "Friendly URL", which should be the same as the category name where possible. Click Save when you're done and repeat with your other product categories.

2 **NOW ADD PRODUCTS** Now we add products. Select Catalog/

Products to bring up the (presently empty) list of products and click the Add New button at the top right. Begin by completing the "global information" screen. The Short description only appears if the customer hovers their mouse over the product thumbnail – the Description field appears once the customer clicks on the product so this is the one to spend time on. Your copy needs to clearly describe the product and encourage your customers to buy now. Click the SEO tab on the left, then the Generate button to create a friendly URL for the product. Click the "Save and stay" button to save your progress.

3 **SET PRICES** Click the Prices tab to set up the costs for this product. If you want to track how profitable each product is, enter the cost of the product to you in the "Pre-tax wholesale price" field. In the "Pre-tax retail price" enter the price you want to charge. If you're VAT registered, this should be the amount before VAT is added, and in that case, make sure "UK Standard Rate" is selected

in the Tax Rule dropdown. If you're not VAT registered, then the "Pre-tax retail price" should be the full amount – with the Tax Rule dropdown set to "No Tax". Click "Save and stay" again and then the Images tab. Add at least two good quality images – pictures sell products! Finally, click Quantities and enter your stock levels, then click Save to go back to the product list.

4 **BE YOUR CUSTOMER** Now, go to your shop in your browser to see it from a customer's point of view. To change the design altogether, go to Preferences/Themes in the control panel and, from there, to the library of themes. To make more minor changes, go to Modules/Positions and click the LiveEdit button on the right. This allows you to move, edit or delete any existing blocks. Once you've done this, the Modules/Positions list allows you to add specific modules to the blocks – to power your newsletter form, for example. And since PrestaShop is open source, you can change it directly using CSS.

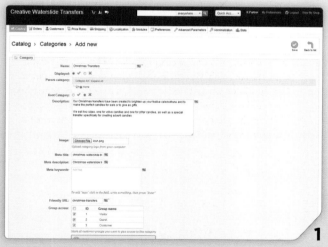

1

2

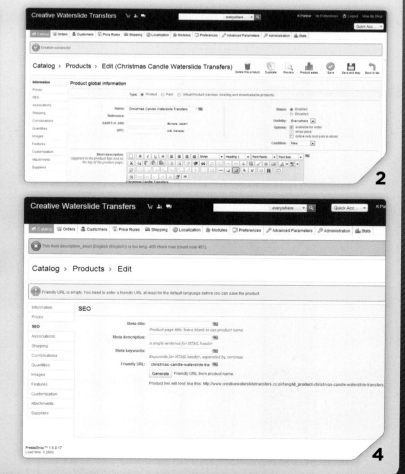

3

4

Going mobile: selling on phones & tablets

Not so long ago, all websites were designed to work on laptop or desktop monitors set to a few standard resolutions. These days, if your site can't cope with the bewildering range of screen sizes, aspect ratios and browsers used by your customers, its conversion rate will suffer.

The biggest challenge is to present a fully functioning online shop or web application that will work on the widest possible range of mobile devices. To put this challenge into perspective, in the two years to August 2011, the proportion of web traffic accessed via mobile jumped five-fold in the UK and by a factor of seven worldwide. Whilst, on average, mobile traffic currently amounts to less than 10% of total visitors, this figure has more than doubled in the past 12 months so there's no sense building an online business today that isn't mobile-ready.

You wouldn't imagine that the target audience for MakingYourOwnCandles.co.uk would be at the forefront of the mobile revolution, but even there over 7% of all visits are from mobile devices. Half of these visitors are using iPhones, but almost as many use iPads.

A Google study conducted in April 2011 showed that 35% of those who use a smartphone to search go on to purchase – perhaps because the effort involved in searching and buying means they don't even start the process unless they're serious. What it certainly means is that if your site isn't optimised for mobile, and so you make it difficult for visitors to buy from you using their mobile device, you're throwing money away. There's also evidence, as the average transaction value rises, that customers are becoming increasingly comfortable with spending money online.

BOUNCE RATE One of the most important site metrics is the bounce rate. This is the percentage of visitors to your site who leave without going to another page within the site. It's one of the main ways in which Google works out whether your site is relevant and therefore how it will rank in search results.

Even more importantly, it indicates whether visitors are engaged with your site. In the case of an online shop, a high bounce rate is the kiss of death since it indicates that visitors are leaving as soon as they arrive rather than buying. Landing pages are an exception to this since their purpose is to get a customer to buy straight away; but even then, there's often more than one page in the buying sequence.

On average, you can expect a site that has not been mobile-optimised to have a higher bounce rate for mobile users than for desktops

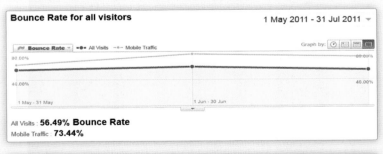

A high bounce rate indicates visitors are leaving your site as soon as they arrive. The site represented by the top graph has a much higher bounce rate for mobiles because it hasn't been optimised...

...while the bottom has been optimised for mobiles, resulting in a minimal difference in bounce rate across devices.

or laptops. Take a look at at the top graph on the opposite page. This shows the bounce rate for mobiles compared with the overall rate for a non-optimised site. As you can see, three-quarters of mobile users leave immediately whereas the figure for all users is closer to a half. So for every 100 users, only 25 will explore the site on a mobile.

The graph below shows the figures for a similar site – but this time the site has been optimised for mobile. Here mobile users are even more engaged with the content than the average. And what do engaged users do? They buy!

Having said all that, for now at least the majority of your visitors will be using laptops and desktops with high-resolution displays. So, the changes you make to your site must improve its effectiveness for mobile users without compromising the majority. After all, it's hardly good business practice to sacrifice your conversion rate today so that it might improve later.

DO YOU REALLY NEED TO OPTIMISE?

You could argue that since tablet devices offer similar display resolutions to laptops, there's no need to spend time and effort optimising your site for them, especially given the fact that despite the success of the iPad, they're much rarer than smartphones. Why not simply offer the standard view of your site to tablet users since, after all, they're designed to be "magical" internet devices?

The longer term answer is to test it both ways but, since time is at a premium when you're setting up in business, I suggest treating tablet and smartphone users similarly. Once you're up and running, Google Analytics will, with a little jiggery pokery, tell you whether you're losing sales to mobile users and can break that down further into specific devices.

For example, looking at the traffic for MakingYourOwnCandles.co.uk, I can see that the iPad is a close second behind its smaller cousin in terms of the number of orders made. However, the average value of each

Whether an iPhone or an Android phone, these devices are a way for you to make money.

> "Google Analytics will tell you whether you're losing sales to mobile users and can break that down further to specific devices."

transaction is almost 50% higher, so tablet users are worth more to us overall. This site has already been optimised, with the main tablets and smartphones receiving the mobile version of the shop.

As a general rule, I recommend optimising information sites such as blogs for smartphones and online shops for tablets since tablet users appear more likely to buy, and spend more when they do. These are early days of course but, by making sure mobile users get a good experience when they visit your site, you will be ahead of the game and, in all likelihood, selling to the frustrated customers of your competitors.

ONE SITE TO RULE THEM ALL

The good news is that modern mobile devices have pretty good browsers and they work fairly consistently across different platforms and manufacturers. The bad news is that, in the main, screen sizes are much smaller than the site was designed for whilst the pointing device (the finger) is much bigger than a mouse pointer. As such, your carefully crafted navigation and buttons might be hard to use.

So, in most cases, you'll want to show a differently styled version of your site to mobile users. Until recently, this often meant using an entirely separate site on a different domain and directing users there. For a small business, the cost of doing this would be ruinous and it also dilutes your marketing because you end up having to promote two separate domains.

Some sites use sub-domains such as mobile.domainname.com or subfolders within the main domain. One famous example is www.bbc.co.uk/mobile/index.html, which presents a mobile view accessed as a link from its main mobile page at www.bbc.co.uk/mobile/web. Indeed these pages illustrate perfectly the problem even the best resourced sites have with catering to all platforms. The mobile view itself works well on a smartphone but is very poor when viewed using a tablet. Non-iPad users are better advised to use the standard BBC site but, given its reliance on Flash, iPadders will have to be content with accessing it piecemeal via apps.

The best and simplest approach for most new online businesses is to have a single site, to detect when a visitor is using a mobile device and, if so, to change the design to suit on the fly. There's a walkthrough describing how to do this in WordPress at the end of this section but, before you jump ahead, you need to check that your site is mobile-ready.

IT'S ALL ABOUT THE CONTENT

The good news is that if you've followed the guidance in this book on how to put a website together your site is already halfway there. By basing your site layout on CSS →

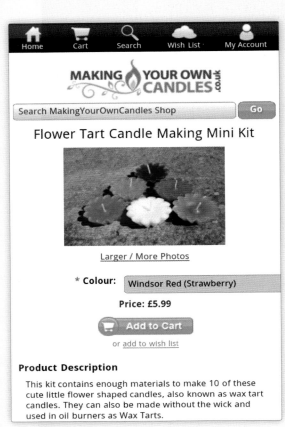

The MakingYourOwnCandles.co.uk shop viewed on an Android phone. This optimisation was done with a few clicks.

IrfanView is an excellent free photo optimiser perfect for minimising the file size of your images.

rather than tables, it's much easier to present different designs to different devices - essentially it's just a matter of swapping CSS files.

Navigation needs to be simple and easy to understand. Since smartphones have a narrower screen ratio than standard displays it's better to have many subheadings beneath a few main headings than the other way around, because this stops your menu from splitting across more than one line. Keep the main section names short (one word each if possible) for the same reason.

If you're optimising an existing site then now's a good time to re-read all the copy and trim it where possible. The smaller the device, the harder it is to read long copy, so get the scissors out. If you're using WordPress, think carefully about where you split the page. The abstract should be just long enough for the reader to be tempted to view the entire article and not a word over: every character counts on a mobile display.

OPTIMISE UNTIL THE PIPS SQUEAK First and foremost, you need to make sure that images and other media are compressed as much as possible without degrading their quality too much. A useful

rule of thumb is to pretend your visitors are using a dial-up connection, because the combination of dodgy mobile connections and slower browser rendering speeds often make the mobile experience feel like a trip down memory lane.

You also need to consider the dimensions of your media. Images more than 480 pixels wide are going to overspill the edges of most smartphone screens; if you don't already have a favourite image editor, I recommend IrfanView (www.irfanview.com).

Video is a little different as users are more likely to turn their phone into landscape orientation to watch a video, so the maximum width increases to around 800 pixels.

Be careful with data tables since they don't usually resize well. Even if the columns do resize (if you've used proportional widths for example), you'll end up with only a few characters per line. Where possible, keep tables small and if they need to be complex consider converting to images.

Taking mobile payments

If you run an online shop, try to incorporate mobile-friendly payment methods. The most widely useful is probably Google Wallet since anyone who's bought an app from the Android Market will have set an account up. PayPal is relatively mobile friendly but never ask your customers to pay by credit card: they're likely to give up long before the purchase is completed.

Making your WordPress site ready for mobile devices

WordPress offers a big range of plugins and themes for mobile sites. Broadly speaking, if most of your visitors will be using smartphones and tablets then pick such a mobile-friendly theme and optimise every aspect of the site for those potential customers. For most sites, however, the majority of visitors will be using big monitors so the primary design should be aimed at them. In that case, pick a plugin.

1 The easiest to use plugin I've found is "WP Mobile Detector". This works by establishing whether the visitor is using a mobile device and, if they are, switching the WordPress theme to one that's mobile optimised. It comes with half a dozen themes so it should be possible to find one that suits.

Begin by going to your WordPress dashboard. Click Plugins and then Add New. In the search box type "WP Mobile Detector" and click Search. Click the "Install Now" link and the plugin will be downloaded. It may take a little time as it's a hefty download. Now, click Plugins in your dashboard again, scroll to find the WP Mobile Detector and click Activate.

2 You'll notice that the plugin has added a new menu to your dashboard on the left. Under that menu, click the Settings item. With the free version of the plugin the only options you have are whether to track mobile statistics and whether to include a credit to the developers. The latter option is entirely up to you, of course, but if you've installed Google Analytics then you don't need or want the plugin to store usage data as you can get the same information from Analytics. Deselect this option.

3 Now select the Mobile Themes submenu and you'll see a whole range of new themes available to you. In fact you're seeing all the site's themes, so make sure you pick one that's mobile optimised. Once you've found one you like, click the Activate link and then test your site on a mobile device. Then double-check that the desktop version still works as before. The thumbnails on this page aren't particularly accurate so you'll need to cycle through the themes, activating each one, to find the one you like the best.

4 Here's how the site looks on an Android smartphone both before the plugin was activated and after. Whilst the user could double-tap to zoom in the standard view, they'd still end up see-sawing down the page as they read. The mobile view, on the other hand, is perfectly sized for a smartphone with big chunky buttons to prod.

3

◄ Before

1

▶ wer

2

4

Making money through memberships

It's one of the oldest commercial models in the book: build, buy or create something you can then charge others to access. It can also be one of the trickiest to get right, and it's becoming harder and harder to convince customers to pay money for something they believe they should get for nothing.

Newspaper publishing, for example, is a model in which readers pay for the "content" via a physical copy. From that point of view, it makes sense that the same content on the paper's website can be charged for. However, most readers are also internet users who expect information to be free.

To build a successful membership business, then, you need to offer one or more resources of value. Many successful membership sites combine the selling of information with other resources including downloads, coaching and access to an exclusive community.

PassYourTheory.org.uk, for example, sells practice tools and videos, plus pure information. The convenience of having it all in one place and access to these extra services means enough people sign up to make it profitable.

 MODEL 1: PAY ON ENTRY The internet equivalent of the turnstile, "pay on entry" websites require visitors to become paying customers before they can access the site. The visitor can see what's on offer, usually in the form of a list of contents or brief abstracts, but to proceed they must sign up. This is the model used by The Times (www.thetimes.co.uk).

For this to work, visitors must be offered a way out if the service doesn't live up to their expectations. This could be a limited-length trial or an unconditional guarantee. Offering payment via PayPal gives some measure of protection for customers since they know they can cancel their subscription or ask for a refund through PayPal.

 MODEL 2: FREE TRIAL Offering a free trial has been around since the days of the travelling salesman and his suitcase of samples. Until recently, this was the dominant method of signing up customers to web applications and membership sites, but it's been overtaken by Freemium. This is largely because of the abuse of the free trial by companies afraid to give

The Financial Times' website uses the Freemium model to offer a worthwhile free membership, which it hopes you'll upgrade at some point. It's clear that The Financial Times has spent a lot of time working out which features to give away and which to restrict to paid members.

meaningful access to the service without payment.

These days, customers are much less likely to invest the time in going through a registration process merely to try out a membership site. That's why a free trial works well if you are prepared to give complete or nearly complete access for a limited time, and if you make accessing the trial as simple as possible.

 MODEL 3: FREEMIUM If you go to www.ft. com and attempt to click on an article, you'll be asked to register. Registration is free and allows you to view up to ten articles per month. All but the most casual visitors will sign up and, during this process, they'll be encouraged to pay for an upgrade to a premium service. Some will pay at this point, some will view the ten articles and decide to pay then, and some will never pay.

Providing a long term, restricted but free membership level like this is the basis of the Freemium model. This gets customers into your sales funnel and onto your autoresponder sequence. The key is to get the balance right: you need enough functionality to get a good percentage of visitors signing up for the free membership whilst holding sufficient amounts back to encourage enough of those free members to pay to upgrade.

For example, let's say your AdWords campaign sends 1,000 visitors to your site at a cost of 10p each. If you persuade 25% of them to become free members (250), each of them has cost you 40p. And if 10% of free members pay to upgrade, that's 25 paid members at a cost of £4 each. That analysis is very sensitive to changes in conversion rate and AdWords cost. If you paid 50p per click, free members would cost £2 each and paid members £20. This is why it's so important to do your research up front – you might make money at £4 per paid member and lose a fortune at £20.

 MODEL 4: CONTINUITY A "continuity programme" is a membership site where subscribers get more value the longer they stay. For example, Terry Dean is an internet marketer who runs a "monthly mentor club". Every month, he will deal with a new topic, and members also get access to one additional archive per month for the first year. These archives cover general internet marketing issues to complement the more topical entries. Members also get a printed newsletter once per month on that topic, along with additional videos and slideshows. As time goes on, this becomes an increasingly thorough resource and this promise of regular new material keeps subscribers paying their membership fee.

Some continuity programmes are of fixed length. For example, a 12-week course on taxidermy clearly ends once the 12 weeks are over. Fixed-length programmes tend to have higher conversion rates than ongoing continuity

programmes because members know exactly what the maximum cost is going to be.

Most continuity programmes of either sort offer a low-cost, or free, initial period. This is partly to give customers a chance to sample the resources on offer but also because simply having the offer reassures them you have confidence in your service. As with all online selling, it's not just about having a great product, you must also convince your potential customers they can trust you. Offering the first month's membership for £1, for example, means you're taking the risk rather than the customer, and this will make it much more likely they'll sign up.

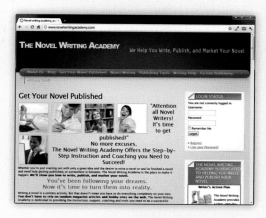

Writing a novel takes time, making it perfect for a continuity membership site.

There are no firm rules with any of these models and many successful sites will incorporate elements of more than one. PassYourTheory, for example, combines aspects of the free trial into its freemium model: we automatically cancel free memberships after two weeks.

 SETTING UP A MEMBERSHIP SITE For a small online business, WordPress makes the ideal platform for a membership site, especially one based on digital resources. Plugins such as MagicMembers, MemberWing and WishList Member add payment handling, account management and content protection. Once you've installed a membership plugin, you can add the resources to your site, which you can then selectively protect.

For example, a "pay on entry" site could be set up very easily since all posts and resources would be protected from all non-members. A "free trial" site would have a special membership category that expires after a specific period and usually also limits access compared with a paid membership. "Freemium" sites would have a free membership level that doesn't expire and one or more "premium" levels. Finally, a "continuity" site would have memberships set up with recurring payments that progressively open up new resources.

By using WordPress, you have a built-in content management system and framework so adding your articles, media and other resources is simple. Although the membership plugins aren't free, they save a huge amount of development time and expense. The main barrier to getting a membership site up and running, then, is creating the content and not building the technology. Create content people will pay to access, find the best membership model, set the right price and build an effective marketing campaign and you might just be onto a winner.

PART 4 Marketing

Find new customers

Introduction to marketing

Marketing your product is more important than getting your website right; arguably, more important than getting the product itself right. It's essential that you set up an effective marketing campaign and keep working on it over time. The good news is that marketing isn't rocket science. In fact, it's mainly about common sense and testing. It's also great fun.

What is marketing? Well, it's more than just advertising, but exactly how it's defined depends on who you ask. Don't ask the Chartered Institute for Marketing, because the definition it gives encompasses just about everything. For an internet-based business, your focus is going to be mainly on direct marketing and, specifically, permission-based direct marketing.

At its most basic, marketing is the process by which you encourage the right customers to find and buy your products. In direct marketing, we do this by interacting with individuals who will then, we hope, buy our product direct from us. Contrast this with Coca-Cola, for example, whose marketing is all about supporting its brand and encouraging people to buy from retailers, who in turn buy their stock from Coca-Cola, thus passing on a proportion of their revenue. Coca-Cola doesn't have a one-to-one relationship with any of its consumers – and this is one way in which the internet, by contrast with traditional retail channels, can make it possible for you to interact more effectively with your customers than the big corporations.

"Permission-based" direct marketing is widely acknowledged as the most effective form of marketing for most internet businesses. As you might guess, this involves getting agreement from customers – and potential customers – to interact with them.

The main benefits of this approach are that your conversion rate increases hugely and that you can establish a relationship that leads to lots of sales over a long period. Indeed, many profitable internet products lose money on their initial sale, because their vendors will make it back over the longer term.

ATTRACTING TRAFFIC The first aim is to attract the right visitors to your site. Note the qualifier there: web traffic is of little use unless the people who visit your site are likely to buy. Indeed, one of the biggest mistakes amateur marketers make is to waste money attracting the wrong people. Get it right and you can find potential customers, either for free via the "organic" search listings or at the lowest possible cost via pay-per-click advertising.

Google's AdWords dominates the pay-per-click market. Get your campaigns right to reap greater profit per sale.

AWeber is one of the leading auto-responder providers, characterised by its simple wizard-based approach.

Once you have visitors arriving at your site, it's essential that you convert the maximum number of them into buyers. This is rarely done instantly, and most successful internet businesses seek to establish a relationship with their potential customers rather than sell to them immediately. This usually involves the visitor giving their email address and permission for you to contact them in exchange for something you provide to them for free.

The organic search results are those that appear in the main listing area of Google, Bing or Yahoo!. These listings are lifted from the database that's created as the search engine scans websites and categorises them according to their content. Appearing high up the listings for your most profitable keywords means you will get free traffic from people who have searched for relevant words and are therefore likely to be interested in your product.

THE JOY OF SEO The process of ensuring your site is as highly ranked as possible is known as search engine optimisation, or SEO. A great deal of mystique surrounds this, but there's a limited range of aspects of your site that you need to work on, and it's possible for the layman to grasp the essentials, despite the claims of some specialist companies.

The first thing to understand and accept is that there's no way of guaranteeing the top spot for any high-traffic keywords. Any SEO company that claims to be able to achieve this is either lying or will only guarantee the top position to a very limited, low-traffic key phrase. Avoid this kind of claim like the plague: there are plenty of reputable companies out there if you feel you need help. As with so many things, you can do most of the optimising yourself, for free – and, in fact, much of the optimisation has to be done by you in any case, whether you hire someone or not.

Second, you need to accept that SEO takes time. Google rewards sites for their longevity in two ways. First, it will rank an older site higher than an equivalent newer site. Second, you earn credit for the number of incoming links to your site (but only links from relevant, highly ranked sites), and these take time to accumulate.

The really good news is that using sensible "white hat" techniques to optimise your site will also improve its effectiveness when it comes to converting sales and make it cheaper to advertise using Google AdWords.

PAY-PER-CLICK ADVERTISING When most people think about internet marketing, they think about Google AdWords. While AdWords can't build a relationship with a client or sell a product directly, it can drive targeted, relevant traffic to your site at a price you set yourself.

The earliest forms of internet advertising were

"The first aim is to get the right visitors. Web traffic is of little use unless the people who visit your site are likely to buy."

paid for per thousand impressions (PPM), whereas with pay per click (PPC) you pay only when a potential visitor clicks the ad and visits your site. Aside from that obvious advantage, this mechanism makes it possible to track the effectiveness of your ad by measuring its click-through rate (CTR), the percentage of those who view the ad that go on to click on it. You can then extend that to tracking the sales themselves, so that you can tell which ads end up with the most profit per sale.

Google stole a march on Yahoo! by introducing a much more sophisticated treatment of PPC, and offers by far the best service to advertisers as well as the biggest market share. In most cases the best technique is to get your ad campaign working effectively via AdWords and then export it to the Yahoo! and Microsoft equivalents.

PERMISSION MARKETING Once a user arrives at your site, you need to make sure you begin a long-term relationship with a profitable percentage. This means giving them something of worth in return for their contact details – usually no more than a name and email address. Over the following days, your customer will receive specially written emails with two purposes: to encourage them to read more emails and, ultimately, to make the sale. Not surprisingly, if you make every email a sales letter, your potential customer will read part of the first one and then unsubscribe.

This automated sequence of emails is called an "autoresponder". In my view, the autoresponder is the most powerful, and most poorly used, weapon in the internet marketer's arsenal. A good autoresponder sequence will convert a far higher percentage of customers than a simple sales page, while building a mutually beneficial long-term relationship that leads to more sales.

How to optimise your copy

Search engines reward "relevance" – how closely the content of a web page matches the search phrase typed in. Your aim is to ensure that the right page from your site appears as high as possible in the rankings. So sensible search engine optimisation (SEO) involves not only getting your content right, but also structuring it in such a way that the mechanised process that the search engines use results in the best possible indexing.

Search engines serve up a link to an entire page, so the page is the fundamental unit you need to think about. Broadly speaking, each page should deal with a single major content area. If you have a range of products, each should be on its own page. For example, the driving theory test comprises a multiple-choice test and a video simulation. To rank well, each needs to be on its own page: this way, the density of the relevant keywords on the page is much higher.

STRUCTURE Within each page, you need to structure your content to reinforce the main messages it contains. Google tends to give extra weighting to the top 25% and bottom 25% of copy on any page. When it comes to deciding if the page is relevant, keywords in those places outrank those in the middle. The lesson is to make sure your main, keyword-dense, messages are near the top and the bottom.

On most web pages, users tend to pay attention to the top of the page, then the bottom, and finally spend the least time on the middle. Google's weighting of the content is designed to mirror this behaviour – one of the ways it succeeds over its competitors by providing the most relevant results. Since visitors look primarily at the top and foot of the page, they are more likely to regard the results of their search as relevant – and therefore continue to use Google – if they find their search terms here.

HTML TAGS Remember HTML is supposed to describe the *meaning* of the content, not how it *looks*. The <h1> ("Heading 1") tag is intended to indicate that this text is the most important on the page. Accordingly, Google gives greater weighting to <h1> text. So your main heading, being <h1>, needs to include your most important keywords. Don't, for example, write a clever or oblique heading that doesn't mention any of your keywords – or if you do, give it a different tag, using <h1> for a more direct piece of copy, even if your CSS then makes this visually less prominent. Google gives proportionate priority to the other headings, <h2> being higher than <h3> and so on. Structure your headings with this in mind, and make sure you have only one <h1> tag, fewer <h2> than <h3> tags and so on.

Within paragraphs, Google prioritises text contained within the <strong> and <em> tags. These usually appear as bold or italic, and Google assumes you think they're more important. There's a case, therefore, for surrounding your keywords with <strong> tags. Again, your CSS determines the visual effect – which could be none.

Keep in mind that Google is trying to second-guess what a human reader will see as the most important words. Google doesn't buy anything from you, so remember the main point of your copy is to talk to humans. Sensible use of tags will make the page more effective for humans and for Google; go overboard and you'll satisfy neither.

IMAGE LINKS Believe it or not, images also impact on SEO. Again, this goes together with making the page useful for humans. For example, the alt element of the <img> tag – a piece of text attached to an image – was originally used to

```
Source of: http://www.passyourtheory.co.uk/hazardperceptionlandingpage1b.php - Mozilla Firefox
File  Edit  View  Help
<h1 class="toptitle" style="margin-top:100px;">
Passing your Theory and Hazard Perception Test: The Inside Track
</h1>
<p><span class="drop">D</span>id you know that around <strong>HALF</strong> th
</p>
<p>The government rakes in over <strong>20 Million Pounds</strong> per year fr
<hr />
<p><strong>Stop Press! Changes for September 2009</strong></p>
<p>If you're worried about any changes to the test for September 2009, don't b
<hr />
<p>
Since 2005 we've helped <strong>307,828</strong> members like you pass their t
</p>
<p>
We must be getting something right as <strong>96%</strong> of our members tell
</p>
<p class="buybutton"><a href="http://www.passyourtheory.co.uk/signup.php"><img
<p>
<h1>How does the theory test work?</h1>
<p>
The theory test has two parts. The first part is a multiple choice test in whi
<p>
To get a pass in this first part, you need to score 43 or more. <strong>That's
Line 42, Col 26
```

Clear, standards-compliant code is easily digested by search-engine spiders. That means you maximise your rankings in the resuilts without paying a penny.

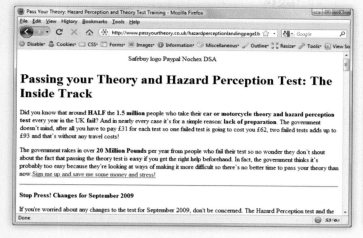

Turn off CSS and images (above left) and you get a good idea of how your site looks to a search-engine spider. Here, the main heading and first part of the copy contain our keywords. On the right is how a table-based site might look to Google. It's not nearly so obvious what this site is about or the relative importance of the keywords – assuming there are any.

describe the image while it loaded. When that was no longer useful, many designers ignored it. But alt text is also used by screen-reader software to describe images to users who can't see them, and is essential for accessibility.

When Google's "spider" visits a page, every text element is read. It sees the text part of an <img> tag as text, so adding your keywords to an alt element will increase the page's keyword density. But this is worth doing only if you can preserve the real purpose of alt, to describe the image accurately. Less obviously, adding your keywords to the URL of the image will also increase keyword density at no cost. All you need to do is change the filenames of your images to include your keywords, inserting hyphens between the words. For example, here's the HTML for an image from a page covering the Hazard Perception test:

was first developed, it described the meaning of the page while including presentational tags such as <b> (bold) and <font> to give more – albeit primitive – design control. More than a decade ago, however, CSS was introduced to allow presentation to be handled outside the HTML, as we explained on pp48-53. Sadly, many people still use outdated presentational HTML to clog up their pages: I strongly advise you to avoid this mistake.

The biggest culprit is the use of tables for layout. The <table> tag was developed to allow the presentation of spreadsheet-style figures, but designers quickly found they could lay out entire pages using table cells. Table-based layouts often have tables nested within tables within tables.

This causes a number of problems. First, the page becomes absolute gobbledygook for screen readers and,

"Google gives extra weighting to the top 25% and bottom 25% of a page. Keywords in those places outrank those in the middle."

```
<img src="/images/screenshot1.jpg"
alt="Test footage" />
```

And here it is after optimisation:

```
<img src="/images/hazard-perception-
example-screen.jpg"
alt="Hazard Perception example screen" />
```

The revised version includes the key phrase "hazard perception" twice, while also making it clearer what the image is about – good for both Google and your visitors.

STICKING TO STANDARDS Your website will be indexed much more effectively by search engines if you strictly separate content from presentation. When HTML

therefore, very hard for search-engine spiders to make sense of. Second, the sheer quantity of <table>,<td> and <tr> tags swamps the copy and messes up your attempts to manage the keyword density. Third, your site is unlikely to work on mobile devices. Finally, the site is almost impossible to redesign without changing every single page (a CSS-based site can be redesigned without touching the HTML). For all these reasons, my advice is to avoid presentational HTML entirely and use CSS for all your design.

An easy way to see how your site looks to Google is to disable CSS and images. For example, using the Web Developer toolbar in Firefox, go to CSS > Disable Styles > All Styles and Images > Disable Images > All Images. You can now check that your headings and other tags include your keywords and, crucially, whether your most important copy is at the top or bottom of the page, as seen by the spider.

Metadata and links

View the source code of any website (see p40) and you'll see, near the top, a series of "meta" tags. The purpose of these is to provide information about the page to search engines. As you might guess, this can be abused to tell search engines what you want them to believe, rather than the truth. But search engines have become more sophisticated, and now index pages based on their actual content, not the web designer's meta tags.

The long and the short of it is that meta tags have practically no impact on your search engine ranking. The most common meta tags are "Description", "Keywords", "Robots", "Generator" and "Revisit-After". The old technique was to stuff the "Keywords" tag with your chosen keywords, but today this is more likely to do harm than good. By all means put your main keywords in there, but don't expect any significant benefit, and don't try to pack hundreds in.

The only meta tag you should always include is "Description". While this doesn't improve your ranking, it does give you control over how your site appears in the search results. All major search engines use this tag as the text that appears beneath the site link. Google and Bing use the text on its own, whereas Yahoo! will pad it out with content from your site to fill the available space. In the absence of a Description meta tag, all search engines will grab some of the content of the page itself and present that instead. That gives you much less control over exactly what appears. Bear in mind that whatever keywords the searcher has typed in will appear in bold in the description section of the results, making your site appear more relevant and therefore more likely to be clicked.

Here's an example from PassYourTheory.co.uk:

```
<meta name="Description" content="The best
Hazard Perception and Theory Test training
anywhere. Official DSA Theory Test question
bank and Hazard Perception video clips">
```

This text is used by Bing as our site description in the search results (Google takes exactly the same approach):

THE TITLE TAG While the meta tags have next to no impact on your ranking, it's essential to get the <title> tag right. This tag is placed in the <head> section alongside the meta tags, and has two effects. First, whatever you type here will appear in the browser title bar. More importantly, search engines use the contents of the title tag as the title of your listing. Including your main keywords in your title tag

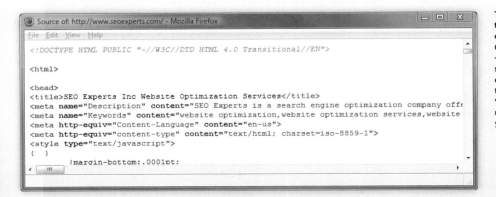

The meta and title tags of a search engine optimisation (SEO) company – after all, they should know. It's essential to get the title and meta "Description" tags right to optimise your listing.

will boost your natural ranking – but take care, as always, to ensure that the title makes sense to humans, too.

INCOMING LINKS Search engines, particularly Google, rank results on three main criteria. The first is *relevance*. As we've said, this is mainly about getting your content to match the search phrases used by your potential customers. The details of the Google algorithm are a closely guarded and ever-evolving secret, but the search giant makes no secret of the fact that, along with relevance, two other factors are highly important. The first of these is *age*: longer-established sites tend to appear higher up the listings. The second is the number and, especially, the quality of *links* on the site.

By acquiring links from other relevant sites, you will improve your ranking considerably. You may have heard of PageRank. This is an algorithm invented by Google co-founder Larry Page to indicate the relative importance of a web page by analysing its links. It results in a number out of ten, which you can see if you download the Google Toolbar. Any incoming link from a site with a higher PageRank than yours will boost your position in the natural search listings as well as increasing your PageRank.

As an example, the BBC home page (www.bbc.co.uk) has a PageRank of 9/10 and is, therefore, considered by Google to be a leading authority. If (by some miracle) you could convince the BBC to link one if its relevant pages to your site – which almost certainly has a much lower PageRank – then that would boost your ranking. On the other hand, if you have a PageRank of 5 and your links are coming from sites with lower PageRanks, that will not have a positive effect on your listing position.

So the aim should be to get incoming links from authoritative sites. You could do this by providing free information of interest to their visitors, offering them discounts, or indeed paying the site for a link. A number of SEO companies offer to submit your site to hundreds of directories in return for a sizeable fee, but the value of these services is debatable.

You should certainly submit your site to the DMOZ directory (www.dmoz.org), as it's well recognised and used by major search engines. Other directories should be chosen with care: make sure they're relevant and have a greater PageRank than you.

OUTGOING LINKS If you have owned a website for any length of time, you've probably received emails asking to exchange links. In other words, the emailer offers to add a link to your site in return for you adding a link to theirs. There's some debate about the effect that outgoing links have on your PageRank, but it seems likely

> **"Meta tags now have practically no impact on your SEO. By all means put your main keywords in, but don't expect any significant benefit."**

Do you find these tags informative, or are they just clutter? Modern search engines feel much the same way about superfluous metadata in web pages.

that outgoing links will have either no affect or a minor negative impact. As with all other matters SEO, it comes down to striking a balance between what's good for your ranking and what's good for your visitors. If you're offered a link exchange by a site with a higher PageRank than you, then generally speaking you should accept it as long as the outgoing link is likely to be of interest to your visitors.

All outgoing links should be set to launch in their own browser tab. To do this, use the following format:

```
<a href="http://www.thewebsite.com"
target="_blank">My link text </a>
```

This is one of the few occasions when I think it's fine to disobey the XHTML 1.0 Strict guidelines, under which the target attribute is deprecated. What this HTML does is to launch the other site in its own window or tab (depending on how the user's browser is set up) rather than overwriting your site in the same window; after all, they might want to come back, and you need to make that as easy as possible.

How much time you spend on link building depends on the importance to you of appearing high in the organic rankings (as opposed to the paid-for "sponsored results"). Yet no matter how hard you work, achieving a high position in the organic rankings will take months or even years. For most new businesses this is simply too long, and they'll focus mainly on pay-per-click (PPC) advertising.

Given that you only have so many hours in the day, it makes sense to get your content as well-optimised as you can, submit yourself to the main search engines and directories, and then focus on your PPC campaign.

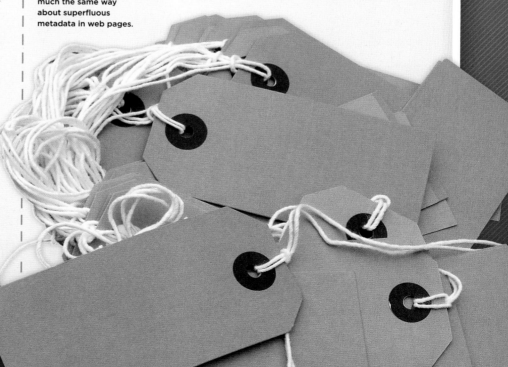

Using Google Analytics

Information is power: you need to know which pages on your site are popular, and track your visitors all the way from arriving at your site to clicking "Buy". Google Analytics does this for free.

4 Marketing Find new customers

This data can help you test and improve every step of the process. If, for example, a high number of users exit your site at a particular page, you can change it and see if it improves. Analytics will tell you where your visitors come from, whether via a pay-per-click ad, organic search results, links from other sites or typing your URL into a browser. This tells you which are the most important sources of traffic and which are most effective.

Analytics will also tell you about the browsers your visitors are using, whether they have plugins such as Flash Player, what languages they speak, whether they're a new or returning visitor and plenty more besides.

SET UP YOUR ACCOUNT To set up Google Analytics for a WordPress site, all you need is a free Google account. Armed with this, go to http://analytics.google.com and click Sign Up. You'll find yourself at the New Account Signup page. Enter your site's URL where requested, give it a name and set your location.

GET TRACKING Click Continue and fill in your contact details. Click Continue again, read the Terms and Conditions and click Yes. Click Create New Account. You're presented with your tracking code. Be sure to use the "New Tracking Code". This JavaScript needs to be inserted into every page on your site. Here's how to do it in WordPress. Run FileZilla and navigate to the /wp-content/themes/theme-name/ folder. You need to find a file called "footer.php" which, as its name suggests, creates the footer for every page. Copy this file to your hard disk.

EDIT YOUR FOOTER Open the file in PSPad or Notepad. Find the entry "<?php wp_footer(); ?>". Switch back to the Analytics page and click on the tracking code. This should select it; now right-click and select Copy. Paste the code after the above line in the footer.php file. Use FileZilla to upload footer.php back to its original location. Click Finish to complete the setup.

FINAL CHECKS Make sure the tracking code is working. From the Analytics Overview, click Edit next to your domain name. You'll see "Tracking Unknown" at the top right. Click the Check Status link to force Analytics to analyse the page. It should confirm that you're all set. Come back in a day or two to see some stats.

1

2

3

4

Beginner's guide to keywords

Keywords help search engines determine if your web pages are relevant to the search terms entered by a user. However, making your pages more relevant is not simply a matter of packing your copy with your chosen keywords. In the early days of search engines this was accepted practice, but now you're much more likely to see your site punished for this rather than rewarded.

Why? Well, search engines such as Google, Yahoo and Bing compete largely on the quality of the results that users get. Google dominates the market because of its obsession with presenting the most relevant search results, and it continues to focus on this as its number one priority. If a page is artificially padded out with keywords it will irritate the visitor and probably result in them clicking the Back button – not the result either you or Google was looking for.

Here's how to assess your keywords properly.

1 **LOAD THE TOOL** Google should be your first target when optimising your site, so start with its keywords tool. Go to www.pcpro.co.uk/links/keywordtool. In the Website field, type the URL of one of your main competitors, enter the Captcha text and click Search.

2 **FIRST RESULTS** This will present a list of keywords, ranked by the number of searches carried out per month on each. This search figure is surprisingly inaccurate in my experience, but it does give a rough indication of the relative importance of each. You can also see the price that Google suggests you bid for the keyword when setting up your AdWords (see p110). You can ignore this figure, but it does show which keywords are more expensive.

Finally, you'll see a graphical indication of the level of competition for that keyword. Pay particular attention to high-volume keywords with low to moderate completion.

Click Download/All to export these keywords as a CSV file, which you can later paste into your AdWords campaign.

3 **FIND THE KEY** Bear in mind that your rivals may be poor at optimising their sites, and their product range may be different to yours, so this isn't a complete list. But it does offer a start. Looking at the list for my candle-making site, I can immediately discount some of these keywords as I won't be stocking those products; I'll also

be adding my most important key phrase, "candle making kits", which this competitor doesn't stock.

4 **KEY PHRASES** At this stage, don't bother with keywords that have a low number of monthly searches. I've drawn the line at 500, and most of my effort will be focused on high-traffic keywords. Equally, avoid very generic keywords that have massive monthly traffic: while this won't cost you anything financially, it signals huge competition and makes it much harder to rank near the top. In most cases, your keywords will actually be phrases. For example, with www.makingyourowncandles.co.uk I won't be focusing specifically on "candle" or "candles", but rather on "candle making" and "candle making kit". Both of these contain "candle" too, and so will rank against that keyword, but I don't expect a high position.

Finally, remember to include the word "buy" alongside your product names in your copy where possible, as many searchers will type "buy candle" rather than just "candle". Similarly, if your product is seasonal, include "Christmas" or "summer" in your copy alongside it.

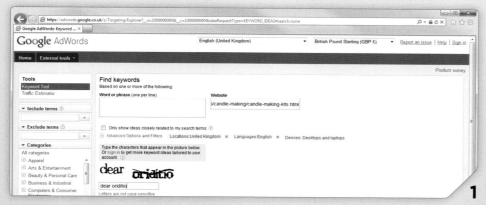

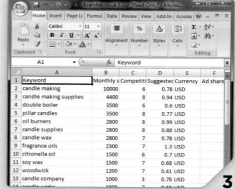

Get blogging!

In this book I've advocated using WordPress to create your business website. As you may know, WordPress was originally developed as a blogging platform, so it's worth thinking about using it for that purpose, too. There are two basic approaches to blogging: publishing under your own name, to express your personal views and perhaps connect with friends and colleagues, and blogging under the identity of your business.

These days the blog as personal web diary is increasingly being replaced by Facebook and Twitter, and for most users is unlikely to achieve anything much from a commercial point of view. Unless you're a celebrity, it's probably much more effective to create a blog under the name of your business rather than your personal identity. WordPress makes it simple to mix posts and pages in the same site, so you can integrate your blog with your main sales website. If you're using hosted e-commerce, a blog makes an ideal companion to attract traffic.

WHAT'S THE POINT? As a businessperson, you'll want your blog, like everything else you spend time on, to have a specific business function that contributes to your bottom line; if you feel the need to vent your spleen on anything, a personal blog is the way to go. Having said that, don't make the mistake of thinking you need to be balanced and neutral with all your company blog entries. Your aim is to have people return on a regular basis or subscribe to your blog, and nothing is more likely to put people off than a bland, corporate-style blog. The key is to keep it on-topic and avoid any really outrageous views that might alienate customers.

To contribute to your profitability, your blog must either make it more likely that your customers will buy your company's products or it must make money for itself.

BRINGING IN CUSTOMERS A well-written, relevant blog will help establish a relationship of trust with potential customers, which can then lead to sales. A blog of this sort establishes you as a figure of authority in your market and the natural choice for the customer. If you've based your business on your interests and expertise, creating a credible, useful blog shouldn't be difficult – but it does take time.

My top seven tips for a successful business blog:

1 Know your audience

In developing your product, you will have defined who is your typical customer. Every blog entry you consider writing should be relevant and interesting to this target audience. You should always be writing to that individual, using a voice that suits and appeals to them.

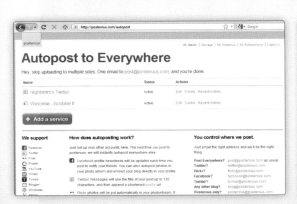

Posterous makes it easy to update your blog and social networks.

Glenn Livingston's blog has great content to entice you to sign up.

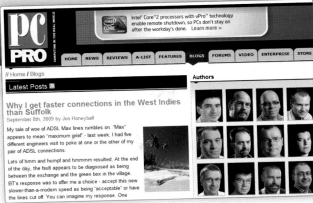

2 Write with personality

Think about the personality you want to project in your blog. It's unlikely to be "boring, middle-aged corporate-speak". Look at some of the best business blogs (see right) and analyse how the way in which they've been written affects how you perceive them and their company. You can also find inspiration in magazines and books that appeal to your target audience.

3 Write what's interesting

Nobody will read a boring blog. Come up with interesting angles or be the first with news or opinions. If you solve a problem that's relevant to your customers, blog about it. Whatever you do, don't start a blog that is nothing more than a list of links to other blogs.

4 Link it to your business

A common mistake is to expect visitors to understand how your blog relates to your business. Most people don't want to think that hard. Make it clear who you are and what your business does. Include obvious links to the business.

5 Capture their details

Blogs should be open to all visitors; it's not a good idea to require them to register to view your posts, unless there's intrinsic value in the information or resources on the protected pages. By writing an eBook, recording an interview or buying resale rights to useful resources, you can offer the visitor something in exchange for their details. Once you have these, you can begin to establish a longer-term relationship that might lead to multiple sales.

6 Keep updating

How many blogs have you come across that look interesting on the face of it, until you notice that they were last updated months or even years ago? An outdated blog is worse than no blog at all. Services such as Posterous (www.posterous.com) make it easy to update your blog, Twitter feed and Facebook page via email. There's no excuse.

Best blogs

If you want to see how it's done, these are some of my favourite business blogs.

www.perrymarshall.com
Combined blog and website of the foremost AdWords and internet-marketing expert.

www.payperclick searchmarketing.com
Glenn Livingston's pay-per-click marketing blog: full of excellent material, and a good example of how to get someone to begin a relationship by offering something valuable. (Also notice the shining example of a keyword-filled URL!)

www.alistapart.com
A List Apart is an excellent and long-established blog aimed at web developers.

www.smashing magazine.com
Smashing magazine's blog is specifically for web designers.

www.pcpro.co.uk/blogs
Naturally, the best technology blog!

7 Host it yourself

Don't use free hosted services such as WordPress.com or Blogspot.com. Like using a Hotmail address for your business, this suggests you're a cheapskate or incompetent.

HOW TO BLOG FOR MONEY First, build an audience. The more relevant people who visit you, the more sales you'll make from your main business and the more potential there will be to make money from the blog itself. Once you've built your blog and populated it with useful articles, you can then drive traffic to it using the SEO techniques we've covered and a low-cost Google AdWords campaign.

You can make money directly from a healthy blog by selling advertising space or selling products as an affiliate. Ads are very simple to set up, especially if you use Google AdSense, but unless you have a massive audience, they'll generate only a small income. On the other hand, many bloggers have built entire businesses around affiliate marketing, not least because of the low setup cost.

Keep in mind that you are creating a blog that people want to revisit and recommend. Making money from advertising or affiliate schemes depends on having a viable blog in the first place. This is increasingly important, as Google appears to be preparing to eliminate blogs that only "review" products for which the blog owner is an affiliate.

If you want to add affiliate products to your site, these are my recommendations:

 DON'T OVERDO IT Make sure no more than 10-20% of posts link to an affiliate product. This will prevent it feeling like a pure sales page.

 BUY THE PRODUCTS There's no excuse for selling a product you haven't personally used. By buying and using a product you will see how it works and be able to write a balanced review (it's essential to include cons as well as pros). This will also ensure you don't recommend duff products to your audience, which will alienate them and could result in costly returns.

STAY RELEVANT Stick to products that are truly relevant to your audience. Your blog will only succeed if it is focused, and your credibility only counts in the areas in which you've built that credibility.

Relationship-based marketing

Would you buy from a stranger? Probably not – yet many web businesses are based on exactly that premise. Create (or buy in) a product, add a shopping cart, run a pay-per-click ad, then sit back and watch the lucre roll in. Or not. Even if customers do buy, most businesses then forget about them. You can do better.

Businesses that don't build customer relationships can make money only if every transaction is profitable. The costs of production, running your business and marketing must add up to less than the price customers pay for an item. This is increasingly hard to achieve as the cost of pay-per-click (PPC) advertising rises, and it's not how successful bricks-and-mortar businesses work. A Tesco Clubcard, for example, is the basis of a long-term relationship with the supermarket that encourages you to shop there. Even your local car mechanic has the advantage of a roadside location and passing traffic. An internet site, unless brilliantly optimised to appear on Google's first page or have a wide network of incoming links, is invisible unless you're running a PPC campaign, and if you are, every click is costing you money.

The internet also suffers from a lack of trust. If I go into my local corner shop, however run-down it is, I know I'll be able to take the contents of my shopping basket home once I've paid. This isn't the case online, so your customers are understandably concerned about handing over their credit-card details to a company they don't know.

This contributes to the low conversion rates of most websites. A website is doing well if it achieves 2% conversion; many languish at below 1%. Think about that: over 98 out of every 100 visitors – who have arrived at your site by clicking on an advert targeted at them – *do not buy*. If you're spending 10p per click and getting a 2% conversion rate, each conversion is costing you around £5. In practice the figure can be much worse, and many, many new web businesses fail because they can't make PPC pay.

Traditionally, marketing has relied almost entirely on "interruption advertising". TV and radio adverts are typical examples of that; they rely on interrupting your chain of thought, making an impression, getting across a message and having you take some sort of action. In the 1950s and 1960s this approach worked because there were few channels through which to advertise, but these days we're all exposed to hundreds of interruptions per day.

Instead, as we saw on p110, successful internet and direct marketing is usually permission marketing. Here, potential customers are attracted to your site by interruption advertising, links or recommendation, but then enter into a mutually beneficial long-term relationship with you. Usually, this begins with you offering something worthwhile in exchange for your visitor's name and email address.

Seth Godin literally wrote the book on this subject. *Permission Marketing: Turning Strangers into Friends and Friends into Customers* (£7.49 from www.amazon.co.uk) is still a bestseller despite being more than ten years old. Godin's blog (http://sethgodin.typepad.com) is also worth reading for advice and analysis.

And for the doubters

I appreciate that many people are suspicious of the internet. Some people will believe that we made up all the testimonials you see around the site or that everything on the internet is a scam. Well, there's not much I can do about that but if you just need a little more convincing then please sign up for our FREE trial membership. This gives you the opportunity to try 3 FREE, fully functional mock theory tests with absolutely no obligation to buy anything.

You'll see how useful and realistic our theory test is before you commit to becoming a member. Add that to our pass pledge (if you become a Premier Member and then fail we will refund your membership twice over!) and our outstanding track record and you've got nothing to lose!

First name & Surname

Your E-Mail :

`Sign Me Up For a FREE Trial Membership`

Consumers are quite guarded about giving away their email addresses – perhaps increasingly so. You must offer something of value to persuade them.

> **"Traditional marketing relies on interruption advertising. These days we're exposed to hundreds of interruptions per day."**

The potential customer is then sent a series of emails, written by you (if you're tempted to buy them in, you're missing the point), at pre-programmed intervals. The ultimate aim of these, of course, is to make one or more sales, but they should be mainly devoted to providing great information to your subscriber.

The key is to ensure your emails are anticipated by people who have volunteered to receive information from you. Your emails are then not junk or spam, but a welcome source of knowledge (and maybe, if you're a good writer, even entertainment). This means the permission you've purchased with your initial freebie needs to be renewed with each and every message. Abuse that trust just once, and your carefully cultivated relationship can be ended instantly.

That's not to say you shouldn't use your auto-responder sequence to sell your product or service. Rather, the sales pitch needs to be relevant to the subject matter and must occupy a relatively small portion of the message. A good rule of thumb is that 80% of your message should be useful, free information, which buys you the right to spend 20% of the message selling. This might be 20% of a single email, or one sales message out of every five emails.

 GETTING THE DEAL RIGHT The biggest single impediment to a successful autoresponder campaign is the site owner's reluctance to give away too much free of charge. If you don't give away something of true value, potential customers won't sign up in sufficient numbers. Let's imagine you're selling aquarium accessories. Your job is to establish your credibility as a trustworthy figure of authority. You may well have set up a blog (see p118), and your autoresponder will reinforce this while giving you the opportunity to sell to the customer.

Algae is a common problem for owners of fish tanks, and among your various product lines you sell anti-algae tablets and gizmos. The email your customers want to receive (especially if they've responded to a PPC ad that mentions solving algae problems) is one that tells them how to prevent algae forming in their tank. But hold on: doesn't that mean they won't buy your anti-algae tabs? Perhaps. If they follow your tips, they won't need your tabs – but they'll almost certainly need some other accessories, and who are they going to buy them from? That helpful person with the anti-algae advice.

By giving something authoritative away for free, you make these people much more likely to buy from you later, particularly if you send a whole sequence of useful emails to them. And thanks to human nature (and laziness), many of your customers won't actually follow your advice on clearing the algae because it's too much like hard work, and will buy anti-algae tablets from you in any case, since your emails show you know what you're talking about.

Autoresponders are the classic quid pro quo: everyone wins. You end up with a long-term, well-informed customer whose multiple purchases outweigh the original cost of attracting them; and your customer ends up with a trusted supplier of the things they genuinely need. ➜

Even when you're selling something that, by its nature, people might need only once – such as advice for a driving test – you can increase your profitability by building ongoing relationships.

Case study
PassYourTheory.org.uk

PassYourTheory.co.uk has a fundamental problem: drivers need to pass their test only once. It might seem, therefore, that we need to make a sale on the user's first visit. In fact, it's hard to make a profit that way, so we use autoresponders to increase our conversion rate.

Think about the way you search for a product. Typically, you'll type a search term into Google, then visit a number of the sites that appear both in the Sponsored Listings and the organic results. Very often you'll want to mull it over before buying, and unless you're very organised, by the time you come back, credit card in hand, you've forgotten which one you liked best. Alternatively, you leave it for a week or two and whatever inspired you to search in the first place has been long forgotten.

Now imagine what would happen if one of those sites you visited emailed you a couple of days later with an informative email and a link to their sign-up pages. Wouldn't you be more likely simply to click the link and buy from them rather than start again?

This is the approach we use at PassYourTheory. As part of the process of obtaining a free membership, the visitor signs up to our email autoresponder. This means that they get a sequence of emails starting a couple of days after signup. These contain sample theory questions along with answers and hints and tips.

At the end of each email is a reminder to upgrade to one of our paid memberships. All of this is entirely automated.

STEP BY STEP Set up an autoresponder

1 **SIGN UP** Go to www.aweber.com and click Order. I would always sign up for month-by-month membership in case I don't get on with a service. Complete your details, sign up and click Let's Get Started. You can now create a "double opt-in" email.

2 **FIRST EMAIL** Current anti-spam regulations require that anyone signing up to your email list confirms their request by clicking a link in an email. The first email you create will encourage them to click the verification link. Note here that I'm using the field {!firstname_fix}. This inserts the user's first name – they will have supplied this on registering – and the "fix" part means it'll automatically capitalise the first letter if they didn't. So, if sent to me, the email would have a subject line: "Kevin, Confirm your subscription".

Some internet marketers believe that adding the user's name to the subject line makes it more likely they'll open the email, but the only way to know is to test it. In my view it does no harm if not overused. The "Confirmation Success Page" is the page on your site that subscribers are directed to once they've verified. This is optional, but a very good idea. If you're using WordPress, create a page specifically for the purpose and enter its URL here.

You can now go on to edit your first email, which subscribers will receive on completing the verification process. You have the choice of sending in HTML or plain-text format (or both). I recommend plain text, as it's much more likely to make it through your users' junk filters, and HTML in email clients is unpredictable.

3 **CREATE A WEB FORM** You can now create a web form that will be used by subscribers to sign up. I strongly recommend the "In-line" format, which creates some code for you to insert in your site with a standard pair of input fields for the user's name and email address. Avoid any form of pop-up or pop-under, as visitors often loathe them.

You can specify a "thank you" page that will tell users to check their email for the verification message. You can also forward variables to the thank you page, which makes it possible, with a bit of coding, to capture suscribers' details and add them to your own database. If, for example, you give away access to specific parts of your site, or a download, then you could have AWeber send the customer's email address and name to your website to facilitate this. Scroll down to the bottom of the page and click Get HTML. This should be copied into your page or post (use the HTML view in WordPress).

4 **NEW MESSAGES** You can now go through the process of adding further messages.
Remember, it's your job to encourage your subscribers to read the next message in the sequence. Your emails must be anticipated and welcomed by your subscribers, and this means including genuinely useful information with the minimum of sales pitch. If you want to see a superb autoresponder sequence, go to www.perrymarshall.com and complete the form to receive "5 Days to Success with Google AdWords". This will give you an idea of how to structure your own sequences.

Search engines:
how to get listed

Any site containing inbound links will eventually be indexed by all the
major search engines, but you can submit it manually to be sure.

Yahoo still offers a £199 service to speed up adding your
site, but with Google and Bing you can manually submit it
free. Google currently represents around 80% of total search
traffic, so make sure your site is set up properly for it first.

1 **ADD YOUR SITE** Go to www.google.com/
webmasters/tools, click "Add a site…" and type in
the URL of your site. Click Continue and you'll see
a verification screen: this is there to ensure you own the site.

2 **VERIFICATION** The best way to verify
ownership is to upload a file to your server. Click
the link to download the HTML verification
file. In FileZilla, upload that file to the root folder of your
site. Click the link in step 3 of the "Verify ownership"
instructions to check that it has successfully uploaded. If so,
click the Verify button and Google will check that it's there.
All being well, you'll be taken to your dashboard. There won't
be much to see, as the site won't yet have been visited by the
spider. In the meantime, create a sitemap to help the search
engines index your site properly. A sitemap is an XML file in

a standard format; WordPress has a free plugin to create it
automatically. From Plugins in your WordPress Dashboard,
search for "Google XML Sitemaps". Click Install.

3 **SUBMIT SITEMAP** Go to Settings > XML-
Sitemap. Ignore all the options for now. Hit "Click
here" at the top to build your map. Then make
sure Google has found it: in the Google Webmaster Tools
dashboard, click Site Configuration > Sitemaps, click Submit
a Sitemap, type "sitemap.xml" and click Submit Sitemap. The
sitemap.xml file also works with Bing: find its equivalent
tools at www.bing.com/webmaster.

4 **CHECK KEYWORDS** Once the Google
spider has visited, you'll see a range of data
that complements Google Analytics (p116).
For example, it shows how Google sees your site, where
incoming links are from, the top search queries and where
you appeared in the organic listings. Note the summary
of keywords found across the site; check the top ones are
your most important.

Getting your keywords right

There's nothing more important to the success of an AdWords campaign than finding the right keywords: they determine who will see your ad. There's clearly no point in having your ad displayed to the wrong people, since that will result in the twin nightmares of low click-through rate and low conversion rate.

The greatest problems come when you focus on keywords that are close to the correct ones but don't attract buyers. For example, imagine you sell candle-making kits, like our example business. If you decide your ads will target searchers who type "candles", you're making an expensive mistake: they may be looking purely for information, or to buy ready-made candles. Maybe a few of them are looking for kits, but the percentage will be tiny, with the result that your click-through will be very low and your conversion even lower. The people seeing your ad are casual browsers, not buyers. And remember, if by chance they do click your ad, but don't buy anything, they've cost you money.

Contrast this with using the key phrase "candle making". A searcher who types this is likely to be looking for information on candle making or a supplier of candle-making materials. This keyword might well be profitable.

Even better, having "candle making kit" as your main key phrase would be much more likely to attract active buyers.

CHOOSE YOUR WORDS WISELY It's essential to start your campaign with a small set of highly focused keywords. Many AdWords "gurus" will encourage you to generate a list of dozens (or even hundreds) of "long tail" keywords that each generate only a small amount of traffic but have little competition. However, doing this from the beginning only cloud the issue. In most AdWords campaigns, the vast majority of profitable clicks come from a small percentage of your keywords.

An 80/20 rule is often cited: 80% of your clicks will come from 20% of your keywords. If you follow that through, you'll see that, in fact, 65% of your clicks come from around 4% of your keywords (20% of the 20%). Of

> ## "Imagine you sell candle-making kits. If you decide to target searchers who type 'candles', you're making an expensive mistake."

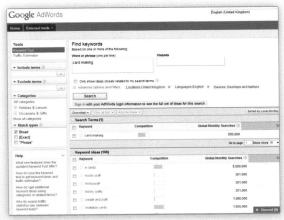

Enter a key phrase to see Google's analysis of related keywords.

Select the checkbox beside each keyword you want to pursue.

Create multiple Ad Groups for different sets of relevant keywords.

course, the actual figures will vary, but the fact remains that it makes sense to work on the most productive keywords.

Begin with your primary keywords: the ones you've used for your company name, domain name, blog title and SEO. For example, with PassYourTheory.org.uk the primary key phrase is "theory test"; for MakingYourOwn Candles.co.uk, it's "candle-making kits"; and for Greeting CardMaker it's "card making". Remember that in part 1 of this guide we established that there was probably sufficient volume in the market for those keywords. Throughout this process, check that each keyword or phrase is aimed squarely at your intended customer.

FIND GOOGLE KEYWORDS Go to https://AdWords. google.co.uk/select/KeywordToolExternal and type your primary keyword phrase into the box (see opposite, bottom left). Make sure "Only show ideas closely related to my search terms" is checked and click Search. If you're selling only in your own country, click on the "Local Monthly Searches" column under "Keyword ideas" to sort the keywords into descending popularity..

You'll now see a list containing your term and all the terms Google thinks are related to your primary keyword phrase. You'll also see the search volume and a bar showing the level of advertiser Competition. Google will also tell you what it expects you to have to pay for an ad based on that keyword to appear in the top three positions. To do this, you need to create an Adwords account (see the walkthrough on p112) and click the "sign in" link on the keyword page.

Having said that, you should take this estimate with a shovel full of salt: Google can't take relevance into account since you haven't, at this point, told it which domain the ad will be linked to, or the ad text. In my experience, the estimated average cost per click can be out by a factor of five or more. Also bear in mind that it's an average. In most markets, the ads in positions 1 and 2 might be disproportionately expensive compared to 3 and 4, so the average is skewed. I've seen examples where the Google estimate was 75p but the actual cost for position 3 was 13p.

What's the point, then? Well, the estimate is a good indicator of the relative cost of each keyword phrase. You can see that our main phrase, "card making", has an approximate CPC of 50p whereas the similar "make cards" is predicted to be much more expensive. You'll also notice that the top few keywords account for a huge proportion of the potential traffic, so we'll concentrate on those for now.

FOCUS YOUR CHOICES You now need to go through the list and click the checkbox next to your primary keyword and those that are closely related and likely to cost a similar amount. In this example, I've chosen "card making", "make

card", "make a card" and "card make" because they are essentially interchangeable. Why not "card making kits" or "card making ideas"? Because searchers typing those keywords into Google are not necessarily looking for the same as those typing "card making", and it's essential to keep your ads focused. You now have your first Ad Group.

AD GROUPS The next step is to find one or more additional Ad Groups based on different sets of keywords. An excellent way of doing this is to analyse what your competitors are advertising against. Click the "Website content" radio button at the top and type in the URL of your main competitor. Google will then trawl its site looking for relevant keywords. Again, list them by local search volume. You need to be careful here if your product is significantly different from the competition (as it should be) and only pick keywords that are relevant to *your* product.

Google helpfully categorises keywords, and I'm drawn immediately to "greeting cards". This is obviously closely tied to "card making", but it's too wide: lots of people searching on that phrase will be looking to buy pre-printed cards. So we're looking for phrases that qualify better. In this case I'm adding "handmade greeting cards", "personalised greeting cards", "blank greeting cards" and "alternative greeting cards" to my list, because in each case the keywords suggest the user wants to customise their card. Some other alternatives, such as "photo greeting cards", have been rejected at this stage because their cost per click is very high.

So these are the keywords for my next Ad Group. Looking down the list, I see keywords related to birthday cards, so I'll also create an Ad Group based on those words.

After all this, you should end up with three to six groups of keywords with between one and six highly focused keywords or phrases in each. My advice is to take your time over this: choosing the right initial keywords will give your AdWords campaign the best possible start. It's then a matter of testing, refining and expanding over time.

Don't look now...

It may well be that there are certain combinations of keywords that you specifically don't want to result in visits to your website. The classic example of this, when you're running a commercial site, is any combination including "free". Searchers who specifically type "free" are relatively unlikely to pay for a product, however persuasive you may be. In these situations, you can specify that any search containing certain keywords should not result in your ad showing. Since every click incurs a cost, the use of negative keywords can be crucial in making your campaign profitable.

Introducing pay-per-click

Print advertising has been the mainstay of the marketing of businesses – large and small – for over a century. For a small firm, it might be an ad in a local paper or the Yellow Pages. But each of these needs to interrupt the reader's flow, grab their attention and get them to buy. This is a lot to attempt in a tiny classified ad that can't be changed until the next reprint and that you pay for up front, whether or not anyone responds.

Pay-per-click (PPC) solves these problems. First, your ad appears when, and only when, a web user types in a word or phrase that's relevant to your product or service. This means the right people are more likely to see your ad. Second, you can amend the ad as much as you like and, indeed, run alternatives alongside each other to test which generates the most profit. Third, you only pay when the user actually clicks; if you get no clicks, you pay nothing.

PPC originated with Goto.com in 1998. Goto later metamorphosed into Overture and then became part of Yahoo, so you might expect Yahoo to be the main force in PPC, but today Google dominates the market with its AdWords programme – which, although it was introduced four years later than Goto.com, accounts for around 80% of the total global "paid search" market share.

The reason for this is linked to Google's success as a search engine. Right from the beginning, Google has focused on the importance of relevance in its search results. Web users quickly gravitated to Google when they started getting more useful results than with Yahoo or MSN.

Google applies this principle to its paid advertising, too. With Yahoo and Microsoft adCenter, the more you bid for your clicks, the higher in the paid results listing you'll appear. It's a bit like traditional advertising, where you'd pay for a better position in the hope – but with no guarantee – of a better response.

With Google, the bid price accounts for only around half of the ranking algorithm. Google also assesses how relevant your ad is to the searcher by examining the ad and its associated website and giving it a "Quality Score". The net result of this is that the more relevant ads will tend to appear higher up (good for the searcher) while also making it possible for focused, content-rich sites with well-written ads to outperform competitors who can afford to pay more per click.

Because of this advantage, we'll spend the next few pages focusing on Google's AdWords system. AdWords not only works better for startup businesses, it also offers the most sophisticated range of tools and reports to help make your campaign a success. So the best approach is

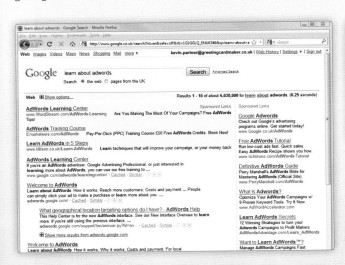

Type "learn about adwords" into Google and you get three full pages of ads by AdWords experts. It's an ideal way to see what's working right now.

Microsoft's Bing search engine tends to deliver fewer targeted ads than Google, as I found when I searched for the same phrase and got only four relevant sponsored links. Bing has only around 10% of the market, but the lack of competition could be an opportunity.

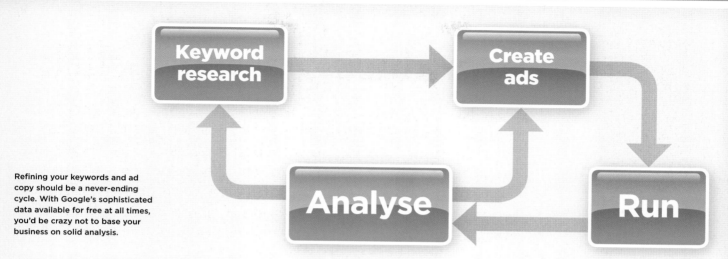

Keyword research → **Create ads**

Analyse ← **Run**

Refining your keywords and ad copy should be a never-ending cycle. With Google's sophisticated data available for free at all times, you'd be crazy not to base your business on solid analysis.

to get everything set up and profitable on Google before expanding into the other PPC systems.

ONE CAMPAIGN, THREE AUDIENCES An advertising campaign is made up of one or more Ad Groups, each of which is made up of one or more PPC ads triggered by a specific set of keywords and phrases. The ads themselves can be displayed in three places: within the Google search results (in the "Sponsored Links" down the right-hand side); within the search results of Google's partners, including Virgin Media and other Google entities such as Google Maps and Google Groups; and in the "Content Network".

The Content Network is made up of all websites signed up to Google's AdSense program, along with bigger

> **"Google AdWords not only works better, it also has the most sophisticated tools to help make your campaign a success."**

advertisers such as newspaper and media sites. Your Google Ads can be shown within this network, but in that context they function more like traditional interruption ads, since the web user is likely to be in "browse" rather than "buy" mode. As a general rule, you need to get your search campaign (Google and its Search Partners) working profitably before tackling the Content Network.

THE PROCESS The PPC process begins and ends with keyword research. In part 1 of this book we established your primary keyword phrase, derived from your company's one-sentence "elevator pitch". This phrase can be used in naming your business, its domain and its website title. It should also appear throughout your site. So your keyword research will begin centred on your primary keyword phrase and

DIY

If, despite my reassurances, you think all this sounds too much like hard work, what about outsourcing your AdWords management? As a rule, I don't recommend it. No-one knows your business (or cares about it) like you, so you're ideally placed to run your campaigns. There are only two situations where external management might be a good idea. First, if you really believe you have too little time. This will be rare, given that marketing is probably your most important activity. Second, once your campaign is up and running profitably, there might be a case for passing the day-to-day chores to someone else. For most of us, however, getting down and dirty with AdWords is an essential skill.

then move outwards, rather than simply picking up every related keyword regardless. Once you've come up with a list of keywords, these need to be split into related groups. Each of these clumps becomes an Ad Group in your AdWords Campaign. You'll create at least two ads within each group.

Typically, you might have three to six Ad Groups in your main campaign, so that's around 12 ads, each being shown to its own set of keywords. You activate the campaign and let it run for long enough to get conversion statistics that can be relied on: usually at least 100 clicks per ad. Then you can compare the performance of the Ad Groups against each other: how profitable is each? Are any burning money?

Within each Ad Group, you'll check the performance of your two (or more) ads, looking at the click-through rate (CTR; the percentage of people who click on the ad) and the conversion rate. This latter figure represents the percentage of people who arrive on your site and then go on to take whatever action you've specified – usually signing up to an email sequence or buying something. This is the key ratio; CTR is money down the drain if you're not converting.

You'll usually find one of the two ads in a group works substantially better. So you'll disable the poor performer, duplicate the winner and alter it in some way so you again have two ads running against each other. Also look at the keywords – Google tells you how each performs – and disable or delete those that are losing you money.

This continues ad infinitum. Initially you will probably see big performance gains in each cycle as you implement improvements, but these will tail off over time, at which point you'll enjoy consistent performance and can concentrate more on other aspects of your sales process.

If all this sounds confusing, don't worry: it needn't be. AdWords is presented as a great money-grabbing mystery machine by marketing gurus who want you to buy their wares. The essentials, however, are very straightforward and can be tackled one step at a time.

STEP BY STEP Creating a Google AdWords account

As you'll have come to expect, it's entirely free to set up an AdWords account. It's simplest if you already have a Google account (for example on Gmail), so if you don't, I suggest you create one before you begin.

1 **NEW ACCOUNT** First you need to set up your account. Go to http://adwords.google.com and click on Try AdWords Now.

2 **ASSOCIATE YOUR GOOGLE ACCOUNT** On the next screen you're asked whether you have an existing Google account. If not, you'll be taken out of the process to create one. If you do, you can elect to use it or create a new one just for AdWords. I'm not sure what benefit there would be in the latter, unless your main Google account is purely for personal use and you don't want to associate it with AdWords. Click Continue.

3 **GEOGRAPHY LESSON** On the next screen you're presented with regional settings. It's absolutely essential you get these right, because Google doesn't allow you to change them later without creating an entirely new account. Click Continue and Google will announce that it's sent a verification email to your email address. Once the verification email arrives, click the link and you'll be taken into AdWords itself for the first time.

4 **TAKE CONTROL** Google helpfully presents a button entitled "Create your first campaign", but we're going to ignore this. Why? Well, by following the wizard-based setup procedure and leaving the options set to the default, you would end up with a campaign that devolves more decisions to Google than is ideal. The option is there for people who want to get up and running as quickly as possible, but I don't believe that such a campaign is likely to be effective. You need to take control from the outset and make choices that make sense for you and your campaign, rather than simply leaving Google to spend up to your daily limit.

So I recommend you click the link for creating advanced campaigns under "For experienced advertisers", even though you're only just starting out. Don't worry: the process is very similar to what you would get by clicking the big button at the top, it's just that you're taking more control.

The key, as I've mentioned in our general discussion of pay-per-click campaigns, is to plan carefully and then experiment methodically. You shouldn't expect your AdWords campaign to "just work". Even if it did reap instant results, there would be every chance you could obtain an even better response by tweaking your adverts and keywords. This is something we'll go into in even more depth over the coming pages.

Take control with Google advertising

For most types of advertising, you pay for people to **see** your ad. With Google AdWords advertising you only pay when they **click** to visit your website. So you get exactly what you pay for – more customers. And because this is pay as you go advertising, you have complete control.

Control how much you spend
You can set a daily spending limit and an amount you're happy to pay for people to click on your ad. The price is chosen by you, not us, so you never have to worry about going over your budget.

Control who sees your ad
Your ad will only appear when potential customers are searching online for relevant terms you've chosen to describe your business.

Control where and when they see it
You can choose to target your audience by location and time: attract local customers during your opening hours or, if you'd rather, promote yourself to a global audience round the clock.

Don't miss out – try it today

We'll **turn your first £25 of advertising into £100***. To start attracting new customers today:

 Visit **google.co.uk/adwords**

 Or call **0800 169 0478**†

---

†Calls to 0800 numbers are free from BT landlines but charges may apply if you use another phone company, call from your mobile phone or call from abroad. Support is available in English only. Offer subject to website and business qualification.

Your promotional code is:

4P6T4-QXDJG-34AE

Redeem immediately; call ☎ 0800 169 0478†
or, to create your own account, visit
🖱 www.google.co.uk/adwords

*Offer is valid until **31/01/2013**

A pocket guide to
DIGITAL PHOTOGRAPHY
Amazing photos every time, everywhere

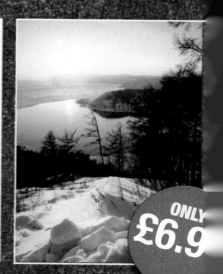

ONLY £6.9

ON SALE NOW!
Order your print or digital MagBook
at magbooks.com

Setting up your AdWords campaign

It's time to roll up your sleeves and get started, beginning with Google AdWords. The "campaign" is AdWords' highest level of organisation. Ad Groups are made up of one or more ads, and campaigns are made up of one or more Ad Groups. Your campaign's settings apply to all Ad Groups and ads within it.

Marketing **4** Find new customers

LOCATION, LOCATION, LOCATION Billing, budgets and regional options are among the choices you need to make for your campaign. Unless you have a truly global product, you should set your location according to your audience. If you're based in the UK and selling a physical product, in most cases you'll want to specify the UK as your target location; if you were living in France, but still planning to target mainly UK buyers, you'd still pick UK.

There aren't many situations in which you would leave the location set to Global. This is because your ads and the landing pages they link to must be optimised to appeal to your target audience, and audiences will vary around the world, requiring different techniques and different language – indeed, different languages! – to achieve a reasonable conversion rate. So even if you have a truly global product, you should normally have one campaign per region.

Generally speaking, Google allows you to target at the regional and country level (along with individual states in the US), and you should specify the most focused location you possibly can. If you offer a service in a local area, you can set your campaign to appear in specific cities.

SEARCH OPTIONS At the campaign level, you can also decide in which search engines your ads will appear and on which devices. You have three basic choices: Google Search, Search Partners (including AOL and Virgin Media) and the Content Network. When setting up a new campaign, Google recommends you have your ads shown across "All available sites and devices". This is a bad idea: Google is the only beneficiary. To begin with, you should set every new campaign to Google Search only. This is because each of the three options should be treated differently.

Begin with Google Search and get your campaign operating profitably before adding Search Partners to that campaign. When your campaign is working profitably across Google Search and the Search Partners, you can then set up a separate campaign for the Content Network. The Content

The dashboard for an AdWords campaign. From the graphs, can you guess when I gave Google experimental control of my ad bidding? It was a very short experiment...

Network (where the ads appear within web pages) is a completely different beast to sponsored listings, and needs to be treated with caution.

Google lets you choose whether to target mobile devices as well as standard computers. Again, when setting up it makes sense to limit yourself to computers initially, unless your product specifically targets the mobile market.

AD ROTATION Once you've created an Ad Group, you'll be able to decide how Google rotates your ads, if you have more than one (as you should). Rotation means that instead of showing the same ad every time someone's search matches your keywords, Google will cycle through all those you've created.

By default, Google will give preference to ads with higher click-through rates, so as some of your ads start to outperform others, they'll appear more often. This might seem logical, but it prevents you testing which ads work best. Instead, instruct Google to show your ads in strict rotation, otherwise you'll end up with a lot of detail about one ad and nothing about the others.

The key point is to think carefully about all your choices when setting up a campaign. Aim to focus closely on your target audience while handling each aspect of the campaign yourself. Don't leave it to Google.

STEP BY STEP Enter your campaign settings

1 **FIRST STEPS** If you don't have a Google AdWords account, see p128. Then go to http://adwords.google.com and sign in with your Google account details. Click "Create your first campaign". Bear in mind that Google is presenting the line of least resistance with this process, and many of its settings won't suit you.

2 **DETAILS** On the Campaign Settings screen, give your campaign a name.
Under Locations, select the narrowest range of locations that will ensure your most profitable audience sees your ad. For example, GreetingCardMaker.co.uk allows users to create cards and print them on their own printer, so it could be used anywhere in the world, but some users will want the cards printed for them (at a cost) and this would only be possible for users in the UK, at least to begin with. It therefore makes no sense to advertise outside the UK.
Under "Networks and devices", click "Let me choose" and deselect all options except "Google Search". You should get your campaign running effectively on the main network before adding Search Partners or Content

Network. Unless you're targeting mobile devices specifically, deselect that. All this reduces the number of variables in the campaign, making it easier to tweak.
Under "Bidding and Budget", again reject Google's recommendation. Select "Manual bidding for clicks" so you can specify how much each click is worth to you, rather than having Google modify your bid using its own algorithms (and to suit its own purposes). Ultimately, you want to pay as little as you can to achieve a good position in the sponsored listings: you can only do this by manually setting bid prices and noting where this ranks you. It's an iterative process that can't be bypassed.
You now need to set your budget. The maxim is simple: never set a budget higher than you can afford. Google spreads it over a month, so on any given day your actual costs might exceed the daily limit set here, but not by much. For most new campaigns, I recommend setting the budget between £5 and £10, unless you're sure a higher amount will be profitable or you feel you can afford to risk more. Remember, if for some reason a lot of users suddenly click your ad, your bill can rise precipitously.

Apocryphal tales are told of advertisers losing thousands of pounds over a weekend. Whether you believe them or not, this is the place to prevent it. If in doubt, err on the low side; you can raise it later.

3 **FIRST AD** Click Save and Continue, and Google will ask you to create your first ad. I recommend putting dummy text in here until you set up your Ad Groups (overleaf). Enter your primary keyword in the keyword box. You need to set a cost per click (CPC); to do that, click Estimate Search Traffic and pick a value below the lowest estimate. Again, err on the lower side. Google will now take you through the billing process. My only advice here is to use a credit card to get up and running quickly.

4 **HOLD ON** Once you've finished with billing, Google will automatically turn on your campaign. You don't want that yet, so immediately click the Campaigns tab, click Enabled and select Pause. You now have a campaign that's inactive but ready for you to add keywords and ads.

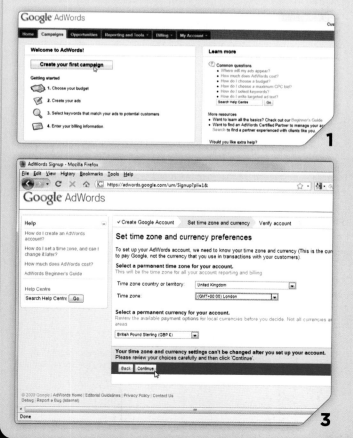

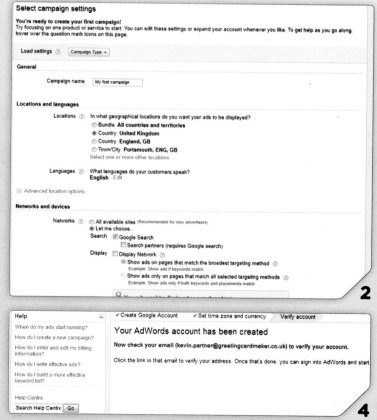

Creating your Ad Groups

The aim of your marketing (and your business) is to make a profit. So you need to attract the maximum profitable traffic to your site for the lowest possible cost. In general, the higher up Google's Sponsored Listings your ad appears, the more clicks you'll get – but, all else being equal, you'll need to bid more for those positions, squeezing your profitability. Fortunes have been lost chasing the top positions purely by bidding more.

The key is to understand how the Google bidding process works. Whenever a search term is typed into Google, it holds an "auction" among the potential advertisers and determines where each ad will appear. Google assigns each ad a "Quality Score" out of ten and then calculates its "Ad Rank" by multiplying the Quality Score by the maximum bid.

For example, let's say there are two advertisers. The first has set a maximum cost per click of £1 and the other 50p. If they both have the same Quality Score (QS), the first advertiser will appear above the second, because they've bid more. However, if the first advertiser has a QS of 2 and an Ad Rank of 2 (£1 × 2) and the second has a QS of 5, then the second will appear above the first, because they have an Ad Rank of 2.5 (£0.50 × 5).

Take a moment to think about that. It's possible to pay half as much as your competition and yet appear above them in the Sponsored Listings. This is why understanding Google's Quality Score is probably the single most important aspect of AdWords: it can singlehandedly turn a struggling campaign into a profitable one.

So how does Google work out the Quality Score of an ad? It looks at three things: the ad's historical click-through rate, the relevance of the ad (there's that word "relevance" again), and the landing page to which it directs the user. But it doesn't give equal weight to each. By far the most important of these three is the click-through rate. Why? Because by using CTR, Google is asking searchers to vote with their clicks to

"Each Ad Group should focus on one of your main keyword groups. The ads will then be more relevant to those keywords."

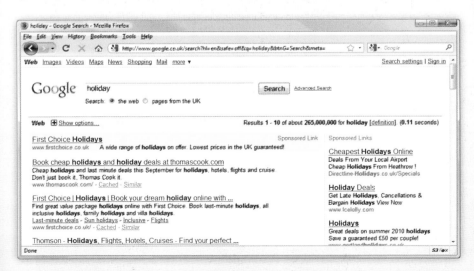

Very popular, broad keywords such as "holiday" are hugely competitive on Google and will rarely be profitable. Avoid them.

Your Ad Here
Use Ad Groups to optimise **your** pay-per-click advertising
www.sortout**your**adgroups.com

decide whose ad is the most pertinent for their search. CTR accounts for around 60% of the QS, relevance around 30%, and the advertiser's landing page only 10%. (Relevance, in this context, relates to how well the text of your ad correlates with the search term.)

To put it another way, 90% of the Quality Score is determined by the ad itself. The quality of your landing page is important for its own reasons (principally conversion), but as long as the main bases are covered, the focus of your attention when it comes to getting economical traffic should be on the ads themselves.

SETTING UP YOUR AD GROUPS Each Ad Group should focus on one of your main keyword groups. The primary reason for this is that if you create an ad group for each main keyword, the ads will be more relevant to those keywords. For example, if you were an aquarium supplier you might decide that two of your keyword groups would be "cold water fish" and "aquariums". Putting each of these into its own Ad Group means you can write ads aimed specifically at people looking for goldfish, and separate ads for those looking to buy a tank.

The result is a more relevant ad that will have a higher click-through rate. This will mean you need to pay less per click to appear high in the Sponsored Listings. You can also point each ad at a specific landing page, which will increase your conversion rate.

There are four "match" types for keywords. The default is Broad Match: in this case, Google will use fuzzy logic to match your ad to the keywords typed in. So "card making" would appear for "card making", "making cards" and "making greeting cards", among many others. Phrase Match (denoted by enclosing your keywords in quotes) requires that the searcher type in the exact phrase, so "making cards" wouldn't appear in the above example, but if the user typed "custom card making", then it would.

Exact Match (denoted by enclosing your keywords in square brackets) requires that only the keyword has been typed in, so a search can contain only "card making" and nothing else. Finally, there's the negative match (denoted by a minus sign), where any search containing that word will not display your ad.

As a rule, begin with Broad Match and narrow it down as you find the most profitable keyword combinations.

WRITING YOUR ADS Remember you're trying to achieve two things with your ad copy. First, and most importantly, you need the highest possible CTR of profitable traffic. Don't make the mistake of thinking that maximum traffic is your aim. Visitors who click on your ad but don't buy anything have cost you money; you need to convert enough of them to make a profit.

The second aim is to make sure your ad appears relevant to Google. Both of these reduce your AdWords costs. Including the keywords in the ad body and title will increase relevance. Usually, it will increase CTR as well because Google will show these keywords in bold, making your ad stand out more. →

Ad Groups let you build clusters of keywords and test multiple versions of the ad you create for each group, enabling you to carry out a comprehensive analysis of exactly which keywords and messages combine to give you profitable CTR and, ultimately, conversion rates.

STEP BY STEP Set up an Ad Group

You've created a campaign with one ad, which is paused (see p115). It's now time to get your ads up and running.

KEYWORDS Go back to your AdWords campaign and click the Ads tab. You'll find your existing ad there. In the Keywords tab, enter your keywords, one per line. For any negative keywords (see p109), add a minus sign: for example, "-free".

Click the pencil icon to open the inline editor and edit the headline, ad body, display URL and destination URL. The display URL is the web address seen in your ad; the destination URL is the one users are actually taken to if they click. Arguably these ought to be the same, but the display URL can have a significant impact on your click-through rate (CTR) and Google's rules are fairly liberal at present, although you are limited to 35 characters. Your ad will be allowed as long as the display URL points to the same domain as the destination URL. You don't need to include "www", you can use capitalisation to make the text more eye-catching, and you can put almost any text after the domain name.

SECOND AD After clicking Save, you can make your second ad by selecting Text Ad from the New Ad drop-down menu. (Get your text ads working profitably before you consider the other types.) Create your new ad using the editor. At this stage you should use substantially different text so that you get a clear result when you split-test the two ads. As

time goes on, you will make smaller and smaller changes. You can see in this example that I've changed the headline and body copy of the ad but left the display URL and landing page the same. The target audience of both ads is exactly the same, but we're looking at which form of wording gets the most profitable traffic.

OTHER VARIABLES In this example I've made four ads. There are only two variations of the ads themselves: the difference is that one points to my site's home page and the other to a custom-made landing page. So we're testing two things at once: the performance of the ads and (once we've set up conversion tracking) the effectiveness of the landing page.

ROTATION Finally, go to Campaign Settings > Advanced Settings. Click Ad delivery, Ad rotation, Frequency capping, and pick "Rotate: Show ads more evenly". You'll be warned that most advertisers leave this set to Optimise. That's because most campaigns aren't actively managed in the way yours will be. If you intend to set the ads up and leave Google to manage them, by all means pick Optimise, but actively managing campaigns is the only way to make them pay in a competitive market. By choosing to have your ads shown evenly, you're ensuring all variations get enough clicks to enable you to choose a winner quickly. You can then delete the losing ad and create yet another variation of the winning ad to test.

→ If there is a true AdWords guru, it's Perry Marshall (www.perrymarshall.com). In his *Definitive Guide to AdWords 2010*, he identifies four stages to go through to create the best-performing ad:

1 Message
2 Word ordering
3 Words
4 Punctuation

MESSAGE Your ad should reflect whatever is unique about your business and what it offers. Do you supply something free that others charge for? Does your product or service give better results than others? Do you have a guarantee? (And if not, why not?) What is the specific deal you're offering?

Take a look at this ad for PassYourTheory.co.uk, which appeared when users did a Google search on the keywords "hazard perception":

> Hazard Perception 2009/10
> Join & PASS. New Official Questions
> DSA Hazard Video. Pass Guarantee!
> PassYourTheory.co.uk/Hazard-Test

This features three of our service's most important features: first, that we are official licensees of the DSA; second, that we have the very latest questions; and finally, that we offer a pass guarantee. How do we know that our potential members are interested in these things? Because we have asked them in a survey and we have tested which features result in the best conversion rate.

Here's an Amazon ad (below) in similar vein. It was triggered by the search phrase "buy Sony A200K". Notice how it's very specific about the free delivery offer (an Amazon feature) and the price. Given the word "buy", Amazon is gambling on being cheaper than the other advertisers, so it shows its price in the headline. As it happens, this ad commits the cardinal sin of leading to a page that doesn't offer what the ad promises: the camera is available (it's an old model) but not for the stated price! Be warned: Amazon may be able to get away with this, but mere mortals cannot.

> Sony DSLR-A200K - £305
> Digital SLR Camera + Lens18-70mm
> Buy Now. Free Delivery.
> www.amazon.co.uk/Sony

WORD ORDERING You should start by running ads that feature various iterations of your product's main features, and test them until you find out which ones trigger the best conversion rate. Once you've done this, you can alter the specific wording. A classic technique is to swap the second and third lines around; you'd be surprised at the difference this can make.

WORDS You should also test the effect of swapping specific words. In general, you should only test one word-swap at a time – otherwise the results will be impossible to analyse – so this stage should be carried out after the other two described above. Getting your message right is likely to yield bigger improvements in CTR and conversion than changes to word order or word selection. Make sure you get your keywords into the message: if at all possible they should appear in the title, in one of the body lines, and in the display URL.

PUNCTUATION Finally, test the effect of adding commas, exclamation marks (Google only allows one per ad) and dashes. Capitalising The First Letter Of Every Word can also be effective in grabbing attention and provoking more clicks – but it must be tested.

There are dozens of tips and tricks you can use to improve your CTR and conversion, but the key is to remember to communicate your main messages – and only promise what you can actually deliver.

CREATING AD GROUPS Google is quite happy if you create only one ad in an Ad Group, but you should always have at least two, and usually more. This is because you need to test both the effectiveness of the ads themselves and the process the visitor goes through after arriving at your site. Clicking on the ad is just the first step; Google lets you track visitors right through the process, whether you want them to buy from you or sign up to a mailing list.

This process has two steps: creating your landing page – the page on your site at which visitors arrive when they click the ad – and setting up conversion tracking. If you're going to use a landing page other than your main home page, it might be worth creating this now (see over-leaf). Alternatively, if you'd prefer to take your time over this, you could get the Ad Group up and running first.

On the opposite page, I'll take you through the vital first steps. You may be tempted to launch your campaign as soon as you finish this and use your home page as your initial landing page. All you'd then need to do is set up conversion tracking. However, if you're serious about your AdWords campaign you should really create a custom landing page from the beginning. My experience is that they're always more effective than your home page.

Good-quality classified ads are an excellent source of inspiration for your online ad copy, since they do the same basic job of getting response from readers.

Designing a landing page

The landing page is the main entry point to your website and probably the most important page on the site. Over the next four pages, I'm going to concentrate on how to get it right. The first thing to understand is that landing pages have two purposes. The first and most important reason is to convert more visitors into buyers. However, in doing this you need to take care not to damage your AdWords campaign.

Remember, Google takes your landing page into account when it works out your Quality Score, and this heavily influences how much your ads will cost. While it's true that the landing page is the least important of the three factors (the others being click-through rate and relevance, as we saw on p130), it represents around 10% of your Quality Score, so it could make the difference between appearing in position 4 or 5 in the Sponsored Listings.

The good news is that Google looks for exactly the same features in your page as your visitors will, so by optimising the page to suit potential customers, you're also optimising it for Google. In the bad old days, landing pages were known as "squeeze pages", and the prevailing wisdom was that they should have no links to the rest of your site and no distractions: their one purpose was to get a visitor to give up their email address. However, both your visitors and Google will respond poorly to such tactics. Visitors will leave in droves, and Google will lower your Quality Score.

ANATOMY OF A LANDING PAGE Generally speaking, each Ad Group in your campaign should lead to its own unique landing page. To be effective, a landing page must closely match the ads that lead to it. Contrast this with your site's home page. Until a few years ago, the home page was considered to be the most common entry point, since most visitors arrived by typing the URL directly into their browser or via an old-style "directory" search engine. Nowadays, search engines index individual pages rather than entire sites, so home pages have become much less important and should not be the destination for your ads.

If a visitor types "natural back pain relief" into their browser and sees an ad saying, effectively, "we sell natural back-pain relief, buy it here", then they expect, when they click the ad, to see a page selling that back-pain remedy – not the front page of a site that might be selling remedies for dozens of different ailments. You need to make the buying process as simple, short and obvious as possible.

Jay Abraham's 100 Best Headlines (http://ypcommando.com/tips/17.html) is an excellent source of inspiration.

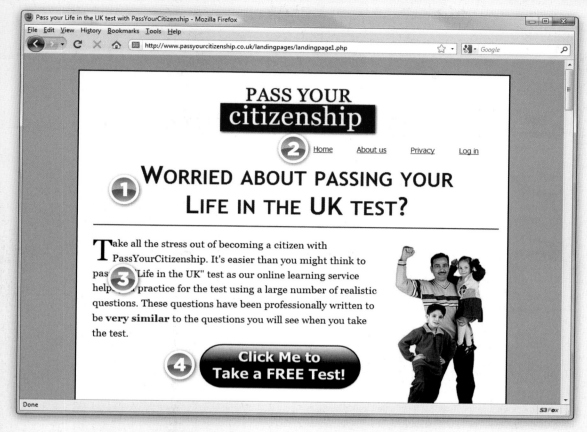

Each landing page is made up of two parts: a series of benefits, whose aim is to allow the customer to evaluate whether your product meets their needs, and, crucially, a very clear call to action. In other words, you need to make it abundantly obvious what action you want the user to take, whether that's to buy now or sign up to a mailing list. The main elements of your page should be:

1 Headline
2 Navigation
3 Copy
4 Call to action

THE HEADLINE It's essential your headline closely reflects the ad. It should include your keywords and make the immediate point that the visitor has arrived in the right place. For 100 excellent headline examples, go to http://ypcommando.com/tips/17.html – but the main thing to remember is that the headline must encourage the visitor to stay for long enough to read the copy.

Your headline should be short, relevant and inviting. If you can make it witty as well, so much the better, but the most important factor is relevance. Using the back pain example, the headline should refer directly to

the solution you offer to back pain: if it doesn't, the visitor, having clicked your ad under the impression that it would lead to back-pain remedies, is likely to click the Back button immediately, and your advertising is wasted.

NAVIGATION Traditional "squeeze pages" had no navigation, and when it became obvious that Google punishes such pages with low-quality scores (because of the lack of links), marketers simply added navigation at the bottom of the page. The thinking behind this is that you don't want people to wander off around your site when you're trying to get them to carry out a particular action. Whether there is any merit in this theory is debatable, and it will vary from site to site, but the fact is that you can't get away without putting navigation in. Specifically, you should include not only links to other parts of your site, but also to your privacy policy and contact details. Users expect it, and if they want a link but can't find one, they'll just click Back.

My belief is that navigation, if it's going to be there, should be at the top of the page, where it's most useful to your visitors, either just above the headline or just below it. As with so many other aspects of your marketing, however, you should test the position (on multiple landing pages) to see if it affects your profitability. ➡

→ **COPY** Internet marketers continue to debate whether "long" or "short" copy is more effective. Again, the only way to be sure is to test it, but my experience has been that long copy tends to outperform short. Why? Probably because people who prefer short copy can always skim through the longer form, whereas those who want to read more before making a decision won't find what they need in a short version.

Landing-page copy tends to be conversational in style, and the best landing pages include elements of storytelling in their construction. This, if done well, has the effect of drawing the reader into the copy and giving a structure within which to outline your benefits.

Having said that long copy tends to be more effective, that doesn't mean the text should be dense. Inserting bullet points and numbered lists, along with graphics and photos, will help to break up the text and keep the reader interested. It also makes it easier for visitors who prefer short copy to skip their way through the page, picking up the important messages.

 THE POWER OF YOU It's essential to write copy from the point of view of your audience. The market research you did when planning your business pays off here: you should know who your customers are and how they talk. I'm not suggesting you mimic their language – people don't necessarily buy from someone who communicates as they do – but you can at least avoid putting them off. For example, if you're selling to teenagers (good luck with that!) then writing your copy in "text-speak" is unlikely to work, but it would make sense to visit sites that are popular with that group and emulate their writing style.

The word "you" should appear throughout, and the features of your product should be expressed as benefits for your target audience. For example, a candle-making kit might include high-quality metal moulds, but what does this mean for the buyer? The benefit of the metal mould is that it can be re-used many times, reducing the ongoing cost of candle making – so say so.

A final note on testimonials. Testimonials (recommendations of your product and/or company from real customers) are unquestionably important to have on your site, and it might seem obvious that you should include them in landing pages. But I have now tested this twice and, for my sites at least, testimonials have actually reduced the conversion rate. It doesn't make sense (which is one of the reasons I've tested it twice), but the page containing testimonials reduced conversions by almost a quarter. My recommendation is to include a few and test against a page without them.

STEP BY STEP
Build a landing page that works

There's a definite generic "look and feel" to the standard landing page. The design tends to be minimal, with a central white rectangle containing the copy, links and pictures. This rectangle is centred horizontally, and narrow enough to fit a reasonable minimum monitor resolution. The only problem, if you've created your site using WordPress, is that it's difficult to have WordPress apply one design to the site as a whole and a different one to the landing page.

Fortunately, this straightforward design makes it quite simple to create your landing page in HTML and CSS. Of course, you can still add links between this page and your WordPress site. Once you've established a look and feel, the same code can be re-used as the basis for all your landing pages. To get started, you can download my landing page template from www.scribbleit.co.uk/landingpages/template.zip.

1 **ADAPT THE TEMPLATE** Unzip the template and you'll find that there are two folders: images and css. Double-click landingpage1.html to view the template. You'll see there are a number of placeholder sections and graphics for you to replace. This should give you the opportunity to concentrate most of your efforts on getting the copy right.

2 **CHANGE THE CSS** Open the file landingpage.css and you'll see it's a bog standard fixed-width centred layout. If you want to change the body copy font, find the "body" type selector. Within that, you can alter the "font-family" attribute, sticking to the range of "web safe" fonts found on most computers (see p48). You can also change the background colour within the body selector – this manifests itself as the colour of the surround – along with the default text colour (using the "color" property).

The heading fonts can be altered in the <h1> and <h2> selectors. If you want to change the width of the main frame, find the outer "wrapper id" selector and change the width value there. It's currently set to

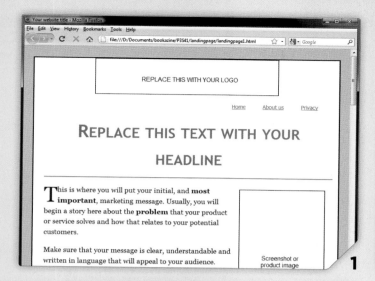

1

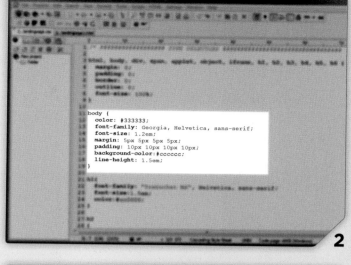

2

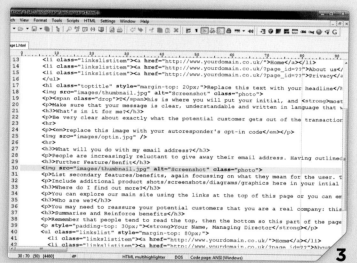

3

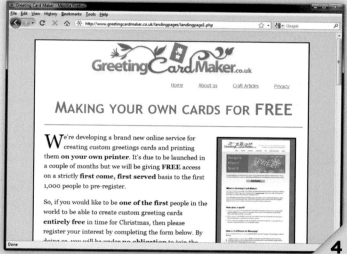

4

800px, which is ultra-safe: it wouldn't be too risky to increase this to 1,000px if you want extra space, although this may be too wide for netbooks, for example.

You'll find a file called logo.jpg in the /images folder: replace it with your own logo or banner. I've also included place-holders for two pictures, both floated to the right-hand side. If you want photos, diagrams or graphics, just replace these placeholders with your artwork and amend the <img> tags within landingpage1.html. It's good practice to include one or more pictures in your initial design and then test whether they are effective.

3 **WRITE THE COPY** Having got the landing page looking right, spend the majority of your time writing compelling copy that sells the benefits of

your product or service. Go through the text in the template and replace it with your own. If you have genuine customer testimonials, I suggest including a limited number at this point and testing their effectiveness. Keep in mind that your purpose is to get your visitor to take a specific action: make sure there's no doubt exactly what this is. Get someone else to read the copy to make sure. You'd be amazed how many landing pages leave potential customers wondering what to do.

4 **UPLOAD THE FILES** Once your HTML and CSS files are complete, use FileZilla to copy the landing page and its folders to your web space. I suggest creating a folder for your landing pages to ensure they remain separate from the files for your WordPress site.

Running your AdWords campaign

Once your campaign is up and running, there are plenty of numbers to keep track of. Some of these are instantly available within your AdWords dashboard, but others aren't. Take it from me: you should never run an AdWords campaign without setting up conversion tracking. It's the road to business failure.

The seven key metrics for an AdWords campaign are impressions, clicks, click-through rate (CTR), cost per click, conversion number, conversion rate and cost per conversion. The first four are always shown in the AdWords control panel, requiring no further work to set up, but the conversion rate and cost-per-conversion figures aren't, and they're by far the most important. Running a campaign without checking the conversion figures means you have no way of knowing how much you're spending in marketing per sale; and without this, you can't tell if your campaign is profitable. So it's essential to track conversions, and I'll show you (on p142) how to set up the code for this.

Here's what to look for in each of the three main categories of data.

IMPRESSIONS Every time an ad is seen, that's an "impression". In the Keywords tab, you can see how many of those impressions were triggered by each keyword. If you order the list by impressions, you'll see which keywords generated the most views of your ad. This is the first time

		Ad group	Status ⑦	Search Max. CPC	Content Auto Max. CPC ⑦	Clicks	Impr.	CTR ⑦	Avg. CPC ⑦	Cost	Avg. Pos.	Conv. (1-per-click) ⑦	Cost / conv. (1-per-click) ⑦	Conv. rate (1-per-click) ⑦
☐	●	life in the uk	Eligible	£0.05	auto	88	3,720	2.37%	£0.04	£3.93	4.2	12	£0.33	13.64%
☐	●	citizenship	Eligible	£0.05	auto	55	1,428	3.85%	£0.04	£2.47	3.8	8	£0.31	14.55%
☐	●	British Citizenship	Eligible	£0.05	auto	47	4,995	0.94%	£0.05	£2.14	9.3	9	£0.24	19.15%
						179	6,013	2.98%	£0.05	£8.11	4	27	£0.30	15.08%

Impressions

		Ad group	Status ⑦	Search Max. CPC	Content Auto Max. CPC ⑦	Clicks	Impr.	CTR ⑦	Avg. CPC ⑦	Cost	Avg. Pos.	Conv. (1-per-click) ⑦	Cost / conv. (1-per-click) ⑦	Conv. rate (1-per-click) ⑦
☐	●	life in the uk	Eligible	£0.05	auto	88	3,720	2.37%	£0.04	£3.93	4.2	12	£0.33	13.64%
☐	●	citizenship	Eligible	£0.05	auto	55	1,428	3.85%	£0.04	£2.47	3.8	8	£0.31	14.55%
☐	●	British Citizenship	Eligible	£0.05	auto	47	4,995	0.94%	£0.05	£2.14	9.3	9	£0.24	19.15%
						179	6,013	2.98%	£0.05	£8.11	4	27	£0.30	15.08%

Clicks

		Ad group	Status ⑦	Search Max. CPC	Content Auto Max. CPC ⑦	Clicks	Impr.	CTR ⑦	Avg. CPC ⑦	Cost	Avg. Pos.	Conv. (1-per-click) ⑦	Cost / conv. (1-per-click) ⑦	Conv. rate (1-per-click) ⑦
☐	●	life in the uk	Eligible	£0.05	auto	88	3,720	2.37%	£0.04	£3.93	4.2	12	£0.33	13.64%
☐	●	citizenship	Eligible	£0.05	auto	55	1,428	3.85%	£0.04	£2.47	3.8	8	£0.31	14.55%
☐	●	British Citizenship	Eligible	£0.05	auto	47	4,995	0.94%	£0.05	£2.14	9.3	9	£0.24	19.15%
						179	6,013	2.98%	£0.05	£8.11	4	27	£0.30	15.08%

Conversions

you'll have real statistics (as opposed to estimates) from Google about the popularity of your keywords.

CLICKS "Clicks" is the number of times the ad was actually clicked. Again, you can see the number of clicks for each keyword under the Keywords tab. Your click-through rate (CTR) is the percentage of impressions that result in a click.

Too many AdWords advertisers concentrate on these three figures, especially the click-through rate. By working on impressions and CTR you can maximise traffic, but remember, you're charged per click. If you drive up your CTR but the percentage of people who buy from you goes down, you can turn a profitable business into a disaster. The classic example is when you put words such as "free" in your ad: this will drive lots of traffic, but the people arriving at your site are unlikely to be in the mood to pay for anything.

CONVERSIONS A "conversion" is when a visitor takes an action you want them to take. This is usually signing up to an email list (which you hope will result in a purchase later) or making an immediate purchase. In many cases, there are numerous steps between the initial search and the purchase, so – unlike the other figures – the conversion rate is affected by much more than just the quality and position of your ad.

However, the number of conversions, the conversion rate and the cost per conversion are by far the most important three figures you can track, and Google's "roundtrip" tracking allows you to see the exact marketing cost per sale. To put it simply, if you sell a product for £10 and your cost per conversion is £20, you're in trouble. If the figures were reversed but you only made two conversions a week, you'd also have a problem. In an ideal world, you're looking for a high number of conversions, a good conversion rate and a profitable cost per conversion.

GOOD NUMBERS Newcomers to internet marketing often ask what click-through rate and conversion rate they should be aiming at. This will vary from market to market and business to business, but you should always be aiming to maximise these figures (except where increasing the CTR reduces the conversion rate) so that you make a profit.

To give some rules of thumb, successful internet businesses tend to have a conversion rate in the range of 0.75% to 2%. Some may be much higher, but very few profitable business are lower. A conversion rate of, say, 0.5% requires 200 visitors per sale; if that traffic has been paid for via AdWords, then clearly the product would have to have a high purchase price to be profitable.

THE GOLDEN TWO Broadly speaking, when it comes to judging whether one ad is performing better than →

What really matters is how many people buy from you and how much profit you make on each sale, taking into account the cost of your marketing. The calculations could get complicated, but if you set it up correctly, Google will do the numbers for you.

→ another, you should be concentrating on clicks and click-through rate. At the same time, you must check that any increase in these figures isn't cancelled out by a drop in conversions.

Overall, the two most critical figures to keep your eye on are the number of conversions and the cost per conversion. These sum up the profitability, or otherwise, of your business, since one is an indicator of your turnover and the other of what is likely to be your main cost of doing business. If you spot that the number of conversions drops or the cost per conversion rises, take immediate action to work out why this might be and what to do about it. More often than not, you'll find something's changed in your marketplace or in the shopping cart process that acts as a barrier to conversions. For example, a competitor might have entered the market or may be running a promotion.

CONVERSION TRACKING Since the conversion figures are so important, you need to set up conversion tracking through AdWords. It's free and pretty easy to do, and it's the single factor that separates the serious, profitable, businessperson from the half-hearted dabbler. After all, if you don't know how much each conversion costs, you're missing out on the most important piece of financial data. You're running an AdWords campaign blind.

Google begins tracking when the user clicks the ad, and registers a conversion when they complete whatever action you specify, whether that's a purchase, a sign-up, or even that the user visits a particular page. Conversion tracking works by saving a cookie to the visitor's computer when they click on your ad. This cookie has a life of 30 days, and any conversion that takes place within that period is recorded. Google will also track multiple conversions – for example, if the user comes back and buys again – and can report this in your AdWords interface.

The conversion statistics are displayed alongside each of your ad variations, so you can see immediately which ads result in the highest number of conversions at the lowest cost. Believe me, once you start seeing the figures, they'll exert an irresistible pull on you – which is a good thing! They also build up a long-term record of your business's performance.

DON'T LEAP TOO EARLY One final word of warning: don't pay any attention to your figures until you have enough to be statistically valid. In most cases, you should have at least 25 conversions before taking any action. At a conversion rate of 1%, this means you'd need 2,500 clicks and, at a typical CTR of 5%, around 50,000 impressions. Patience is needed. Once you do have enough data, however, don't delay acting on it: in the beginning you will usually see a definitive winner when comparing ads, so the first step is

How to track conversions in Google AdWords

The only way to know if your marketing is profitable is to set up conversion tracking. It's a reasonably straightforward task, but you need to get it right.

1 **NAME YOUR ACTION** From your AdWords Control Panel, select Reporting and Tools and, from the dropdown box, select Conversions. Click the "+ New conversion" button. Give your action a name – you can track multiple conversion types so it's important to differentiate between them – and choose the most appropriate action type from the Tracking Purpose list. Click "Save and continue".

On the next page, select the security level of the page. Generally this will be HTTP but ecommerce websites often use HTTPS. If the conversion has a set value (for example, a purchase of a specific product) you can type it in the "Revenue for your conversion" box. In most cases, though, this will be left blank. Select the Page Language from the dropdown. It's set to Arabic by default so make sure you change it!

The rest of the page can be left as it is. Note that Google suggests you notify your customers that you're adding a cookie. These days most users are happy to accept them but bear in mind that recent EU regulations might make it a legal requirement to get the permission of your users when using such cookies (keep an eye on www.ico.gov.uk). For now, the easiest way to notify customers is to use one of the text formats offered here. Click "Save and get code".

2 **GET THE CODE** Google now provides you with the JavaScript code to insert in the page of your site on which the action occurs. If it's an email list sign-up, for example, it'll be the confirmation screen that the user reaches when they've completed the sign-up process. If it's a purchase, you would insert the code on the order confirmation screen. Make it something that the user must see if they actually complete the action, but will never see if they don't. Select the code shown in Step 2 and copy it to the clipboard by pressing <Ctrl-C>.

3 **INSERT THE CODE** This code needs to be inserted between the <body> and </body> tags of the action page. In WordPress, the simplest way to do this is to open the page in your Dashboard, click the HTML tab and paste in the

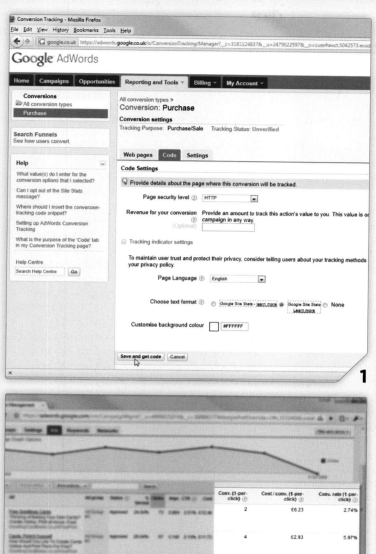

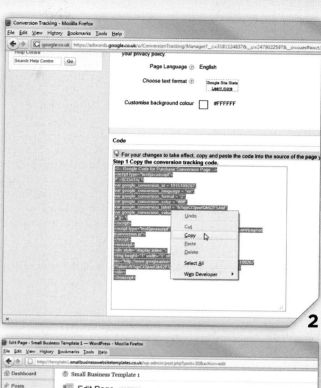

1

2

3

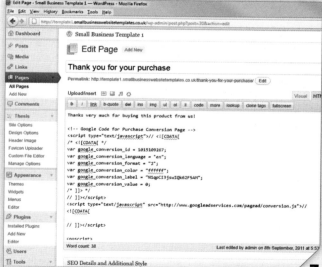

4

JavaScript, then save it and test that it isn't visible. If it is, you've accidentally pasted it into the visual editor: make sure you use the HTML view!

4 **AND NOW WAIT...** That's all there is to it. Unfortunately, conversion tracking doesn't perform any immediate checks to see if the code is in the right place, so you'll need to wait a day or two to make sure you have some data coming through. How long this takes will depend on how busy your site is. To check your figures, click the

Ads tab in your Campaign Management panel on the Google AdWords site and you should see figures appearing in the Conv, Cost/Conv and Conv.rate columns (assuming you've sold anything, of course).

Don't jump to any conclusions until you have enough conversions to make a judgement. The more ads you have, the longer this will take. In this example, the cost per conversion of one of the ads is three times more than one of the others. That may seem like a conclusive result, but there simply haven't been enough conversions yet to be sure.

The importance of split testing

Today's internet business technologies offer previously unimaginable ways to test your marketing. The simplest, and one of the most effective, is A/B split testing. You try one approach on half your audience and another on the other half, and see what happens. The results can be very surprising.

A typical use of this kind of testing is when you want to optimise your landing pages – the pages where visitors arrive after clicking your ads. Instead of bringing every user who clicks a particular ad to the same web page, you send them at random to one of two different pages. Then you wait and see which route gets you the most conversions. It's just one of a seemingly infinite number of methods to refine your marketing. You don't have to rely on "gut instinct" or accepted wisdom to dictate the way you sell: you can try alternative ideas and see within a few weeks exactly how they perform.

Landing-page split testing can be set up using the Website Optimizer, part of the Google AdWords toolset. The process is slightly more involved than setting up conversion tracking, but it's easy enough if you follow the steps closely, and won't interfere with your conversion tracking code.

1 START THE EXPERIMENT Begin by selecting Website Optimizer, which you'll find under either Tools or Reporting. You may be prompted to create a Google Analytics account if you don't already have one (see p116).

Click the "Create another experiment" link and select A/B Experiment from the options presented. (The other option, Multivariate, should only be attempted once you've broadly optimised your landing page and you're getting lots of traffic to provide statistically meaningful data.) The next page presents the series of steps you must already have completed. Click the checkbox and select the Create button. On the setup page, give your experiment an appropriate name and then tell Google which two pages to test. In this case I'm testing the home page of PassYourCitizenship against my first try at a landing page.

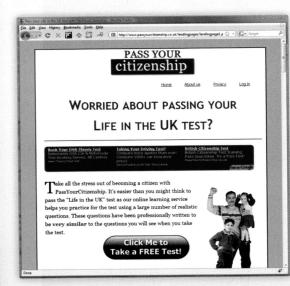

On my PassYourCitizenship website, the landing page (left) hugely outperformed the home page (right) when tested with Google's tools.

Finally, tell Google which page the user has to reach to qualify as a conversion. Here I'm testing which of the two is more effective at getting the user to the sign-up page. Once I've got the landing page broadly working, I'll change the conversion page to my PayPal confirmation page, so I'm only including paid members in my figures. I won't do that immediately because fewer visitors will reach that point, so it would take much longer to get useful results.

On the next page, select "You will install and validate the JavaScript tags" and click Continue.

2 **ADD THE CODE** Google now presents the code that needs to be copied into the various pages of your site. The first two blocks are for the top and bottom of your "original" page (the home page in this case, as opposed to the variation you're testing). The first block controls whether the user sees the original or the variation. It makes the choice randomly, but will present the same page to the same visitor if they come back later.

If you're not using a content management system, you'll have to copy and paste this code manually into your pages. If you're using WordPress, install the Google Website Optimizer for WordPress plugin (which you already have if you followed our guide to conversion tracking on p142).

3 **VALIDATE** The "variation" page (the landing page in this case) needs only one block of JavaScript: paste this immediately before the closing <body> tag. If you're using the WordPress plugin, just go to your landing page via the WordPress Dashboard and paste the code into the appropriate box.

Finally, you need to add the conversion page tracking script to your sign-up or "thank you" page (or whichever page represents a conversion). Once this is done, click Validate Pages and Google will check to see if the code has been installed and is working.

You should now preview your experiment to check that the correct pages are showing up. It's very difficult to change experiments once they're running, so make doubly sure before clicking Start Experiment.

4 **MEASURE OF SUCCESS** You now need to give Google time to collect and process the results. Leave it a day or two, then go back to the Website Optimizer and you'll see your experiment listed. Click View Report to see how it's doing. In all likelihood, it will tell you that it hasn't yet collected enough data to reach a conclusion, so it's a case of checking back to see at which point Google declares a winner: it usually needs at least 100 conversions. In this example, my landing page has outperformed the home page by over 40%. Imagine what a 40% improvement could do for your business!

Home truths

The first split test you should do is create your first landing page and test it against your site's home page. A landing page should almost always be more effective than the home page, so if it isn't, you need to work on the landing page until it is. As an example, I set up an experiment recently where the home page surprisingly performed much better than the landing page – only to find that I'd miscoded the "Sign me up" button on the landing page. With that fixed, the home page was quickly trounced.

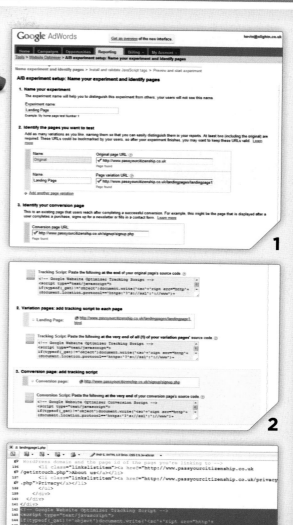

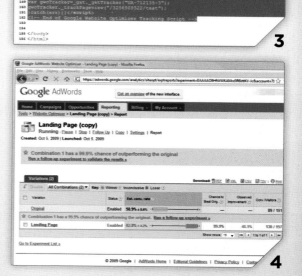

Watching them watching you

Uninformed preconceptions are the enemy of effective marketing. Never assume anything about how your customers will react to your website or your product. Over the years I have been surprised (and sometimes shocked) so many times that I now take nothing for granted – and nor should you.

As we've seen, you can split-test your AdWords ads to see which are the most effective and use Google's Website Optimizer to test landing-page variations on your website. But what you're doing there is comparing one version against another and selecting whichever is better. This results in step-by-step improvements, but if you want to radically change your understanding of how your site is used by your customers, you need something more.

What if you could see which parts of a page visitors spend longest looking at? Where they scroll to? Or which links on the page they click most often? Until recently this involved running "usability lab" experiments where you watched (or videoed) a limited number of typical visitors interacting with your site, but this is expensive and tends to be a one-off rather than ongoing.

Clicktale (www.clicktale.com) is a JavaScript-powered technology that records the mouse movements of your visitors. By doing this, it can tell how long users spend on specific parts of the page, where they scroll to and what they click on. The results of this tracking can be displayed in "heat map" form: the redder the colour, the more time was spent on that part of the page.

If you know which parts of your landing pages visitors spend more time on, for example, you can ensure your most important messages appear there. You can also see which of your "calls to action" are working: which "sign-up" buttons attract the most attention, whether users prefer links or buttons, which colours work best... You're certain to learn something that will improve effectiveness.

You can also spot logjams and misunderstandings. For example, you might notice visitors clicking on a graphic that you intended just as an illustration. That means they're interested in learning more about whatever it represents. It's as if someone is asking you to tell them more, and by taking them up on it (in this case by linking the graphic to another page) you will connect with your visitors better, build trust and interest, and convert more to sales.

Clicktale offers a free trial version of its service, and setting it up is a matter of copying two small JavaScript code snippets to the top and bottom of each of the pages you want to track. A few days later, you can view your heat maps, click maps and even Flash movies that show how an individual user has interacted with your page. You won't look at your visitors in the same way again.

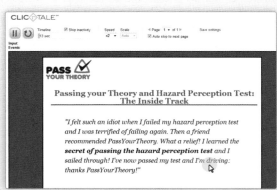

Clicktale's heat map shows which parts of your pages generate the most interest, while movies look over the shoulder of individual users.

Hiya,

Thanks for your ace program, I signed up Monday night for the 3 days and took my test today (Thursday) and passed! Woo hoo! Last time I took the test I failed miserably and thought I would this time too, but after doing the questions time and again and practising on your clips I passed with flying colours, well worth £3.50!!!

Thanks again, Julia

What do they think of you?

Lack of trust is one of the main reasons potential customers don't become buyers. Credit-card fraud, email spam and spyware all work to reduce trust in internet-based businesses. For some customers, if something goes wrong their first instinct is to assume the service they're using is attempting to rip them off. Others won't even consider buying online. So what can you do to increase trust in you and break down those barriers?

SECURITY People do worry about credit-card fraud when they buy online, so reassure them. Your best protection comes from the services you outsource to. If you use PayPal, Nochex or WorldPay, for example, your users' credit-card details are never stored on your server but only on the super-secure servers of those service providers, each of whom has policies to protect customers from fraud.

You will store the email addresses of users who sign up, but by using licensed, reputable autoresponder services and obeying the anti-spam regulations you will ensure that the customer's details remain on your system rather than being stolen by shysters.

All this protection for your customers is of little use from a marketing point of view unless you tell them about it. The simplest way is to include the company logos on your site and, most importantly, on your landing pages. Link the logos to the service providers' consumer protection policy pages (but make sure the link opens a new window or tab rather than overwriting your page – see p115) and, if you meet its requirements, consider joining the SafeBuy (www.safebuy.org.uk) accreditation scheme to further reassure potential buyers.

Incidentally, you must also notify the Information Commissioner's Office that you will be storing personal data, at a cost of £35: see www.ico.gov.uk/what_we_cover/data_protection/notification.aspx.

TESTIMONIALS Nothing builds trust like personal recommendation. Most successful businesses actively encourage word-of-mouth marketing, both by asking their customers to recommend them to friends and family and by asking them directly for testimonials. However cynical you might imagine visitors to be, genuine testimonials can be highly effective. Don't make them up: users will see through it, and this destroys your credibility (as well as constituting false advertising).

The simplest way to get testimonials is to ask customers what they think of you as part of a satisfaction survey. Ask what aspects of your service they value most (and least) and request basic demographic information such as gender and age. This in itself can be priceless: when we first surveyed customers of PassYourTheory.co.uk, we found the people who actually bought from us were not the ones we'd been aiming at. As you can imagine, this radically altered the service and the way we subsequently presented it.

Include in your survey a question asking the customer to summarise what they think of your service, making it clear that you may use their comments on your website while reassuring them that their full name will not appear. The effect of this is that people often write their comments with the intention of them appearing on the website. Clearly, you shouldn't include negative comments, and you should edit any testimonials that are very poorly written – but take care not to change them too much, beyond correcting spelling mistakes: after all, these testimonials are written in the language of your customers.

While I've found that testimonials have a variable effect on my landing pages, other testing has proved beyond any doubt that a dedicated testimonials page significantly increases trust and, therefore, conversion. Potential customers like to know that other people have chosen your product or service and were happy with it. Never underestimate the power of the herd mentality.

Marketing through social media

You've heard of social marketing and its main platforms, Facebook and Twitter, but are they just so much hype or can they genuinely contribute to the growth of your business?

Facebook's growth over the past couple of years has been phenomenal. It took the social-networking site five years to acquire its first 200 million users but less than a year to double that. And its growth looks set to continue, especially in the emerging Asian and South American markets. Twitter was set up in 2006, two years later than Facebook, and by April 2010 had 105 million users, with 300,000 signing up every day.

Two huge platforms growing exponentially, yet they differ fundamentally from each other and, as a result, the business opportunities they offer are also markedly different. Facebook resembles an online club, in most cases a "club of Joe Bloggs" to which only those chosen by Joe Bloggs are invited. Joe's Facebook page functions like a noticeboard of his life and those of his friends, but Joe's thoughts are not exposed to the entire audience, just to those he chooses.

Twitter, on the other hand, is more like sitting in a cubicle in an open-plan office with all your associates announcing to the floor in general what they're doing at any particular moment by shouting across the partitions. In the way it's experienced, Twitter is more ephemeral and less personal: it's about "what I'm doing now", whereas Facebook is more a record of "what I've been doing recently and what I'm going to do".

Another major difference is that whereas the heart and soul of Facebook is its website, which hosts all pages, personal and business, Twitter is largely accessed via third-party applications such as TweetDeck (www.tweetdeck.com) and various mobile apps. This reflects both the inadequacies of Twitter.com as a destination and the flexibility it offers via its API (that is, its application programming interface: the way other programs can interact with Twitter's own software).

The business network LinkedIn is "Facebook for suits" and is more about connecting than revealing the minutiae of your life.

DOWN TO BUSINESS So what does this mean for your business? I don't believe it's a sensible policy to attempt to build a small business entirely around social media. However, I do believe that social media can make a strong business stronger.

If you think of the social networks as places your customers might gather, then you need to consider which of the networks your customers are most likely to use. Facebook has the wider demographic, although over half of all UK users are aged 18-34, with slightly more female users than male. The fastest-growing group of Facebook users are middle-aged women, and it's likely that this trend

A Facebook page is easy to set up and can be used to aggregate information from several social media platforms into one place. But how many people actually see it?

The Twitter.com interface isn't up to the task of keeping track of the thousands of tweets per day that tumble through the average Twitter user's feed.

to "fill up the corners" will continue until all age ranges are well represented. Facebook users also have a wider range of technical capabilities; part of the site's appeal is that it's relatively easy to use.

You could argue that Twitter is even easier to use: it's basically a matter of going to Twitter.com and typing in an SMS message. However, Twitter's a bit harder for the wider public to get their heads around and is therefore more popular with technically literate people. It also has a slightly older demographic and is less popular with the under 25s.

Taking MakingYourOwnCandles as an example, our customers are predominantly women in their 30s and above. Not many will be Twitter users and, as a group, "crafty" people are likely to be less technically interested than the average so Facebook will probably be their social media home, if they have one.

THE FACEBOOK APPROACH Facebook allows you to have a page for your business, such as www.facebook.com/MakingYourOwnCandles. It's easy to pull data into this page from your Twitter feed and blog and, to be honest, this is all most businesses do. There's so little effort involved in getting a Facebook page up and running for your business that there's no excuse for not doing it.

In my view, Facebook as a platform is most useful where you're trying to form a community of fans around a product. Testimonials are a very powerful form of persuasion and a Facebook page, if actively promoted, can be the ideal way to demonstrate "social proof". Because of the nature of Facebook updates, if a fan of your product comments on it this message will be seen by all their friends as a personal endorsement. Facebook's modular nature also means that it's possible to integrate some shopping carts (including BigCommerce) into the page, making it possible to sell your product directly from Facebook.

SHOULD YOU JOIN TWITTER? Unlike Facebook, where you effectively create a network of friends or customers, Twitter is one big community with each person following the updates of other, personally selected, people. It's much harder to build a community around a product with Twitter, but it does have its benefits: because it's one big community, it's much easier to discover when your product or service is mentioned by searching on the entire feed.

Twitter can be used to establish your credibility as a provider of a service or product, as a method of providing information about it, to provide customer service and general market information after the sale.

It really comes into its own when it's used creatively. For example:

- To send out special offers specific to Twitter followers.

- To allow a company to interact in real-time and in a public manner with its customers.

- Spreading testimonials or experiences of the product or service.

The sane way of managing Twitter. Using TweetDeck you can easily follow tweets from those you're most interested in, while also spotting when you're mentioned in the Twitterverse.

Quantifying the impact of social media on your bottom line is difficult. You can distribute voucher codes via Twitter or Facebook and see how many times they're used and how responsive your audience is to promotion via social media. Similarly, it should be possible to establish whether specific leads were generated via Twitter especially.

But its real impact is in giving you, as a business owner, a long-term way to interact with your customers and potential customers. For Twitter, this means using tools such as TweetDeck and HootSuite (www.hootsuite.com) to monitor keywords relating to your product or service. By providing help to users via the public Twitter network rather than direct message, you're not only solving a specific problem but also demonstrating your responsiveness to potential customers and raising your profile.

Having said all that, in my view social media marketing is something you do seriously when your product, website and Pay Per Click campaigns are all solid. For example, working on your AdWords campaign is likely to have an immediate bottom-line impact on your business. Split-testing new headlines, URLs or ad copy against the original control has more or less immediate results – you'll either be more profitable or less. Building a Twitter or Facebook following is more akin to search engine optimisation – it's a long-term game. Your first job should always be to ensure that the fundamentals of your business are solid before spending time on social media.

Marketing your business using Facebook

The great advantage of Facebook is the way its users interact. When someone writes an update, it appears on the walls of all their friends. If those friends like it, it will appear on their friends' walls as well. The potential is there for your message to be propagated far and wide, if it's interesting enough.

Whereas Facebook was originally developed as a means of personal interaction, any hope it has of making any money is based on encouraging businesses to use it. The recently introduced Facebook Ads system is an attempt to achieve this, and the business "Page" is one way Facebook sees of closing the loop: you create your business page and advertise it via Facebook Ads. Personally, I think this is a ludicrous approach: the idea that you'd be prepared to launch a business that uses a Facebook page as its main web presence and then pay for traffic to this page via Facebook Ads is madness.

Whether you should use Facebook Ads to push traffic to an independent website is another matter. In principle, Facebook's system is intriguing since it uses the information users have told it about themselves to attempt to serve up relevant ads. For example, I indicated in my profile that I'm a fan of Fleetwood Mac. Some time later, an ad appeared that said "If you like Fleetwood Mac you'll love Vandeville Falls". I was impressed enough to click the link and ultimately bought Vandeville Falls' album, so the advertising worked.

The principle, then, seems sound. The problem is that, however clever they are, Facebook's adverts are an

Facebook Ads are a big source of revenue for Facebook, but that doesn't mean they're good for your business.

example of "interruption marketing", other examples of which include banner ads and Google's Display network. Users of Facebook aren't looking for a product, so for an interruption to be successful, it has to be relevant and very lucky. Compare this with Pay Per Click advertising in Google, Yahoo or Bing. If I'm selling a product, I can write an AdWords ad that includes keywords that make it more likely my ad will appear only when a searcher is looking for a product to buy. For example, "buy candle making kit" is more likely to drive traffic to the shop than "candle making", which will include both buyers and those simply interested in learning about the subject.

So, when using a search engine, I can expose my ad to people in a buying mood. When using Facebook Ads, the people who see my ad are more likely to be in a sociable mood, interacting with family and friends and not looking to buy at all. Aside from the one success with Vandeville Falls, I've been singularly unimpressed by the other attempts to part me from my cash; "credit card for 45 year olds" is a pretty pathetic use of my basic profile information.

Most small businesses would benefit from having a Facebook page, although the amount of work you put into publicising and maintaining it will depend entirely on the nature of your business. One thing to bear in mind is that a link back to your main site from your Facebook page won't help with your search engine ranking because Facebook links use the "nofollow" attribute.

Used correctly, Facebook can give your business a real sense of personality and create its own community.

STEP BY STEP Build a Facebook page for your business

1 **FIRST STEPS** It's essential to create a separate identity for your business, not only because your personal postings might not enhance your professional credibility, but also to access the powerful marketing tools of Facebook Pages.

To create your first Facebook Page, log into your personal Facebook News Feed. In the left hand column, under your profile picture, you'll see a section labelled "Pages".

2 **CREATE A PAGE** You now need to select the type of page you want to create. In your case the right option will probably be "Company, Organisation or Institution". If you sell from a physical location, however, select the "Local" option, while if you plan to use third party retailers to distribute your product, select "Brand/Product". For this example,

choose "Company, Organisation or Institution" – you can always create product pages later.

Facebook will now prompt you to select the appropriate category for your business and to type its official name. Click the Facebook Pages Terms checkbox (having, of course, read them) and the "Get Started" button.

A little known fact is that, once set, you can use the short form fb.com/yourvanityURL to attract visitors

3 **ADD A NEWS FEED** Next, upload the company logo as your profile picture and click "Next". You're now prompted to enter some details about the company, which you can skip for now if you wish. Finally, you can select a custom web address for your page. Until

recently, you needed at least 25 fans before being allowed to assign a vanity URL, but that has now been dropped. Select the name with care, though, as it can't be changed later, and bear in mind the URL must be unique across all of Facebook – if someone else has already registered the same name, you'll have to use a variant.

A little known fact is that, once set, you can use the short form fb.com/yourvanityURL to attract visitors to your page – perfect for marketing through leaflets and email signatures, for example. Click Set Address and Facebook will create your page.

4 **IMPORT & CONFIRM** The first thing you'll want to do is invite the friends from your personal account to become fans of the page, and also to ask them to share the page with their friends (don't forget to "like" the page yourself!). This way, you can very quickly acquire the 30 fans needed to turn on the analytics functions and for Facebook to consider you a serious proposition. Just as with your personal profile, you can, and should, add a cover picture and you should certainly spend some time filling in your company details. If the business has been set up for some time then make use of the milestones feature within the Timeline to mark up important moments in your history.

It's then a case of running the page in a similar way to your personal account but with the focus on providing value and interest with each status update, rather than posting cute photos of your new niece. Share links to web pages that might interest your audience (including your own blog posts), photos of your products and tutorial videos. Don't be afraid to be humorous, but take care – one person's harmless joke is another's offensive comment.

At fb.com/MakingYourOwnCandles we've found visitors respond best when we give insights into our day-to-day business – when we ship to an unusual location, for example. The long-term aim is for your Facebook page to become the heart of a community and the more active you are, even early on when it feels like you're talking to yourself, the more you'll get out of it.

1

2

3

4

Advertising on Facebook

Facebook is an excellent example of how not to start a business. Begun in 2004 as a programming exercise by Mark Zuckerberg, Facebook was, for a long time, a great platform looking for a way to generate profits. In other words, the product was developed first, and only then was thought given to how to make money from it.

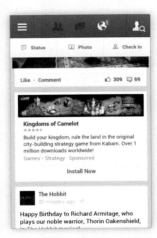

Ads are now being incorporated into Facebook's smartphone apps. Here's an example of a paid-for invitation to install a game.

This might seem counterintuitive given that Facebook floated for $100 billion in 2012, but for every Facebook, there have been thousands of other startups whose only aim is to build up enough users to attract funding. In almost every case, they fade out of existence.

Facebook has identified advertising as its main income source and this has become much more urgent since its flotation. The good news for online businesses is that the only way Facebook can increase its revenues is to make its advertising more and more effective for us. When first introduced, Facebook's ads aped those of Google by directing users to the external website of the advertiser. Since then, Facebook has experimented with many different forms and begun to tackle the thorny problem of advertising on the smaller screens of mobile devices.

Because of this, Facebook now offers a wider range of advertising than Google – this means that for many businesses, Facebook advertising is now a viable choice, especially if they've already built up an audience.

THE OPTIONS Each of the different types of Facebook ad targets a different audience. If you want to drive traffic to your online shop or website, you'll most often use an AdWords-like ad that will appear in the right-hand column. Later on, when you have more than 400 fans, you'll also be able to use Facebook to support a coupon-based campaign via Facebook Offers.

This is a very powerful resource as it allows you to create a coupon in your ecommerce package, for example, and have that publicised to your fans. When the user clicks, Facebook sends them an email containing the offer code and instructions. Crucially, it also alerts all their friends (who may not necessarily be fans of your page) that they've "claimed" the offer, which encourages these people to also participate.

Typically, however, your earliest campaigns will be aimed at getting more fans of your page. Remember, though, that this is the sort of advertising that has a long and uncertain gestation period – it only turns into money in your pocket if those fans and their friends buy from you. Contrast this with Google AdWords campaigns, which drive traffic direct to a sales page.

It takes a while to build a worthwhile Facebook community, so building this is best done in conjunction with your main AdWords campaign – but with a much lower budget. As soon as you've got AdWords running effectively (and assuming you've chosen Facebook as one of your promotional channels), you should then focus on gently building your fanbase using Facebook ads alongside the techniques we covered on the previous pages.

Here, we provide three steps to building a commercial audience.

Facebook Offers – just one of the many ways you can promote your online business on Facebook.

Kevin Partner likes
makingyourowncandles.co.uk.

makingyourowncandles
👍 Like

With the Page Like, friends of your fans are notified when they Like your page.

1 THE SCATTERGUN

Let's assume you've built your page, you've invited everyone you know to "like" it and have begun posting regular, interesting, status updates and photos – this should give your page a good start at no financial cost. As a general rule, however, a page only starts to come to life when it has more than 100 fans, so that should usually be your first target. Remember that every new fan also connects you, indirectly, to their network of friends.

Facebook has two main ways to attract fans to a page. With a Sponsored Story, you write a standard status update and, when a fan "likes" the update, an ad appears in or alongside their Timeline (and therefore the News Feeds of their friends) proclaiming they "liked" it. You've probably spotted the flaw in this approach for a new page: unless you already have a reasonable number of fans, the number of "likes" of the original story is going to be too low.

So, to build your initial audience you must use the second approach – directly advertising the page to the Facebook audience. In this case, you create an ad that will appear in the right-hand column of the News Feeds of the people you target. One of the strengths of Facebook's advertising platform is that it uses the information we type in about ourselves to help advertisers target. If you followed the process outlined in this book, you'll have a very good idea of your target audience and you can use this to focus the ad on a smaller, more responsive audience. You can see a step-by-step guide on this subject over the page.

One very effective strategy for attracting new fans is to make a statement and ask people to agree with it.

Kevin Partner likes
makingyourowncandles.co.uk's offer.

Get 10% Off Everything At
MakingYourOwnCandles.co.
Exclusive to Facebook!
Ends 30/9

Get Offer · 5 claimed

With the Post Like, friends of your fans see when they like a specific post on your page.

Facebook users are so used to "liking" posts that they often do it without really thinking. For example "Click Like if you could do with a warm, candle-lit bath".

Lots of people will see the message, immediately get a picture in their mind of relaxing in the tub and click Like. One word of warning though – there's little point attracting people with no interest in your business. As with AdWords, quality is much more cost effective than quality.

2 FRIENDS OF FRIENDS

Once you have 100 or so fans of your page, you can then use Sponsored Stories to grow the number gently over time at very low cost. Sponsored Stories work best when they promote a really interesting post. Examples of how your product solved a problem are ideal, especially if they've been submitted by a fan of the page.

We promote blog posts covering candle-making projects, especially if we've shot a supporting video. We also promote updates containing special offers. The updates get seen by a fair percentage of the friends of your fans (as well as the fans themselves) and has the double effect of promoting your page and, if the status update was a special offer, promoting that also.

3 DRIVE TRAFFIC TO YOUR SHOP

The ultimate aim is to make sales. Most ecommerce packages include an integration with Facebook so you can incorporate your shop into your Facebook Page, but there's little evidence to suggest they're effective. Indeed, you'll achieve a much higher conversion rate from your main shop because you have greater control over the whole process.

Once you have 400 fans, you can branch out into Promoted Posts (you pay to have any post appear higher in the News Feeds of your fans than it otherwise would) or Facebook Offers. However, if you do publicise special offers on your Page, make sure you create a coupon code specifically for Facebook. That way, you can check how effective your campaign was – independently of any other marketing activity. You should also use Google Analytics to track where your sales come from; Facebook Ads don't have conversion tracking built in.

400 is the magic number

Some of the most effective options for placing ads on Google are only available to Facebook Pages with 400 fans or more. This is a fairly blunt instrument Facebook uses to prevent fake pages or those with a nefarious purpose distributing ads. It's not a perfect system but it means that your first target, if you intend to advertise, should be to attract 400 fans – even if that means spending money on those ads that are available to you to get people to like your page.

STEP BY STEP Advertise your website with Facebook ads

1 **CREATE AN AD** We're going to use a standard Facebook ad to drive traffic to our website, but you could also use this form to encourage people to become fans of your page. Begin by going to your Facebook Page and clicking the Ads Manager link on the left. You'll need to create an Ads account if you don't already have one. Once done, click the green "Create an Ad" button at the top right of the Campaigns & Ads screen. Facebook now gives you three choices. If you're promoting an external site, enter the URL in the text field. To advertise your Page, select it from the list below or type its name. In this example, once the website address is typed in, Facebook displays the appropriate details page.

2 **POLISH IT UP** Pick a headline for your ad that will catch the attention of potential customers. The Text area contains the main body of your ad. This should be enticing and contain a "call to action" so that users know what you want them to do – in this case, choose a gift. Finally, you can pick a 100 x 72-pixel image to go alongside your ad. As a general rule, if you can use a photo of someone or something relevant then do so, but we've chosen to keep things simple by using our logo.

3 **HIT YOUR TARGETS** Scroll down to find the Targeting section. If you only ship to certain locations, enter these into the Location box. Since you've researched your audience, you know their

demographic profile, so use this to make the appropriate selections from the Age, Gender, Interests and Relationship fields. This level of targeting is one area in which Facebook Ads are superior to Google's AdWords, and it pays to limit visibility so only your target audience sees your ad. Facebook will update its estimate of how many users will see the ad each time you make a change, and getting this right can be tricky. Generally, you'll want an audience of over 10,000, and anything up to 10 million, to get enough data quickly.

4 **WORK OUT YOUR COSTS** Finally, complete the Campaign Details section. It's essential to limit your budget to the minimum needed to prove whether the campaign is profitable; usually this means setting it to between £5 and £10 per day. Facebook offers two pricing models: CPC and CPM. With Cost Per Click (CPC), you only pay when a Facebook user clicks on the ad, as opposed to Cost Per Thousand Impressions (CPM) billing, where you pay a fixed rate each time the ad is seen.

CPC will almost always be the better choice, because it lets you know the user has actually responded. Facebook will suggest a bid price. The more you pay, the more often the ad will appear and the more prominent its position. It's generally a good tactic to bid slightly below the lowest end of the suggested range; you can always raise it. Once done, click Review Ad to see a preview and then Place Order. Facebook's ads team manually reviews each ad so it will usually be a few hours before it goes live.

How to manage your Facebook ads campaign

Facebook ads are a good way to drive traffic to your website or Facebook Page but, unless you have an unlimited budget, you must monitor their performance to make sure they're profitable.

Begin at the campaigns control panel by clicking the Ads Manager link, then select the ad you want to manage. If you need to rename the campaign, pause it or alter the budget, you can use the shortcuts along the screen, but it's the data near the bottom of the page that you're mainly interested in. Let's look at each of the figures in turn.

CAMPAIGN REACH is the number of individual Facebook users who've seen your ad during the past seven days (if you're using the default period).

FREQUENCY is the number of times, on average, each of these users has seen your ad so far. Placing a higher bid-per-click will increase this number, so seeing too high a number here suggests you're paying too much.

The **SOCIAL REACH** value only applies to certain ad types: it shows how many of the figure shown in Campaign Reach saw information about whether any of their friends "liked" the Page or site. Usually, this will be because this friend was already a fan of the Page – ads displayed with social information tend to perform better. Here, around 10% of our ads qualified.

ACTIONS and **CLICKS** are related and vary according to the ad type. If you were promoting a Facebook Page, then Actions represent the number of people who became fans, for example, whereas Clicks is simply how many people clicked the ad itself. This ad promotes an external site and we can see that 24 people visited it, whereas one person became a fan of the page.

CTR stands for click-through rate. If you've run an AdWords campaign before, you'll notice immediately that the CTR for Facebook ads is tiny in comparison. This is because an AdWords ad appears in direct response to the user's search for information whereas users see Facebook ads when they're merely browsing the social network. Chances are they're not looking for what you have to offer. However, if you've chosen to pay per click, you're not paying for the huge majority that doesn't respond and the Facebook audience is so vast that you can achieve reasonable traffic despite a tiny CTR.

Finally, take a look at the table beneath the summary figures. This shows the stats for that particular ad (you could have several ads in a campaign). The most important number is on the end: the Price. This is the amount you've paid for each visit to your site; in other words, the cost per click.

The one piece of information you don't have is the conversion rate once the user reaches your website. Facebook hasn't built this functionality in, so you need to track this in some other way. The simplest method is to set up a free Google Analytics account. Analytics provides very comprehensive information about the behaviour of visitors to your site. For example, you can set up Goals in Analytics to see how many of your visitors from Facebook ended up at the order confirmation page, and from this it's a simple matter to work out the conversion rate.

Managing Facebook advertising follows the same rules as any other marketing: it must generate more profit than it costs to run. This is harder at the beginning as you build up a Facebook following, but that shouldn't be at all expensive. Once achieved, you can experiment with different ways of driving profitable traffic to your main site.

Facebook grants you excellent targeting options, but click-through rates will always be low.

Making Twitter pay

Twitter began with the simple concept of sending status updates in SMS format. This quickly developed into an online system that used the 140-character SMS limit to send what was, and to a large extent still is, pointless babble. However, you'd be foolish to dismiss this potentially valuable business tool.

In fact, whether you, as a business owner, should use Twitter is a bit of a no-brainer in my view. Even if it does nothing other than provide a medium through which you can vent the frustrations of running a business, it will have performed a valuable service. How much of your time you devote to Twitter, on the other hand, depends on how you intend to use it to support your business.

 ## Sell products directly

Twitter can be an effective channel for self-promotion, but only once you've attracted a loyal and relevant following. Even then, promotional tweets should be kept to a minimum or people will stop following you in droves.

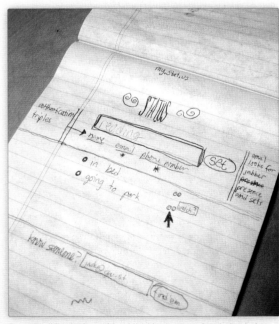

From small beginnings: the original brainstorm sketch that led to the phenomenon that is Twitter.

 ## Find customers for products

You can search for tweets about your products and the general marketplace. People tweet about their frustrations, which means an effective search of the Twitter feed can reveal the sort of language customers use and exactly what they're asking for. Having found customers expressing a need for a product such as yours, you can then interact with them to find out what they need and sell it to them.

 ## Enhance your credibility

If you sell a service, Twitter can be used to establish your reputation. If you sell a product, tweeting about it can create a following. For example, an author might find it worthwhile to build up a Twitter following by providing updates and tips while writing their next novel. In my view, establishing and supporting your credibility in your field is probably the most important role Twitter can play in most businesses.

 ## Provide support

Whenever I have a problem with a piece of software, I'll Google it first and then, if I want the makers to know about it, tweet about it. If the company is on the ball with Twitter, it will pick up on your comment and can then provide support in a much more interactive and instant way than even email offers. For example, I had a problem with the screen-capture software Snagit recently. Having Googled the problem to no avail, I tweeted about it and, a few hours later, I had a response that was not only personalised but also contained a link to a video Snagit's makers TechSmith had made demonstrating a potential solution. This sort of interactivity builds customer loyalty, and in my case this came at a moment when I was considering upgrading to the latest version of its flagship product, Camtasia.

HOW TO GET A FOLLOWING IN TWITTER

Succeeding in Twitter is a matter of achieving critical mass. Your target is to have a large number of relevant followers – people who will respond to your promotions or offers of help. The more followers you have, the more likely it is that others will follow you. The challenge with Twitter, if your aim is to use it to boost your business, is to build up some momentum, and the difficulty of this is what causes many Twitterers to abandon the platform after a month or so.

The key to making a success of Twitter is tweeting. Tweet often, tweet original content, tweet controversial and interesting information, retweet generously, link to external information, add media where possible. There is something slightly weird about tweeting to yourself, as you will be at the beginning, but bear in mind that your tweets join the main Twitter stream; it's just that no-one at this stage has indicated they specifically want to hear from you.

Begin by writing at least 100 good-quality tweets; you can then go looking for followers. To do this, search on Twitter for keywords that relate to your market. Find the most interesting tweets and pick a few Twitter users. Check their profiles. Have they written lots of tweets? Are they interesting, relevant and original? If so, follow that user. In their profile, look at who they follow and repeat the process, following those that meet your criteria. Limit this initially so that you follow 50-100 people. Don't follow anyone who has written only a handful of tweets, since if they have lots of followers they've achieved this by using automated software and by completely missing the point of Twitter.

Conventional wisdom says that if you've picked the right people, around half of the people you follow will follow you back, but my testing shows a figure closer to around 25%. As you write more of the right tweets and attract more followers, this percentage should increase. Of course, some people will be doing the same thing as you and will find you among the followers of people they're following, so you will attract some new followers that way. The more you have, the more you'll get.

The more active you are on Twitter, the more success you will have, and this includes being a genuine follower yourself as well as encouraging others to follow you. Twitter can be a fantastic way to learn about your market. The quality of your tweets will improve hugely if you analyse what it is about tweets you read that makes you pay attention to that update above the general noise.

Use TweetDeck or HootSuite to organise your interaction with Twitter. Set up lists of those you want to actively follow, bearing in mind that if you follow hundreds of people you can't possibly pay attention to all of them. Keep your lists down to no more than 50 or so people and interact with them where appropriate. The key to Twitter is keeping your view of it down to a manageable level.

ACCELERATING YOUR PROGRESS Building up a following this way can be a slow process, depending on how much time you're willing to devote to it. Plenty of online services will claim to offer an easy (though usually expensive) way of attracting new followers, but these followers will often be of poor quality and, perhaps more worryingly, these services often flout the Twitter terms of service, which could result in your account being suspended.

As an experiment, I signed up with the Twiends service (www.twiends.com). With Twiends, you purchase credits that are then offered to the Twiends community. Anyone who follows you gets credits, and others will follow them to get credits, with one credit being deducted each time: it's like a Twitter marketplace. The advantage of this approach is that human beings are choosing who to follow, so the quality of the followers you pick up is a little higher than through purely automated techniques. Having said that, they're still of a much lower quality than those achieved organically.

The best-value plan currently offers 300 credits for $5.95 (around £3.75). It took me eight months and 800 tweets to attract 409 followers by using the organic process of following others and tweeting. It took an additional seven working days and around £26 to end up with over 1,000 at a cost of just over 4p each. Looking at a sample of the people who've followed me through Twiends, only around 10% are, in themselves, useful as followers, 70% are not much use but not a problem either, whereas 20% are the sorts of people I don't want following me and these I've blocked. Interestingly, over half of these undesirable followers had posted very few tweets, if any.

In other words, the worthwhile users cost me 40p each. Depending on your business, you might think this is a reasonable cost, but with a conversion rate of 5% that would translate into a cost per acquisition of £8 – probably not a million miles away from the cost of Google AdWords.

For most businesses Twitter can be a useful extra communication channel, but it usually makes more sense to spend time on it once your Pay Per Click marketing is working effectively. In the meantime – tweet!

Eight months, a lot of tweets and a little money have brought me a four-figure following, but how much is it worth to the bottom line?

What the ? is Google+?

Google may be a giant in search but it's a latecomer to social media. After failing to take on Facebook with its first two attempts (Orkut and Buzz), Google+ was launched in June 2011 and, within a year, had 250 million accounts – a milestone Facebook took almost three years to achieve.

Given its record, though, is there a danger that Google's latest social network experiment will be pulled like the two before it? This seems unlikely. Google+ already has more users than either of its predecessors and the social giant has integrated its new social network deeply into its other services, including search and email. There are no guarantees, but it would be a major surprise if Google backpedalled on its new baby.

But there are only so many hours in a day: why should a busy entrepeneur consider Google+? Well, each social network has its own audience, so selecting the right one is largely a matter of working out which network your customers frequent. Generally speaking, if you're selling direct to consumers, you should focus mainly on Facebook, with Twitter as your second line of attack.

Who's using Google+? In its early days, Google+ attracted mainly techies and, whilst this has now broadened out, the average Google+ member uses the service to follow their interests rather than posting family photos or playing games. These interests tend to be technical, political,

creative (photography is very popular) or business-related, and Google+, at present, appeals mainly to this information-seeking demographic.

Contrast this with Facebook which, as a mature platform, has a much more representative slice of the population. Facebook, at its core, is about posting status updates for friends and family to consume – whether these take the form of text, photos or video. Google+, on the other hand, is much more about engaging in conversation and debate, so the people using it are more actively involved in using the platform.

HOW DOES GOOGLE+ WORK? Google+ is often described as a hybrid of Facebook and Twitter. And it is like Facebook in that you have a "home" page with a stream of posts you can dive into, along with a personal media library and the ability to selectively share content with different people depending on your relationship with them. On the other hand, it's like Twitter in that you don't have to be a "friend" of a user to see their posts. Facebook is somewhere

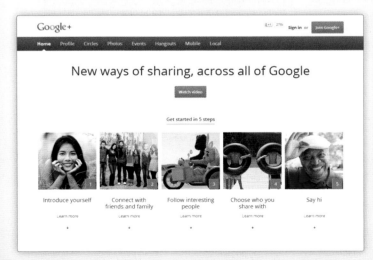

Google+ is not just a social network but acts as a layer on top of a wide range of Google services.

Circles allow you to organise your content by topic or person. Here's a News Circle I've created – note I've contributed to the top discussion. This is how to attract new followers and enrich your experience.

that people with an established relationship come together and share, Twitter and Google+ are for finding new and interesting voices.

But Google+ is more than just a synthesis of Facebook and Twitter. It's perhaps best seen as an umbrella product that links together many existing Google products and services – with this integration getting tighter and spreading to new products over time. For example, if you join a conversation on a topic in Google+, you can continue the conversation in Gmail. Contrast this with Facebook which, whilst it will notify you of posts and comments, requires you to jump back into its platform before continuing any discussion.

YouTube, another brand Google owns, is also very closely integrated – indeed if you have a YouTube account already, it's likely you've already been "invited" to have it merged into your Google+ account. Maps, Local, Picasa and Blogger are all stitched together using Google+ (in many cases becoming part of Google+). Many websites now include sharing options, usually in the form of a +1 button which works in a similar way to the Facebook Like.

The heart of Google+, however, is the Home page. When you first sign up, you'll see nothing much here because you haven't yet followed anyone. Click the Explore button and you'll be shown a list of the most popular topics on the network at that moment. If you see something that interests you, you can either jump right in and comment immediately or hover over the poster's name and click the Add button that appears. You'll be asked to choose a Circle to add the user to. Each account begins with a selection of default circles but you'll probably want to create a new one.

SQUARING THE CIRCLE If the Home page is the entry point to Google+, circles are its gatekeeper. Their first function is to organise the content you see on your home page since, by clicking the appropriate button at the top, you can force it to display only the posts from that particular circle. In this way, it's similar to Twitter's list function.

It's entirely up to you how you organise yourself but most users split their circles into two types: people and interests. For example, you might add family members or close friends into appropriately named circles – as with Facebook. You could also create circles representing your

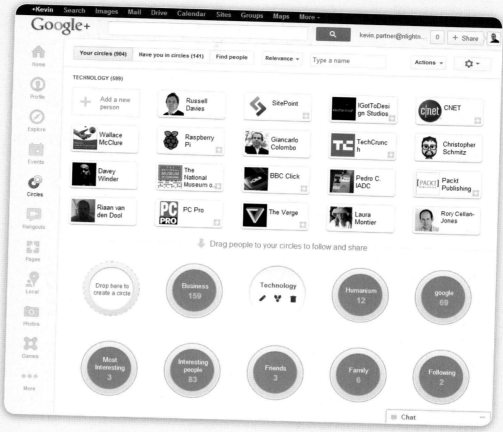

interests and add people who post interesting content in those areas to those circles. The key thing to remember is that you don't need the user's agreement to add them, so you can explore and use Google+ immediately, without needing to send out friend requests.

Circles can also be used to specify who sees your status updates. Only those people who've followed you (added you to their circles) will see your posts in their stream automatically – organised in whatever way makes sense to them. If you wanted to share a photo of your latest holiday with your relations, you would select the Family circle and only those members of that circle who had also followed you would see it. For business purposes, you will almost always set your posts to "public" so that they get the widest possible distribution – that way your followers see it and it goes into the overall Google+ stream where it will be discoverable by all users.

Once you've added a few interesting accounts to your circles, you can use the search box to find people writing about subjects you want to follow. For example, you might type "raspberry pi" or "online business" and then follow those that are posting useful information or having worthwhile discussions.

Google+ provides an excellent interface for managing your Circles – much better than those of Facebook.

Getting followed on Google+

As with Twitter, your public postings will be broadcast to all but will only appear automatically in the streams of people who've followed you. Increasing the number of relevant followers, then, should be an early aim. Quality trumps quantity every time.

Whatever your ultimate strategy with Google+, whether it's to help build a brand, sell directly or access a community of like-minded individuals, you must begin by establishing yourself as a personal user of the platform. The first step is to create an interesting profile. Think carefully about how you want to be perceived by potential followers – if you're selling a product or service then make your profile relevant to this. If you're building your profile more generally so that it supports your business by increasing your credibility then you can afford to have a more personal profile. Remember, people follow interesting people.

Now, set up a circle containing people active in your industry, especially if they could become customers. Get actively involved in discussions, making sure you contribute something positive to the debate. If you're responding to a specific comment, type + and the commenter's name to ensure they're notified of your contribution. Some of these people will look at your profile and, if they think you'll add to their experience of Google+, they'll add you to one of their circles.

You should also be posting interesting content.

Not only does this get broadcast into the Google+ universe, it also appears under the Posts heading in your profile. This is one of the main factors a visitor to your profile uses to decide whether to follow you.

There are three main ways to add content. The first is to type it directly into the stream, along with any pictures or videos. The second is to create the content as a blog entry and add a link to it from your status update; the Google-owned Blogger.com is probably the best choice for this if you don't have an existing blog. Finally, you can link to third-party content and introduce it with your own text.

In the early days, it might feel as though you're talking to yourself, but bear in mind that these posts remain indefinitely and are indexed by Google so nothing is wasted. Make sure you use hashtags (#onlinebusiness, for example) to make it more likely that your post will be listed when a Google+ user searches.

FOUR GOOGLE+ STRATEGIES We've covered how Google+ operates and how it differs from Twitter and Facebook but, as with all activities, there has to be a

A good profile attracts followers. Dave Chaffey uses his cover photo to show the books he's written and his tagline and introduction to give interested visitors good reasons to follow him. The green box shows he's in my Business circle.

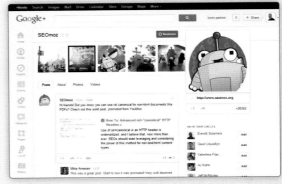

Google+ Pages work almost identically to personal profiles. SEOmoz has over 18,000 followers because it provides excellent content. That may sound unmatchable, but start posting interesting content and your numbers will shoot up.

business benefit to make spending time on it worthwhile. Here are four approaches to Google+, each requiring a different investment of time and attention – which could apply to your business?

1 Business Intelligence and Networking

Having set yourself up on Google+ and established a personal presence, you need to think carefully about what you want to achieve with the social network. You might want to use it largely to keep abreast of the latest techniques, market trends and technology as well as educating yourself – this sort of business intelligence can be very valuable. Once you have a few hundred followers, you'll find yourself invited to events and given the opportunity to become more involved in your industry. In this sense, Google+ works very much like Twitter.

2 Building a community

Unlike Twitter, however, Google+ can be used to create a community around a product or company. Once you've established a personal identity, consider setting up a Google Page. These are essentially the same as Facebook Pages except that the posts you make are available to every user through search rather than being restricted to followers. Those who add your Page to a circle will see your content in their stream. Google+ users tend to be freer with their follows because of the extra organisation that circles bring – they can keep each stream a manageable size rather than being swamped. Because of this, it's not uncommon to see users with the maximum 5,000 profiles in their circles.

3 Promoting external sites

Incorporating the +1 button into your sites enables you to bring traffic in from the general web. The +1 button also functions in a similar way to Facebook's Like button to provide social proof and reinforcement of your product or service. You can also drive traffic the other way – from Google+ to your external site.

As an added bonus, links from Google+ to your site would probably boost your search engine optimisation efforts. However, as with other SEO techniques, this

shouldn't be your primary aim. Google is becoming better and better at sniffing out attempts to game the system so you should engage in Google+ in a natural way – just make sure you include links to your sites when appropriate.

4 Hanging out

Hangouts are a unique feature of Google+.

Essentially, a hangout is a form of built-in video conferencing that uses clever algorithms to enhance sound and switch between attendees as they speak. It's more or less a friction-free system that requires little setup. The original metaphor was to offer a virtual equivalent of "hanging out on the porch". Because of this, hangouts are limited to a maximum of ten active participants, which would seem to make them of limited use to businesses.

However, in 2012, Google introduced Hangouts On Air. In a nutshell, this allows you to host your own broadcast show or webinar to an unlimited audience. Furthermore, Google will automatically record the show and post it to YouTube. From there you can perform basic edits and publish the recording. Taken to the extreme, there's no need to have anyone watch your broadcast live, you can use the system to create a presentation and then use YouTube to distribute it.

Used properly, this could be extremely powerful – not only as a marketing tool but also for training, support and education. It also offers the basic functionality included in paid-for services such as GoToWebinar free of charge, along with the major benefit that all of this activity is integrated into a big social network.

For many businesses, having access to broadcast hangouts alone makes it worthwhile investing in Google+. When married to the Events functionality, which ties together Google+, Gmail and Google Calendar, you get the benefit of a complete marketing process – from organising a live hangout via Events, through publicising it in Google+ and Gmail, holding the Hangout and then offering the recording either free of charge or for a fee.

Make your business thrive

Once you switch on your pay-per-click advertising campaign, you are immediately visible to your customers and, if you've judged your market properly, the orders will begin arriving. Congratulations: your business is alive, and the initial job of getting up and running is done. From here on, there are many factors that will contribute to your success – luck not the least of them – but following some golden rules will help ensure it.

The three rules we've covered in this book are:

1 **You must choose or develop the right product**

2 **You must build an effective platform to sell it**

3 **You must find and connect with enough of the right customers**

For any individual product or service, steps 1 and 2 take place only once. You'll come back and tweak the product specification or the website, but, assuming you've followed an effective process, your product and site will remain essentially as they are for some time.

Step 3, however, is a never-ending, iterative process. The concept of "build it and they will come" has no place in modern business, if indeed it ever did. If you don't market your product or service effectively, it might as well not exist: no-one will ever know about it, much less buy it.

Having said that, if you've followed this book through, the bulk of the grunt work is behind you. Your AdWords campaign is set up, conversion tracking is installed and you're split-testing your landing pages. All you need

An easy-to-use accounting service such as FreeAgent helps you manage your finances without getting bogged down (see p156).

to do is build time into your day to check your AdWords control panel to see if enough data has been gathered to enable you to make a decision. If it has, don't delay: delete the underperforming ad or landing page, make a copy of the winner, change it and split-test it against the original.

As time goes on, the results of this process will become less and less clear-cut. You may hit the "AdWords ceiling", which is where your changes begin to perform consistently worse than the existing ad or landing page. If you get there, congratulations: you can consider that aspect of your marketing to be optimised, for now at least.

However, there are more tools available to help you drive your business on to even greater success.

THE ONE REPORT Google AdWords offers a sometimes bewildering array of reports, but the most useful is the Search Query Performance Report (see opposite). This tells you what searches your visitors typed in to find you. You can use this to find new keywords, along with a very good idea of how profitable they're likely to be, as you can see the conversion rate and cost per conversion.

Begin by clicking the Reporting tab in your control panel. Select New Report and, on the Create Report page, select Search Query Performance. The Level of Detail should usually be set to Ad Group and the View to Summary. Set a reasonable date range, depending on traffic but no more than a month.

Under Campaigns and Ad Groups, select "Manually select from a list" and click the "Add link" next to the Ad Group you want to look at. Under Advanced Settings you can add or remove any columns you don't want to include. The most important figures to include are impressions, CTR and conversion stats.

Give the report a name and opt to "Save this as a new report template" to avoid the rigmarole of going through this process again. Optionally, you can have the report run automatically and the results sent to you by email, but make sure you've got it right before you enable that. Now click Create Report. Google will return you to the Report Center view, and after a few seconds your report will be completed. Click its name to view it.

Initially, you should order the report by Impressions, with the most at the top. Take a look at the "Cost/Conv" figure: do any numbers leap out at you as being either much lower than the others or, more worryingly, much higher?

In our example (see right), compare lines 1 and 3. The conversion cost for line 3 is more than twice that of line 1. Yet it has a higher click-through rate and an almost identical conversion rate. The reason is immediately obvious: the cost per click (CPC) for line 3 is twice that of line 1.

I can see that ads triggered by "british citizenship" are appearing in a higher average position than "life in the uk test", and this is likely to be the reason for the higher CPC. My first step should be to reduce the bid price for that keyword phrase, and in that way push it down the list a bit.

If you see keywords that have reasonable traffic, high click-through rate and low to moderate cost per conversion, consider splitting them off into separate ad groups. You can then target a specific ad and landing page at them and thus drive down the conversion cost.

KEEP YOUR EYE ON THE DATA Don't feel overwhelmed by the amount of data available. Keep a

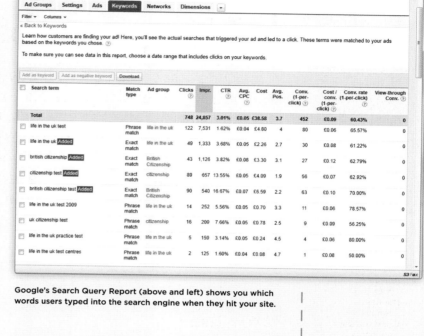

Google's Search Query Report (above and left) shows you which words users typed into the search engine when they hit your site.

regular eye on the key figures outlined in "Running an AdWords Campaign" (p140). You can do this directly within the AdWords control panel or by generating an Ad Performance report. This needn't be onerous.

When you first start up a campaign, you should check it carefully every day and set your daily budget low. Most campaigns are not immediately profitable, and your first aim is to ensure you're breaking even, bearing in mind the long-term value of your new customers.

As you make improvements to your click-through rate and cost per conversion, you'll find it takes less time to identify problems and opportunities and you develop a much better idea of what is likely to work for your business and its customers. However, you should never rely on intuition: always test.

CLICKS FOR FREE There's more to marketing than just getting your AdWords campaign working profitably. At the core is getting inside the conversation your customers are having inside their own heads. What are they thinking when they type their search phrase? What do they think when they see your ad? What do they do when they arrive at your landing page? What do they make of your product or →

→ service? You can answer these questions by regularly surveying your customers, especially in the early days, when you may well experience a forehead-slapping moment as you discover your customers don't see your product in the same way as you do, or they're not the customers you expected.

As far as possible, you should be open in your communication with customers. Make it easy for them to get in touch, even if this means exposing your support email on your website. If your product is an online service, install a support ticket system such as Hesk (www.hesk.com) so you don't end up playing email ping-pong. Questions that are regularly asked should either be added to your FAQ page or should result in changes to the site: remember, for every one visitor who bothers to ask a question there might be 20 who simply left your site unimpressed.

By developing an open dialogue with customers, you'll find they suggest improvements to your product or service. You need to work out if their ideas will actually improve your sales and profits, but new ideas are what push companies to continuing success.

Having a good product and proving there's a real person behind the website is the best way to garner priceless word-of-mouth recommendations. A Facebook user may have hundreds of "friends"; imagine the marketing potential of having them recommend you. As Mark Knopfler (almost) sang: "Money for nothing and your clicks for free".

FIVE STEPS TO SUCCESS I'd like to leave you with five tips that, in my view, differentiate successful businesses:

1 Do what you love, love what you do

If you've been following this book, you'll have picked a business based on your interests. It's much easier to devote the required mental and physical energy if you're naturally interested in what you sell. Setting up and running a business is challenging: you owe it to yourself, and the business, to choose a product or service that gets you excited.

Having said that, there are bound to be aspects of running a business that turn you on less than others. You have two options: either learn to love that task or outsource it.

Take bookkeeping, for example. Few of us enjoy it, so you can either hire someone to take care of it or find a way of doing it that's (relatively) enjoyable. In my case, the online accounting service FreeAgent (www.freeagentcentral.com) is so easy to use that I really don't mind doing my accounts, and I enjoy the control it gives me.

2 Never stop learning

Keep an open mind at all times, and don't assume you know anything without evidence to back it up. This applies to every aspect of the product development process as well as marketing, but also to the day-to-day running of the business.

Having started a business providing a service or product in a field you already had some expertise in, don't let that stop you improving. Nothing stands still, whether it's window cleaning, candle making or driving theory test services. Right now, on my desk, I have a book on Ajax (the increasingly popular group of web technologies) and another on Facebook application development. The first because it's a gap in my skills that needs fixing, and the second because it's a potential new platform for PassYourTheory to exploit.

I read books on marketing – most recently *Free* by Chris Anderson and *What Would Google Do?* by Jeff Jarvis – along with classic and contemporary fiction to "sharpen the saw". Any of these might inspire me; all will provoke me.

What can you do to improve your core skills beyond their current level? What can you do to bring those things that you are poor at up to an acceptable level?

3 Work on the business, not just in the business

This is the credo of the E-Myth series of books ("E" for "entrepreneur"). If you've started a business that plays to your technical strengths, the danger is you'll end up spending all your time working on your product and doing administrative work, rather than working on making your business more successful.

Marketing and leadership are examples of tasks that can easily get neglected in the excitement of cranking out the next great product; without them your business has no chance of success. Your reaction might be to protest that you started your own business so that you could indulge your love of that particular business. Fine – just don't expect to make any money. It's a hard fact that you can't spend all your time playing with your toys. Learn to love marketing!

Of course, if you have the support of a partner or employees, you can farm out the aspects of running a business that you find less pleasant. But I don't recommend outsourcing marketing at the start: no-one knows your business like you do.

"Marketing and leadership can get neglected in the excitement of creating a product, but without them you have no chance of success."

4 Always look on the bright side of life

Entrepreneurs are positive, "glass-is-half-full" individuals. Quite apart from the sheer amount of work required to bring a business into being and apply heart massage until it can breathe on its own, you'll also find yourself up against government bureaucracy and the inevitable naysayers.

How you deal with disaster is much more important than how you react in the good times. Captain Cock-up is the best instructor you could wish for, as long as you learn from it. Your business reflects *you*: if you're enthusiastic and confident, your business will seem that way to your customers, peers and suppliers.

A key element of this attitude is "never give up, never surrender". In short, don't let problems undermine your confidence in your own ability. Take comfort from the fact that all business owners mess up on a regular basis. If you can combine the willingness to learn with an unshakeable belief in your own ability, you'll stay confident without becoming arrogant – the ideal combination.

5 Work your nuts off

There's no getting away from it: setting up your own business is hard work. If it isn't, you're either unbelievably lucky or missing opportunities. While it's important to retain a sense of balance, there's no doubt that in the early days you'll be devoting much of your time to your business, whether you're setting up full-time or running it alongside your job.

Of all the qualities of the great entrepreneurs, a work ethic is shared by just about all of them. That's not to say hard work on its own guarantees success: effort expended without a plan is a waste of time. But without hard work, the greatest plan never sees the light of day.

BONUS TIP: GET A DOG See what I did there? Promised you five tips and then sneaked in a free bonus. "Get a dog"? I'm completely serious. If there's one action that has had more impact on my performance as a businessperson than any other, it's the regular walks Dizzy is subjected to. The size and breed of dog is unimportant (Dizzy is a Cairn terrier/Westie cross) as long as they like, or even demand, walks.

There are three reasons I recommend having a dog on the payroll. First, it makes you take exercise. If you work full-time for yourself, especially from home, the temptation is to sit at the computer all day pounding away at the keyboard without a break. This isn't good for you or your business. A brisk walk with the dog and you'll return refreshed and ready for the next challenge.

Second, running a business is a lonely activity. Even if you have a supportive family, friends and even

employees, being the boss is a lonely position. Having a dog sitting asleep in the corner of your office makes you feel less alone and lowers the blood pressure – and heaven knows running a business can often do the opposite.

Finally, by far the most important reason is this: the vast majority of good ideas I've had in the past few years have popped into my head as I've been walking the dog. It's essential not to listen to your MP3 player or to be distracted by anything else. Just start walking and either ponder a particular problem or think about nothing at all. Relaxing the analytical part of your brain allows the creative subconscious and right-brain to get your attention.

It is no exaggeration to say that Dizzy and her predecessor Ozzy have earned me many thousands of pounds from ideas that have dropped into my head during a walk. If you're a dog owner already, you probably don't need convincing. If not, why not borrow someone else's dog (with their permission, of course) and see what pops up?

And finally...

It's an exciting time to be starting a business, and doing so can be a life-changing experience. Work hard on generating a great product, build an effective platform and market your socks off and you have success in the palm of your hands. Good luck, and welcome to the club!

Daft as it may sound, a canine companion could make all the difference to your entrepreneurial career. Other domesticated animals are also available, but lack the crucial desire for walkies.

MakingYourOwnCandles three years on

We set up MakingYourOwnCandles.co.uk while writing the first edition of this book in 2009. The site went live in November 2009 as we attempted to benefit from the Christmas rush predicted, as part of our research, by Google Insights. Since then, the business has developed a popular range of products and an enthusiastic and loyal group of customers.

We went into MakingYourOwnCandles pretty confident that it represented a worthwhile business opportunity, and it's interesting to look back at the predictions made during the research phase.

Our research predicted we'd attract 5,000 visitors per month. The actual figure for 2010 was 4,666. We predicted a cost per click of 10p to achieve a front page AdWords ad and that turned out to be spot on. The click-through rate was slightly higher than the 5% predicted, which made up for the fact that Google's prediction for the number of searches on my keywords was a little low.

In other words, the critical parts of the research proved to be correct. However, these predictions assume most of your business is going to come from new customers who find you through a Google ad. This is why encouraging customers to come back, and to tell their friends about you, is so important: it's essentially free money.

In 2011, then, we've spent much of our marketing effort on fostering good relations with our customers and encouraging a sense of community. It's certainly paid off as more and more of our customers are coming to us through recommendations, Facebook and organic search – as well as the same people buying again and again.

All of this marketing work would be pointless if we hadn't made the ongoing effort to truly understand what our customers want, to use that knowledge to develop products that meet those needs and to create an online environment they trust. That, in a nutshell, is what makes a successful company.

So what specifically have we learned since 2009?

THE RIGHT SYSTEMS Make sure you have the right software to back up your business. We launched using ekmPowershop, purely because I was familiar with it. While it was adequate as a shop front, the order management, product management and reporting wasn't up to the job so, as part of the relaunch in 2010, we moved to BigCommerce. We now have a professional site with built-in customer accounts, a live postage calculator, and easy product and order management. BigCommerce 6 also added integration with the MailChimp mailing list service, which means customers can join our list when they purchase from us.

MailChimp provides sophisticated ways to interact with and understand your customers.

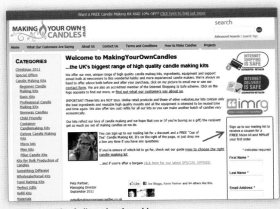

The end result of all our hard work!

We've moved from using PayPal Website Payments Standard to the Pro version. This costs £20 per month but allows the transaction processing to take place entirely within our shopping cart rather than having the user sent off to PayPal. Indeed, the customer doesn't have to know we're using PayPal at all. It's much neater and more professional, but it takes at least a week to get approved by PayPal. Integrating it into your BigCommerce store, on the other hand, is a matter of a few clicks.

IT'S ALL ABOUT YOUR CUSTOMERS Take every opportunity to sign up your visitors to a mailing list. We have two lists at present. The first is for prospective customers and the sign-up form for this list appears both on our blog and the main site. We offer a free candle-making kit and a discount on their first order. While this might seem extravagant, the cost of the micro-kit in question is only around 40p to us and well worth it if it results in a purchase.

One important tip: make sure your sign-up box is prominent. I was concerned recently that our sign-up rate had dropped off a cliff only to find that moving the box to the top right of the home page increased the rate tenfold!

It's vital you understand what your customers are using your product or service for. Based on our survey, we originally thought most people would be buying for their own personal use, except at Christmas. While most orders are like this, the biggest orders come from people seeking to make their own candles to sell, shop-owners wanting to create bespoke kits, and schools looking for activities.

Once your business has been up and running for a while, use your relationship with your customers to find out what they want – it doesn't have to be guesswork! Of course, when it comes to specific products there's a certain risk involved: we're assuming from the market that our customers will want to buy our Christmas Advent Candle kit and, because we know that our most valuable customers make candles to sell, we also offer it as a bulk kit.

Innovate, improve and experiment to create new products without forgetting your original aims as a business. We wanted to offer an easy way for candle-makers to find professional products, so it's essential that we don't overcomplicate things or have too wide a selection.

TAKE STOCK OF YOUR STOCK Make certain you secure your supply, especially of hard-to-obtain items, and identify backup suppliers in case your main source stops stocking the item. Once you're confident that you understand the likely demand, buy in bulk to get a discount. One of the reasons we can make a profit on our kits is because we buy wax in huge quantities.

If you're creating bespoke products, try to keep the number of stock items needed to a minimum. There are many types of wax, for example, but we've identified the best container wax, mould wax and beeswax, and only supply those in our kits. We also try to keep the quantity the same in each kit so the wax can be pre-packed.

SPEND TIME ON MARKETING However good your product or service, if you can't get customers in through your virtual door, you don't have a business. Of the time I've spent working on MakingYourOwnCandles at least half of it has been marketing-related. The first step was to develop a cost-efficient AdWords campaign because we needed to establish whether we could attract business profitably during the quieter months of February to August.

We've spent a lot of time building up a sense of community through our blog and our Facebook page. We get comments from customers delighted and excited by candle making: they ask questions, make suggestions and enter competitions. All this gives a sense of life to the business and, especially, ensures we're close to our customers.

It may also help to give your site a personality. MakingYourOwnCandles is run day to day by my wife Peta. Almost all emails are sent from her, she writes some of the blog entries and interacts with our Facebook fans. I take on the persona of technical support geek and lab rat. For our market, the idea of buying from a small family firm is attractive and reassuring, so it works. However, this may not be the case with, for example, professional services.

Joining a trade body can also boost business. PassYourTheory.org.uk (another of my sites) saw its conversion rate jump 10% when we joined the SafeBuy scheme. MakingYourOwnCandles is a member of ISIS (Internet Shopping Is Safe) and IDIS (Internet Delivery Is Safe) because these issues are especially important to our audience. Reassurance is critical: whether through schemes such as these, testimonials or human interaction on Facebook, it all boosts the conversion rate.

Finally, run regular promotions. If you've set your prices right, you can afford to knock off a percentage and still make a profit. How much? Test it! In our case, we've found that 20% off the price works better than, for example, free delivery, and results in a big boost in business.

To find a product suitable for children, we bought beeswax sheets in bulk, worked out the best method and packaged it into a heat-free kit that has proven a consistent seller.

How to set up an online business

EDITORIAL
Author
Kevin Partner
Editor
Tim Danton
Design & Layout
Adam Banks, Sarah Ratcliffe
Production
Martin James

LICENSING & SYNDICATION
To license this product please contact Carlotta Serantoni on +44 (0) 20 7907 6550 or email carlotta_serantoni@dennis.co.uk. To syndicate content from this product please contact Anj Dosaj-Halai on +44 (0) 20 7907 6132 or email anj_dosaj-halai@dennis.co.uk

ADVERTISING & MARKETING
Advertising Manager
Ben Topp 020 7907 6625
MagBook Account Manager
Katie Wood 020 7907 6689
Digital Production Manager
Nicky Baker 020 7907 6056

MANAGEMENT 020 7907 6000
MagBook Publisher
Dharmesh Mistry
Operations Director
Robin Ryan
Managing Director
John Garewal
MD of Advertising
Julian Lloyd-Evans
Newstrade Director
David Barker
Commercial & Retail Director
Martin Belson
Chief Operating Officer
Brett Reynolds
Group Finance Director
Ian Leggett
Chief Executive
James Tye
Chairman
Felix Dennis

RWC Online Business

ONLINE BUSINESS

Is video going to kill the SEO star?

Kevin Partner investigates video marketing for online businesses, and learns that even ham-fisted techniques may conceal a good idea

"Success requires credibility to persuade customers to do business with you"

Each issue of PC Pro includes Kevin's Online Business column, packed with topical advice. UK users can sign up for three issues of the magazine and iPad edition for £1 by visiting www.dennismags.co.uk/pcpro or calling 0844 844 0083, quoting code G1110BUS4. Non-UK customers should visit subscribe.pcpro.co.uk for digital-only offers.